COLLECTOR'S ENCYCLOPEDIA OF

Fiesta

NINTH EDITION

Plus Harlequin,
Riviera, and
Kitchen Kraft

**Bob & Sharon
Huxford**

COLLECTOR BOOKS
A Division of Schroeder Publishing Co., Inc.

The current values in this book should be used only as a guide. They are not intended to set prices, which vary from one section of the country to another. Auction prices as well as dealer prices vary greatly and are affected by condition as well as demand. Neither the authors nor the publisher assumes responsibility for any losses that might be incurred as a result of consulting this guide.

Front cover:
    Cobalt onion soup bowl, $650.00 – 725.00.
      Dark green salt shaker, '50s color, $40.00 – 45.00 pr.
      Red juice pitcher, $550.00 – 600.00.
      Light green bud vase, $72.00 – 85.00.
      10" cobalt vase, min. value, $950.00
      12" turquoise vase, min. value, $1,100.00
      10" yellow plate, $28.00 – 32.00.
      13" medium green chop plate, $325.00 – 375.00.
    15" rose chop plate, $125.00 – 145.00.

Cover design by Beth Summers
Book design by Beth Ray

Searching For A Publisher?

We are always looking for knowledgeable people considered to be experts within their fields. If you feel that there is a real need for a book on your collectible subject and have a large comprehensive collection, contact Collector Books.

COLLECTOR BOOKS
P.O. Box 3009
Paducah, Kentucky 42002-3009
www.collectorbooks.com

Contents

Acknowledgments

The most difficult part of any new edition is the Acknowledgments. Difficult because we can never find words that can adequately convey how very much we appreciate the outpouring of good will and enthusiasm that so generously comes our way when we undertake every new update. Especially difficult because we don't want to leave anyone out and are afraid that we will. If your name should be here and isn't, we hope you will forgive us and know that the omission is unintentional and much regretted. Our list of acknowledgments grows every year; almost two hundred are included this time, and keeping track of all those names is not an easy task!

We've added several new photographs this time, all of which were sent to us by various collectors. Some struggled with doing it themselves, often working for hours, in some cases days. Others packed up their treasures and carried them off to have professionals take the photos. Either way, it was time consuming and hard work. Many people sent in one or two photos — all were wonderful and much appreciated, and we've tried not to omit any of them in the alphabetical listing on the following page. But there were several in particular who deserve special recognition. We really can't fully express our gratitude, not just for the many photographs they sent but for that spirit of giving and kindness we found in every one of them. Our special thanks go out to: Kathy Garrels (great go-alongs), Patt Hart Keats (Art China, Apple Tree bowls), Sandy Levine (World's Fair), Chuck Denlinger (Fiesta, Art China), Harvey Linn, Jr. (new Post86 Fiesta, Riviera, original packaging), and David Schaefer (new Post86 Fiesta, experimentals). Without new photos, this update could not have been done.

In the last edition, we included about ninety new photos, and most of them were retained for this book. So we still want to recognize the people who provided them: Mick and Lorna Chase (Fiesta Plus), who drove up from Tennessee to Kentucky — actually volunteered to do it — with box after box of wonderful things that were photographed by one of the country's finest photographers, Richard Walker, and Collector Book's own Charley Lynch; Terry Telford, John Moses, Gus Gustafson, and Mike Haas along with Dave Prichard (Gray Barn Photography) sent many shots of Kitchen Kraft, Amberstone, Mexican lines, and others; Mark Rumbolo, Ray Vlach, and Jack and Treva Hamlin need to be recognized as well for the photographs they contributed.

Pricing is a difficult job, but if it weren't for our survey team it would impossible. There were nearly thirty who took part this time, all busy people willing to give of their time and experience to benefit us all. I'm sure this time it was even more of a struggle for them, since the solid, controlled structure of the antiques market as we have have always known it to be has been turned head over heels by the influence exerted on it by Internet auctions. Those sales defy interpretation and yet still must be reckoned with. Our thanks to each and every one of you.

A heartfelt "thank you" to Joel Wilson, who not only provided most of the photos of the new Post86 Fiesta but the text as well. Those of you who know Joel know what a special, talented person he is. It has been great to have someone so willing and able to provide answers to my many questions.

Thanks, Pat Bunetta, for all the phone calls to keep me current on new finds, and for "listening" to my "theories" via e-mail. Patt Hart Keats (what a go-getter), thank you for the research I asked you for — fine job. Thanks to Mary Flick, another great researcher. Jo Cunningham — we love you, thanks for everything. To Sam and Jennifer Skillern, we appreciate your help very much as well. Thanks to our long-time friend, Lucille Wilson — she and her late husband Austin made very substantial contributions to our earlier books, and we wouldn't dream of not including them this time.

We extend our thanks to the Homer Laughlin China Company for their continued cooperation and to our contacts there over the years, Ed Carson (now retired) and presently Dave Conley.

Last, but by no means least, we want to thank Beth Ray for the fantastic job she did on layout — the book is absolutely beautiful! Beth Summers is the designer of the wonderful new medium green cover. Both are very gifted, talented people and they deserve a lot of praise for the super work they did on this edition. Lisa Stroup and Billy Schroeder, you're both great, and I want you to know how much I appreciate your sweet attitude in allowing me so much latitude with my ideas.

To Fiesta collectors everywhere, the time we've spent communicating with you all via our books has been an unforgettable part of our lives. We wouldn't have missed it for the world. We've been so blessed to have been a part of the Fiesta phenomenon. Thank you and may God bless you all!

Sharon and Bob

Don and Pat Adlesperger
Joe and Char Alexander
Millie Allen
Adam Anik
Mary Apgar
Philip Azeredo
Christina Baglivi
Mike Bainter
Wayne and Laverna Baker
Sandra and Tim Baldwin
Jerry Barberio
Rita Barg
Bill Beck
Dave Beck
Gary Beegle
Michael and Lisa Belcher
   (Sit-a-Spell Antiques)
Rick Benning
Gabriele Benson (Memory Lane)
Deane Bergsrud
Dennis Bialek
Donald G. Biellier
Sue Lynn Bishop
Ida Bonner
Dave Bowers
Robert Bowers
Greg and Kristen Bowman
Dennis Boyd
Paul Brache
Noel and Jennifer Brodzinski
Joyce Brooks
Ken Brown
Sharon C. Browning
Ben Brian C. Buckles
Patrick Bunetta
Gloria and George Burkos
Dave Burrows
Jim Campbell
Tom Chanelli
Mick and Lorna Chase (Fiesta Plus)
Emily Chipps
Phillip and Joyce Clover
Don and Gail Contrell
Doug Dann
Mary Delagardelle
David Delaune
Mildred Delaune
Chuck and Margaret Denlinger
   (Dancing Girl)
Michael Desjardins
Bob and Michelle Detterick
Carolyn Dock
Frank and Rita Dow (Fiesta and More)
Mike Drollinger
Glenn Edmond
Robin and Bud Fennema
Darcy Fitspatrick
Mary Flick
Steven P. Fonder

Terry Franks
Dale Gallis
Cinda Gambil
Kathy Garrels
Jo Ann Giovannelli
Leona Gonzales
Robert Green
William and Donna Griglock
Gus Gustafson
   (chromatics@Buttzville Center)
Mike Haas
   (chromatics@Buttzville Center)
Jack and Treva Hamlin
David Hanrahan
Patt Hart Keats
Ted Haun
Mark Hoaglin
Margaret and Charles Huddleston
Jill Hughes
George and Mary Hurvey
Shel Izen
Lynette Janssen
Jim Jenkins
Troy Jenkins
Edward and Linda Jennings
Doug Jensen
Everett and Gladys Johnson
   (Blue Spruce Antiques)
Phillis and Ray Johnson
Paul Joyner
Alice Kahn
Shirley Keller
Kathy Lange
Florence and Leo Keopple
Ann Kerr
Thomas Kiehl
Jack and Norma Kinion
   (White River Red's Antiques)
Lori Kitchen
Jean Kocmond
Frank and Liz Kramer
Hardy Kristopher
Ruth Kulhanek
Kathy Lange
Lois Lehner
Sandy Levine
Gena Lightle (As Time Goes By)
Ron and Joan Lillquist
Annette Littman
Juliana Lloyd
Patricia Logan
George and Deanna Longnecker
Mrs. M.J. Lucas
Jack and Norma Majewski
Grant and Carole Martin
Donna Matherly
Thomas Maybury
   (Maybury's Antiques)
Cathy McCulty

Brad and Diane McHenry
Jim Mederios
Margaret Merryman
Jane Millett
Ronna Miltmore
Mary Mims
John Moses
Hugh Mosher
Donald and Lela Mutch
Fred Mutchler
Larry and Bonnie Newlin
Bob Novak
Donna Obwald
Florence and Lyle Ohlendorf
Janet Parks
Judie Perez
Ron Perrick
Jill Peterson
Diane Petipas (Mood Indigo)
Leonard Pilch
   (Yesterday's Rainbows)
Stephen Ponder
Lori Pratt
Dave Prichard
   (Gray Barn Photography)
Steven Prickett
David Reardon
Charles and Pam Reed
Jim Rodgers
Charles Roehm
Mark Rumbolo
Frank Sargent
Linda Saridakis
Randy Sauder
David Schaefer
Barbara Seimsen
Robert Sell, Jr.
Steve Sfakis
Terry Sfakis
Peter Shalit
Kathleen Shields
Greg and Rose Shinkel
Ronald Sidel
Rick and Joanne Simpson
Sam and Jennifer Skillern
Helen R. Skinner
Sam Smith
Susan Soultanian
Jean Stack
Dennis Stasiak
Marlyn Stampados
Tom and Toni Staugh
George Stecker
Randy Stephens
William Straus
Ora Strock
Mike Sullivan (As Time Goes By)
Jan Sweet

Acknowledgments

Lois Szemko	Kay and Joe Vahey	Gail Wical
Tom Taylor	Bill and Jo Ann Van Voorhies	Donald Williams
Terry Telford	Joan Vermette	Joy Willems
Les and Brenda Tesch (III)	Dr. Geraldine Vest	Joel Wilson (China Specialties)
Gregory Thompson	Vance and Amy Vogeli	June Wilson
Lorna Thornton	Elaine Walls	Rod Wilson
J. Taylor	Lorraine Walker	Ann Wise
David Tiedman	Charles Walter	Ronnie and Jean Woods
Charles Tomlinson	Christine Walter	Michael and Carol Wowk
Dan Tucker	Carole Watkins	Catherine Yronwode
Ernest Tucking	Clyde Watson	
Aural Umhoefer	Harry Weitkemper	

Collector's Clubs and Tradepapers

The Fiesta Collector's Quarterly Newsletter
PO Box 471
Valley City, OH 44280

Sample copy on request and receipt of long SASE. For collectors of old and new Fiesta. Features regular updates of new colors and items added to new Fiesta line.

Depression Glass Daze
Teri Steel, Editor/Publisher
Box 57
Otisville, MI 48463
810-631-4593

The nation's marketplace for glass, china, and pottery.

Homer Laughlin Collectors Club (HLCC)
PO Box 16174
Loves Park, IL 61132-6174

Dues $20.00 per year, includes *The Homer Laughlin Glaze*, issued quarterly.

Homer Laughlin China Collector's Association (HLCCA)
PO Box 26021
Crystal City, VA 22215-6021

Dues $25.00 single; $40.00 couple or family, includes *The Dish* magazine (a 16-page quarterly), free classifieds.

Sources for Post86 Fiesta

Betty Crocker (premium catalog)
Bloomingdale's Department Stores
Bon Marchè
Dayton-Hudson Department Stores
Elder Beerman's
Homer Laughlin Factory Outlet
   Store (304-1300, ext. 668)
House of 1776 (catalog)

JC Penney's (catalog)
Kay's Merchandise
Lazarus Department Stores
Macy's Department Stores
Roots Department Stores
Speigel's (catalog)
Table Top Direct (330-225-3684)

The Laughlin Pottery Story

The Laughlin Pottery was formed in 1871 on the River Road in East Liverpool, Ohio, the result of a partnership between Homer Laughlin and his brother, Shakespeare Laughlin. The pottery was equipped with two periodic kilns and was among the first in the country to produce whitewares. Sixty employees produced approximately 500 dozen pieces of dinnerware per day. The superior quality of their pottery won for them the highest award at the Centennial Exposition in Philadelphia in 1876.

In 1879 Shakespeare Laughlin left the pottery; for the next ten years Homer Laughlin carried on the business alone. William Edwin Wells joined him in 1889; and at the end of 1896, the firm incorporated. Shortly thereafter, Laughlin sold his interests to Wells and a Pittsburgh group headed by Marcus Aaron.

Under the new management, Mr. Aaron became president, with Mr. Wells acting in the capacity of secretary-treasurer and general manager.

As their business grew and sales increased, the small River Road plant was abandoned, and the company moved its location to Laughlin Station, three miles east of East Liverpool. Two large new plants were constructed and a third purchased from another company. By 1903 all were ready for production. A fourth plant was built in 1906 at the Newell, West Virginia, site and began operations in 1907. In 1913 with business still increasing, Plant 5 was added.

The first revolutionary innovation in the pottery industry was the continuous tunnel kiln. In contrast to the old batch-type or periodic kilns which were inefficient from a standpoint of both fuel and time, the continuous tunnel kiln provided a giant step toward modern-day mass production. Plant 6, built in 1923, was equipped with this new type kiln and proved so successful that two more such plants were added — Plant 7 in 1927 and Plant 8 in 1929. The old kilns in Plants 4 and 5 were replaced in 1926 and 1934, respectively.

In 1929 the old East Liverpool factories were closed, leaving the entire operation at the Newell, West Virginia, site.

At the height of production, the company grew to a giant concern which employed 2,500 people, produced 30,000 dozen pieces of dinnerware per day, and utilized 1,500,000 square feet of production area. In contrast to the early wares painstakingly hand fashioned in the traditional methods, the style of ware reflected the improved mass-production techniques which had of necessity been utilized in later years. The old-fashioned dipping tubs gave way to the use of high-speed conveyor belts and spray glazing, and mechanical jiggering machines replaced for the most part the older methods of man-powered molding machines.

In 1930 W.E. Wells retired from the business after more than forty years of brilliant leadership, having guided the development and expansion of the company from its humble beginning on the Ohio River to a position of unquestioned leadership in its field. He was succeeded by his son, Joseph Mahan Wells. Mr. Aaron became chairman of the board; his son, M.L. Aaron, succeeded him as president. Under their leadership, in addition to the successful wares already in production, many new developments made possible the production of a wide variety of utilitarian wares including the oven-to-table ware, OvenServe and Kitchen Kraft. Later, the creation of the beautiful glazes that have become almost synonymous with Homer Laughlin resulted in the production of the colored dinnerware lines which have captured the attention of many collectors today — Fiesta, Harlequin, and Riviera.

On January 1, 1960, Joseph M. Wells became chairman of the board, and his son, Joseph M. Wells, Jr., followed him in the capacity of executive vice president.

Homer Laughlin continues today to be one of the principal dinnerware producers in the world.

Plate 1

In January of 1936, Homer Laughlin introduced a sensational new line of dinnerware at the Pottery and Glass Show in Pittsburgh. It was Fiesta, and it instantly captured the imagination of the trade — a forecast of the success it was to achieve with housewives of America.

Fiesta was designed by Fredrick Rhead, an English Stoke-on-Trent potter whose work had for decades been regarded among the finest in the industry. His design was modeled by Arthur Kraft and Bill Bersford. The distinctive glazes were developed by Dr. A.V. Blenininger in association with H. W. Thiemecke.

This popularity was the result of much planning, market analysis, creative development, and a fundamentally sound and well-organized styling program. Rather than present to the everyday housewife a modernistic interpretation of a formal table service which might have been received with some reservation, HLC offered a more casual line with a well-planned series of accessories whose style was compatible with any decor and whose vivid colors could add bright spots of emphasis. Services of all types could be chosen and assembled at the whim of the housewife, and the simple style could be used compatibly with other wares already in her cabinets.

Plate 2

In an article by Fredrick Rhead, taken from the *Pottery and Glass Journal* for June 1937, these steps toward Fiesta's development were noted: first, from oral descriptions and data concerning most generally used table articles, a chart of tentative sketches in various appealing colors was made. As the final ideas were formulated, they were modified and adjusted until development was completed. Secondly, the technical department made an intensive study of materials, composition, and firing temperatures. During this time, models and shapes were being studied. The result was to be a streamline shape, but not so obvious as to detract from the texture and color of the ware. It was to have no relief ornamentation and was to be pleasantly curving and convex, rather than concave and angular. Color was to be the chief decorative note; but to avoid being too severe, a concentric band of rings was to be added near the edges.

Since the early '30s, there had been a very definite trend in merchandising toward promoting color. Automobiles, household appliances and furnishings, ladies' apparel — all took on vivid hues. The following is an excerpt from Rhead's article:

The final selection of five colors was a more difficult job because we had developed hundreds of tone values and hues, and there were scores which were difficult to reject. Then there were textures ranging from dull mattes to highly reflecting surfaces. We tackled the texture problem first. (Incidentally, we had made fair-sized skeletons in each of the desirable glazes in order to be better able to arrive at the final selection.)

We eliminated the dull mattes and the more highly reflecting glazes first, because in mass production practice, undue variation would result in unpleasant effects. The dull surfaces are not easy to clean, and the too highly reflecting surfaces show "curtains" or variations in thickness of application. We decided upon a semi-reflecting surface of about the texture of a billiard ball. The surface was soft and pleasant to the touch, and in average light there were no disturbing reflections to detract from the color and shape.

We had one lead with regard to color. There seemed to be a trade preference for a brilliant orange-red. With this color as a keynote and with the knowledge that we were to have five colors, the problem resolved to one where the remainder would "tune in" or form appropriate contrasts.

The obvious reaction to red, we thought, would be toward a fairly deep blue. We had blues ranging from pale turquoises to deep violet blues. The tests were made by arranging a table for four people; and, as the plate is an important item in the set, we placed four plates on various colored cloths and then arranged the different blues around the table. It seemed that the deeper blues reacted better than the lighter tones and blues which were slightly violet or purple. We also found that we had to do considerable switching before we could decide upon the right red. Some were too harsh and deep, others too yellow.

With the red and blue apparently settled, we decided that a green must be one of the five colors. We speedily discovered that the correct balance between the blue and the red was a green possessing a minimum of blue. We had to hit halfway between the red and the blue. We had some lovely subtle greens when they were not placed in juxtaposition with the other two colors, but they would not play in combination.

The next obvious color was yellow, and this had to be toned halfway between the red and the green. Only the most brilliant yellow we could make would talk in company with the other three.

The fifth color was the hardest nut to crack. Black was too heavy, although this may have been used if we could have had six or more colors. We had no browns, purples, or grays which would tune in. We eliminated all except two colors: a rich turquoise and a lovely color we called rose ebony. But there seemed to demand a quieting influence; so we tried an ivory vellum textured glaze which seemed to fit halfway between the yellow and the regular semi-vitreous wares and which cliqued when placed against any of the four colors selected. It took a little time to sell the ivory to our sales organization; but when they saw the table arrangements, they accepted the idea.

In the same publication a month earlier, Rhead had offered this evaluation of the popularity of the various colors with the public:

When this ware first appeared on the market, we attempted to estimate the preference for one color in comparison with the others. As you know, we make five colors ... Because the red was the most expensive color, we thought this might affect the demand. And also, because green had previously been a most popular color, some guessed that this would outsell the others. However, to date, the first four colors are running neck and neck, with less than one percent difference between them. This is a remarkable result and amply bears out...that the "layman" prefers to mix his colors.

Company price lists have always been our main source of information. Over the years as more and more have been found, we have been able to pinpoint important production changes more accurately. Lists found as recently as this decade have clarified some misconceptions that resulted simply from not having them available for our original study. Our earliest is dated May 15, 1937; it lists fifty-four items. An article in the August 1936 issue of *China, Glass, and Lamps* reported new developments in the line since it had been introduced in January:

New items in the famous Fiesta line of solid-color dinnerware include egg cups; deep 8" plates; Tom and Jerry mugs; covered casseroles; covered mustards; covered marmalades; quart jugs; utility trays; flower vases in 8", 10", and 12" sizes; and bowl covers in 5", 6", 7", and 8" sizes.

By the process of elimination, then, in trying to determine the items original to the line, these must be subtracted from those on our May 1937 price list. A collector who has compiled the most complete assortment of company price lists that we are aware of tells us that the 10-ounce tumbler, the 6-cup (medium) teapot, and the 10½" compartment plate that are listed on our May '37 pamphlet were not yet listed on the fall of 1936 issue which he has in his collection; so these would also have to be eliminated. These items remain, and until further information proves us wrong, we assume that they comprised the original assortment: coffeepot, regular; teapot, large; coffeepot, A.D.; carafe; ice pitcher; covered sugar bowl; creamer; bud vase; chop plate, 15"; chop plate, 13"; plate, 10"; plate, 9"; plate, 7"; plate, 6";

compartment plate, 12"; teacup and saucer; coffee cup and saucer, A.D.; footed salad bowl; nested bowls, 11½" to 5"; cream soup cup; covered onion soup; relish tray; compote, 12"; nappy, 9½"; nappy, 8½"; dessert, 6"; fruit, 5"; ashtray; sweets compote; bulb-type candle holders; tripod candle holders; and salt and pepper shakers.

Adding to the selling possibilities of Fiesta, in June 1936 the company offered their Harmony dinnerware sets. These combined their Nautilus line decorated with a colorful decal pattern, accented and augmented with the Fiesta color selected for that particular set. N-258 featured yellow Fiesta accenting Nautilus in white decorated with a harmonizing floral decal at the rim; N-259 used green Fiesta to complement a slender spray of pine cones. Red Fiesta, in N-260, was shown in company catalogs with Nautilus decorated with lines and leaves in an Art Deco motif (see Kitchen Kraft, OvenServe for matching kitchenware items); and blue (N-261) went well with white Nautilus with an off-center flower-filled basket decal. These sets were composed of 67 pieces in all. Of the Nautilus shape there were 9" plates (eight), 6" plates (eight), teacups and saucers (eight), 5½" fruits (eight), a 10" baker, and a 9" nappy. Fiesta items included 10" plates (eight), 7" plates (eight), 6" plates (eight), a 15" chop plate, a 12" compote, one pair of bulb-type candlesticks, a pair of salt and pepper shakers, and a creamer and sugar bowl. Retail price for such a set was around $20.00. This offered a complete service for eight and extra pieces that allowed for buffet and party service for as many more in the contrasting items.

For some time during the earlier years of production, beautifully accessorized "Fiesta Ensembles" were assembled — you will see a picture of a display ad showing such a set in the color plates. It contains 109 pieces, only forty of which are Fiesta: 9" plates (eight), 6" plates (eight), teacups and saucers (eight), and 5" fruits (eight). Accessories included a 24-piece glassware set with enameled Mexican motifs. There were eight of each of the following: 10-ounce, 8-ounce, and 6-ounce tumblers; color-coordinated swizzle sticks; and glass ashtrays. A flatware service for eight with color-coordinated Catalin handles, a red Riviera serving bowl, a 15½" red Riviera platter, and a sugar and creamer in green Riviera completed the set. The flatware and glassware in these ensembles were manufactured by other companies and merely shipped to HLC to be distributed with the ensemble. Records fail to identify the company that may have manufactured these complementary accessories. Included in the packing carton was a promotional poster advertising this set for $14.95.

Plate 3

Originally all five colors sold at the same price; bud vases and salt and pepper shakers were priced in pairs. But on the May '37 price list, red items were higher than the other colors. For example, a red 12" flower vase was priced at $2.35; in the other colors it was only $1.85. A red onion soup was $1.00, 25¢ higher than the others. New to the assortment at that time were the three items mentioned earlier — the 6-cup (medium) teapot, the 10½" compartment plate, and the 10-ounce tumbler. Bud vases and salt and pepper shakers were priced singularly.

A few years ago a mid-1937 price list told us that the sixth color, turquoise, was added then and not in early '38 as we had previously reported. There is a 5" fruit on the May list; however, by mid-'37 the listing shows a 5½" and 4¾" fruit. Possibly the 5" and the 5½" are the same size fruit, with the so-called 5" listed actual size in mid-'37 due to the addition of the 4¾" size. (In comparing actual measurements to listed measurements, we have found variations of as much as ¾".) At this point, the first item had been discontinued; the 12" compartment plate was no longer available. The covered onion soup (evidently much more popular with today's collectors than it was then) was the second item to be dropped; by late that year it, too, was out of production. Two new items were added in the fall of 1937, the sauce boat and the 11½" low fruit bowl. The assortment remained the same until the following July when the disk water jug and the 12" oval platter made their first appearance on company listings. No further changes were made until October 1939, when the stick-handled creamer was replaced by the creamer with the ring handle.

From 1939 through 1943, the company was involved in a major promotional campaign designed to stimulate sales. This involved several special items or sets, each of which was offered for sale at the price of 75¢ to $1.00. An ad from the February 1940 *China, Glass, and Lamps* magazine provides us with the information concerning the campaign.

...dollar retailers in Fiesta ware include covered French casserole; four-piece refrigerator set; sugar, creamer, and tray set; salad bowl with fork and spoon set; kitchen set; casserole with pie plate; chop plate with detachable metal holder; and jumbo coffee cups and saucers in blue, pink, and yellow.

But it also presents us with a puzzling question: what were the jumbo coffee cups and saucers? Sit 'n Sips perhaps? (See Miscellaneous.) The colors mentioned, though dark blue and yellow were in production in 1940, sound pastel with the inclusion of pink. Anyone have an answer? We don't!

Another item featured in the selling campaign is described in this message from HLC to their distributors:

JUICE SET IN FIESTA . . . To help increase your sales! Homer Laughlin is offering an unusual value in the famous Fiesta ware . . . a colorful, 7-piece Juice Set, calculated to fill a real need in the summer refreshment field. The set consists of a 30-ounce disk jug in lovely Fiesta yellow, and six 5-ounce tumblers, one each in Fiesta blue, turquoise, red, green, yellow, and ivory. Sets come packed one to a carton, and at the one dollar minimum retail price are sure to create an upward surge in your sales curve. Dealers who take advantage of this Juice Set in Fiesta will find it a potent weapon in increasing sales of other Fiesta items. At a nominal price, customers who have not yet become acquainted with Fiesta can own some of the ware which has made pottery history during the past few years. The result? They'll want to own more!

Although the other promotional items are relatively scarce, the yellow juice pitcher is very easily found. This flyer is the only mention of it being for sale during this period; neither it nor the juice tumblers were ever included on Fiesta price lists. A few pitchers have been found in red, and only recently has evidence surfaced to explain that at least some of them were special ordered by the Reliable Tea Company, who offered the juice sets (red pitcher and six assorted juice tumblers) as premiums to their customers during the 1940s. In 1952 the promotion was repeated — the juice pitcher in gray, the tumblers in dark green, chartreuse, and Harlequin yellow. Either this issue was not extensively promoted or proved to be a poor seller, judging from their scarcity in these colors. Juice tumblers in rose are not at all rare, yet they were not mentioned in this color in any of these promotions. A factory spokesman explained this to us: while rose was not a standard Fiesta color until the '50s, it had been developed and was in use with the Harlequin line during the '40s. Since it was available in the dipping department, it was used to add extra color contrast to the juice set.

The French casserole, individual sugar and creamer on the figure-8 tray, and the 9½" salad bowl were also never listed except in this promotion. Each is standard in a specific color; on rare occurrences when they are found in non-standard glazes, their values soar! (See pricing information in the back of the book.) French casseroles were all to have been yellow; however, two dark blue bases and two complete casseroles have been reported, and a lid and base have been found in light green. Before the fifth edition was published, we received a letter telling us that an ivory one existed, and since then the owners have written to us to verify its existence. Yellow was also standard for the 9½" salad bowl, but a very few rare examples have surfaced in dark blue, red, ivory, and light green. The individual sugar and creamer in the *China, Glass, and Lamps* ad were described as both being yellow on a cobalt figure-8 tray, but in a jobber's calatog dated spring 1940 that was discovered since the last edition, this set is described as containing a red creamer, a yellow sugar bowl, and a cobalt tray. This explains the few red creamers that have been found over the years. One sugar and at least two creamers have been found in turquoise, a cobalt creamer has been reported, and trays in yellow and turquoise exist as well, but these are very rare.

One of the most exciting discoveries of this decade is the three-piece Fiesta Kitchenware Set referred to in the promotions as "casserole with pie plate." See the Fiesta color plates for a look at this exciting set photographed with its original carton. We're sure it's authentic, since it was originally found in the unopened carton in exactly the colors described in the ad: casserole body — green, casserole cover — red, 9½" plate — yellow.

Other items that have never been included on any known price list are the syrup pitcher and the very rare flat 10" cake plate. It was only recently that we found a list containing the four smaller sizes of the nested bowl lids that were mentioned in Rhead's article. A butter dish was never listed with Fiesta, but the consensus of opinion after so many years of collecting is that the Jade/Riviera butter dish (see Plate 188 for more information) was dipped to go with the Fiesta line as well, since it may be found in cobalt and ivory, both standard colors in only one of HLC's lines, Fiesta.

More changes occurred in the fall of 1942. Items discontinued at that time included the tripod candle holders, the A.D. coffeepot, and both the 10" and 12" flower vases.

In 1943 our government assumed control of uranium oxide, an important element used in the manufacture of the Fiesta red glaze. As a result, it was dropped from production — "Fiesta red went to war." Perhaps the fact that Fiesta red had been listed separately and priced proportionately higher than the other colors was due to the higher cost of raw material plus the fact that the red items required strict control during firing; losses that did occur had to be absorbed in the final costs.

Plate 4

The color assortment in 1944 included turquoise, green, blue, yellow, and ivory. The nested bowls no longer were listed. The rate of price increases over the seven years Fiesta had been on the market is hard for us to imagine: ashtrays were still only 15¢, egg cups were up to 35¢ from 30¢, relish trays were up only 15¢ to $1.80 complete.

Although the colors are listed the same on the 1946 price list, the following pieces were discontinued: bud vase, bulb-type candle holders, carafe, 12" compote, sweets compote, 8" vase, 11½" fruit bowl, ice pitcher, marmalade and mustard, 9½" nappy, relish tray, footed salad bowl, large teapot, 10-ounce tumbler, and utility tray.

A price list from November 5, 1950, helps us pinpoint the time of the radical color change that had taken place by October of 1951. Though the 1950 price list still offered the original colors, by fall of 1951 light green, dark blue, and old ivory had been retired; their replacements were forest green, rose, chartreuse, and gray. Turquoise and yellow continued to be produced. These four new colors have been dubbed "'50s colors," since they and the listed assortment remained in production without change until the end of the decade.

Prices listed in 1956, twenty years after Fiesta was introduced, were higher, of course; but still the increase is so slight as to be quite noteworthy to us in the '90s. Ashtrays sold for 40¢, teacups that were 25¢ were up to 65¢. Dinner plates had little more than doubled at 90¢, and coffeepots sold for $2.65. They, too, had about doubled in price.

The big news in 1959 was, of course, the fact that Fiesta red was reinstated. It was welcomed back with much ado! The Atomic Energy Commission licensed the Homer Laughlin China Company to again buy the depleted uranium oxide, and Fiesta red returned to the market in March of 1959.

In addition to red, turquoise, and yellow, a new color — medium green — was offered. Rose, gray, chartreuse, and dark green were discontinued; and the following items were no longer available: 15" chop plate, A.D. coffee cup and saucer, regular coffeepot, 10½" compartment plate, cream soup cup, egg cup, 4¾" fruit bowl, and the 2-pint jug. A new item made an appearance — the individual salad bowl.

By 1961 the 6" dessert bowl was no longer listed. Aside from that change, the line and the color assortment remained the same. Though retail prices had risen in 1965; by 1968 some items stayed the same while others actually dropped slightly.

In the latter months of 1969 in an effort to meet the needs of the modern housewife and to present a product that was better designed to be in keeping with modern day decor, Fiesta was restyled. Only one of the original colors, Fiesta red — always the favorite — continued in production (see chapter on Fiesta Ironstone).

The big news of 1986 was the exciting new line of Fiesta ware that was introduced in the spring. How better to celebrate its fiftieth birthday! We'll tell you all about it in one of the following chapters.

Exactly when the first rumors began circulating, hinting that the red Fiesta could be hazardous to your health, is uncertain. In most probability, it was around the time that Fiesta red was reintroduced after the war and was no doubt due to the publicity given to uranium and radioactivity during the war years. Clearly another case where "a little learning can be a dangerous thing."

In any case, this worry must have remained to trouble the minds of some people for several years. Even today the subject comes up occasionally and remains a little controversial, though most folks in this troubled age of acid rains, high unemployment, cholesterol-free diets, and constant reminders that "cigarettes are hazardous to your health" don't really seem too upset by it anymore.

The following letter appeared in the *Palm Beach Post Times* in February 1963. It was written tongue-in-cheek by a man who had evidently reached the limit of his patience. HLC sent it to us from their files; it has to be a classic.

> Editor:
> After reading about the radioactive dishes in your paper, I am greatly concerned that I may be in danger, as I had a plate with a design in burnt orange, or maybe it was lemon.
> This plate was left to me by my great-grandmother, and I noticed that whenever she ate anything from it, her ears would light up; so we all had to wear dark glasses when dining at her house.
> I first became suspicious of this dish when putting out food for my dog on it I noticed the dog's nose became as red as Rudolph's; and one day a sea gull fed from it, and all his feathers fell off; then one night when the weather was raw I placed it at the foot of my bed, and my toenails turned black.
> Using it as a pot cover while cooking eel stew, the pot cracked; and reading the letters in your paper last week have concluded I am not the only person having a cracked pot in the house; so perhaps some of your other readers used a plate for a cover.
> I finally threw this plate overboard at a turn in the channel, now a buoy is no longer needed there, as bubbles and steam mark this shoal.
> Will you please ask your Doctor or someone if they think this plate is radioactive, and if so am I in any danger, and if so from what?
>
> (Name Withheld)

Several years ago we were allowed the opportunity to search through old company literature in the event that some bit of pertinent information had escaped our notice. It was obvious from letters contained in these files that HLC had always been harassed with letters from people concerned with the uranium content of the Fiesta red glaze. Their replies were polite, accommodating, and enlightening. Here in part is one of their letters:

> Before 1943 the colorant (14% by weight of the glaze covering the ware) is uranium oxide (U-308), with the uranium content being made up of about 0.7% U-235 and the remainder U-238. Between 1943 and 1959 under license by AEC, we have again been producing a red glazed dinnerware. However the colorant now used is depleted technical grade U-308 with the uranium content being made up of about 0.2% U-235 and the remainder U-238.

Studies were conducted for us by Dr. Paul L. Ziemer and Dr. Geraldine Deputy (who is herself an avid Fiesta collector) in the Bionuclionics Department of Purdue University. The penetrating radiation from the uranium oxide used in the manufacturing of the glaze for the red Fiesta ware was measured with a standard laboratory Geiger Counter. All measurements are tabularized in units of milliroentgens per hour (mR/hr).

Item	Surface Contract	4" Above Surface	Along Rim
13" Chop Plate	0.8	0.35	0.1
9" Plate	0.5	1.5	0.07
Fruit Bowl	1.5	0.5	0.1
Relish Tray Wedge	0.8	0.2	0.02
Cup	1.3	0.2	0.03

In order to compare the above values to familiar quantities of radiation, we calculated the exposure of a person holding a 13" chop plate strapped to his chest for twenty-four hours. This gives twenty milliroentgens per day. Safe levels for humans working with radiation is one hundred milliroentgens per week for a five-day week or twenty milliroentgens per day as background radiation.

Some other measurements of interest for comparison purposes are:

Item	Radiation
Radium Dial on a Watch	20mR/hr
Chest X-Ray	44 mR per film
Dental X-Ray	910 mR per film
Fatal Dose	400,000 mR over whole body

Back in May of 1977 on an eastern television station, an announcement was made concerning the pros and cons of the safety of colored-glazed dinnerware. Fiesta was mentioned by name. We contacted the Department of Health, Education, and Welfare, FDA, in Chicago, Illinois. This in part is their position, and it is supported by HLC:

> The presence of lead, cadmium, and other toxic metal in glaze or decal is not in itself a hazard. It becomes a problem only when a glaze or decal that has not been properly formulated, applied, or fired, contains dangerous metals which can be released by high-acid foods such as fruit juices, some soft drinks, wines, cider, vinegar, and vinegar-containing foods, sauerkraut, and tomato products.

The FDA report continues:

> Be on the safe side by not storing foods or beverages in such containers for prolonged periods of time, such as overnight. Daily use of the dinnerware for serving food does not pose a hazard. If the glaze or decal is properly formulated, properly applied, and properly fired, there is no hazard.

Note: Testing is ongoing on vintage dinnerware, and some scientists believe the threat of lead, cadmium, uranium, and other metals leaching out of the glazes is enough to cause concern. They especially warn against putting it into the microwave, since this may accelerate the process.

Identification of Trademark, Design, and Color

Fiesta's original design, colors, and name are the registered property of the Homer Laughlin China Company. Patent No. 390-298 was filed on March 20, 1937, having been used by them since November 11, 1935. These four seem to be the most common.

The indented trademark was the result of in-mold casting; the ink mark was put on with a hand stamp after the color was applied and before the final glaze was fired.

As many other manufacturers were following the trend to brightly colored dinnerware, the wide success and popularity of Fiesta resulted in its being closely copied and produced at one time by another company. Homer Laughlin quickly brought suit against their competitor and forced the imitation ware to be discontinued. To assure buyers they could buy with complete confidence, the word "Genuine" was added to the hand stamp sometime before 1940. Genuine Fiesta was the exclusive product of Homer Laughlin.

There are some items in the Fiesta line which were never meant to be marked — juice tumblers, demitasse cups, salt and pepper shakers, teacups, and some of the Kitchen Kraft line (though a rare few have been found with the ink stamp). Sweets compotes, egg cups, ashtrays, and onion soups may or may not be marked, and many plates that are normally stamped by hand carry no mark as well. Never pass up an unmarked item if you can verify that it is genuine Fiesta. As you become more aware of design and color, you will be able to recognized it quite easily.

Fiesta's design is very simple and therefore very versatile. The pattern consists of a band of concentric rings graduating in width, with those nearer the rim being more widely spaced. The rings are repeated in the center motif on such pieces as plates, nappies, platters, and desserts. Handles are applied with slight ornamentation at the base. Vases and tripod candle holders, though designed without the rings, are skillfully modeled with simple lines, geometric forms, and stepped devices that instantly relate to the Art Deco mood of Fiesta's clean uncluttered shapes. Flat pieces and bowls are round or oval; hollow ware pieces are globular, and many are styled with a short pedestal base decorated with the band of rings.

But, of course, it's Fiesta's vivid colors that first capture your attention. The wide array of color provides endless possibilities for matching color schemes and decor. And if you find you love all eleven, you'll surely enjoy collecting a place setting in every color — Fiesta red, yellow, rose, old ivory, gray, dark blue, turquoise, forest green, light green, medium green, and chartreuse.

Plate 5

Dating Codes and
English Measurements

Many HLC lines often carry a backstamp containing a series of letters and numbers. The company has provided this information to help you in deciphering these codes:

In 1900 the trademark featured a single numeral identifying the month, a second single numeral identifying the year, and a numeral 1, 2, or 3 designating the point of manufacture as East Liverpool, Ohio.

In the period 1910 – 20, the first figure indicated the month of the year, the next two numbers indicated the year, and the third figure designated the plant. No. 4 was "N," No. 5 was "N5," and the East End plant was "L."

A change was made for the period of 1921–1930. The first letter was used to indicate the month of the year such as "A" for January, "B" for February, "C" for March. The next single digit number was used to indicate the year, and the last figure designated the plant.

For the period 1931 – 40, the month was expressed as a letter; but the year was indicated with two digits. Plant No. 4 was "N," No. 5 was "R," No. 6 and 7 were "C," and No. 8 was listed as "P." During this period, E-44R5 would indicate May of 1944 and manufactured by Plant No. 5. The current trademark has been in use for approximately seventy years, and the numbers are the only indication of the specific years that items were produced.

Collectors have long been puzzled over the origin and meaning of such terms as oval "baker" and "36s bowl" — not to mention the insistent listings of 4" plates, when it has become very apparent that 4" plates do not exist! We asked our contact at HLC for an explanation. He told us that each size bowl was assigned a number. Smaller numbers indicated larger bowls, and vice versa. The word "baker" as used to describe a serving bowl was an English potting term. It was also the English who established the unfortunate system of measurements based on some rather obscure logic by which a 6" plate should be listed as 4". The 7" "nappies" (also an English term) actually measure 8¾"; 4" fruits are usually 5½"; and 6", 7", and 8" plates are in reality 7", 9", and 10".

This practice continued through the '50s (though more in connection with other HLC lines than Fiesta) until it became so utterly confusing to everyone involved that actual measurements were thankfully adopted. However, these may vary as much as ¾" from measurements listed on company brochures. For instance, 9" and 10" plates actually measure 9½" and 10½", and the 13" and 15" chop plates are 12¼" and 14¼".

The small incised letters and/or numbers sometimes found on the bottom of hollow ware pieces were used to identify a pieceworker — perhaps a molder or a trimmer — and were intended for quality control purposes. More likely to appear on Harlequin, these are sometimes seen on Fiesta as well.

The Rhead family was prominent among the finest ceramists of nineteenth-century England. Fredrick Hurten Rhead came from a long line of English Stoke-on-Trent potters and must without doubt be considered one of the most productive artisans in the history of the industry. At the age of 19, he was named art director at the Wardel Pottery. After leaving his home in Staffordshire in 1902, he worked at the Vance/Avon Faience Co. in Tiltonville, Ohio, for a term of about six months before moving on to the Weller Pottery in Zanesville, Ohio. By 1904 he was awarded the position of art director at the nearby Roseville Pottery. The many lines of artware he produced for these companies earned him widespread recognition. Inspired by nature and influenced by both Art Nouveau and the Arts and Crafts Movement, he became well known for dramatic sgraffito work, which he executed in intricate detail. An element he often favored was a styl-ized tree, variations of which he used frequently throughout his career.

Plate 6

In later years, he designed a set of nested mixing bowls for Homer Laughlin; they were decorated with embossed trees reminiscent of his earlier work.

Leaving Roseville in 1908, he went to the William Jervis Pottery on Long Island. In 1909 he accepted the post of instructor in pottery at the University City Pottery in St. Louis. From 1911 to 1913 he was associated with the Arequipa Pottery in Fairfax, California. There, with the assistance of his wife, Agnes, he taught ceramics to patients at the Arequipa Sanatorium. Leaving Arequipa, he organized the Pottery of the Camarata in Santa Barbara, later to be incorporated as The Rhead Pottery. Never a confident thrower, Rhead involved himself fully with developing new glazes. One of his finest achievements was Mirror Black, a re-creation of the sixteenth-century black-glazed pottery of the Orient, which earned him a Gold Medal at the 1915 San Diego Exposition.

In December of 1916, Rhead published *The Potter*, a monthly magazine dealing with the progress of the industry. The editor of the historical department was Edwin A. Barber, whose death was reported in the third issue (February, 1917). With that, the paper was abandoned.

Freed of the pressures he had felt at the commercial potteries in Ohio, Rhead utilized this time to

develop his creative capabilities to their fullest, but as a business man he was unable to keep his pottery afloat. He encountered financial difficulties, and his pottery failed. Returning to Zanesville in 1917, he joined the American Encaustic Tiling Company. Loiz Whitcomb, a fellow artisan from his California pottery (with whom he had fallen in love after his first marriage was annulled), came back to the Midwest to join him; they soon married. Rhead served at AE Tile as director of research. In 1927 he moved to the Homer Laughlin Company where he designed his famous dinnerware line, Fiesta. He remained there until his death in 1942. No other ceramic artist made more of an impact on this country's pottery industry. From the early days of his career to the last, Rhead's work evolved effortlessly, leaving behind a legacy still enjoyed by thousands today.

Shown are examples of only two of the lines Rhead developed for Roseville and Weller — Della Robbia on the left, and Weller Rhead Faience above.

Plate 7

 *Dinnerware*

Plate 8

Ashtray. Shown here in dark green, these were made from 1936 until the Fiesta Ironstone line was discontinued in 1973, and they can be found in all of the old colors plus the Turf Green and Antique Gold of Ironstone. They measure 5½" in diameter.

Plate 9

Covered Onion Soup Bowl (left foreground). Imagine a lifestyle that required a soup bowl with a lid! Just one of the little amenities that have gone by the wayside since "stay-at-home" moms went to work. They're very scarce today, so even back in the more formal '30s they probably were never good sellers. They're found in ivory, red, light green (shown), dark blue, turquoise, and yellow. (See an example of each in Plate 10.) Since they were discontinued by fall of 1937, only a few weeks after turquoise was added to the color assortment (mid-'37), they're very scarce in that color. Across the handles, it measures 6" (quite a bit larger than the sugar bottom that new collectors tend to confuse it with.)(See Plate 94 for a cream soup bowl in ivory with a red stripe decoration.) *Dessert Bowl (upper left).* This was also in the original line. Shown here in dark blue, these were produced in 1961 in all colors, but they are scarce in medium green. Note that unlike the fruit bowls in this picture, there is no flat rim flange. They're rather shallow with vertical sides, and they're 6" in diameter. *Individual Salad Bowl (center back).* A later addition, these were not produced until 1959 and were, of course, only made in the colors of that period — red, turquoise, yellow, and medium green. They're easier to find in red

and medium green; nevertheless expect to pay a premium for medium green, regarded by collectors as Fiesta's most desirable color. Occasionally you may find one with no rings in the bottom, probably produced toward the transition into Fiesta Ironstone when such modifications were finalized. Collectors are also reporting bowls in all four colors as well as the brighter Harlequin yellow with no inside rings at all. *Fruit Bowl, 5½" (upper right).* Probably the bowl listed as 5" in the original assortment, this item was made until the restyling in 1969 and is available in all eleven colors. One example has been reported in the blue of the Skytone line. *Fruit Bowl, 4¾" (right foreground).* This was probably the bowl that was added to the assortment in mid-'37. We have price lists that are dated 1956 and 1959; they show it as still available in 1956, but it does not appear on the price list for 1959 when medium green was introduced, and only a few have been found in that color. It's rather scarce in red as well; here you see it in the rose of the '50s assortment.

18

Plate 10
This is the complete color assortment of the covered onion soup bowls. The very rare turquoise example in the front row is especially noteworthy.

Plate 11
Alongside the standard onion soup bowl is a one-of-a-kind example of what is probably the first model. It was replaced less than a year later by the one more familiar to us. Shown here in light green, it differs from the regular version in several ways: note that the handles are flat rather than rolled under, the bowl flares at the rim above the handles, and the foot is wider and shorter. The lid is less rounded and ½" wider. It's marked "Fiesta HLC" in the mold, and it's the only example of its kind to have ever surfaced.

Plate 12
Cream Soup Bowl. These were part of the original line and continued to be made until sometime in 1959. They're found in all colors but are very, very rare in medium green, the newcomer to the color assortment that year. (See Plate 63.) Quality examples, especially in red, have appreciated significantly.

Plate 13

Mixing Bowls. Stacked together, a set of seven weighs just about twenty pounds. Almost gives you a kinder regard for Tupperware, doesn't it? These bowls were made in only the original six colors, since they were in production from 1936 until around 1943. Each bowl is numbered in sequence on the bottom: #1 being the smallest at 5"; #2 — 6"; #3 — 7"; #4 — 8"; #5 — 9"; #6 — 10"; and #7 — 11½". An ad dated December 1938 indicated that as a Christmas season promotion, for $2.50 you could purchase a Rainbow Mixing Bowl Set — a four-piece assortment that contained a yellow 7", a green 8", a

dark blue 9", and a red 10". Collectors tell us that the #7 (11½") bowl is difficult to find, perhaps because it wasn't included in this promotion, perhaps simply because fewer sold, since its size likely made it unwieldy to use. The #1 (5") bowl is also scarce, and that may also be contributed to its size. It might have been just right for storing leftovers, but as a mixing bowl, it's very small! The only bowl lids ever officially offered on a company price list were the four smaller sizes, 5", 6", 7", and 8". Although the list we refer to is undated, we can place it after August 1936 (our price list bearing that date makes no mention of them) and before 1937 (because turquoise was not yet being offered on the list in question).

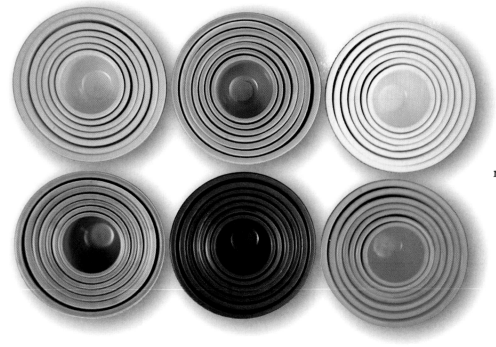

Plate 14
Here's a fantastic view of a complete collection of the nested bowl sets, one in each of the six original colors.

Plate 15
Bowl Lids. They're extremely rare in any size! The #5 nested bowl lid remained undiscovered until just before our 1994 update. Since then, at least three #6s have finally been unearthed, including the one in this fantastic, pristine all-red set. Is there a #7? According to old HLC records, there may just be! There are rumors that suggest that somewhere there are two ivory test lids, but it is generally agreed that the #7s were never marketed.

Plate 16
Nappy, 9½" (left).
This bowl was part of the original assortment and was still listed on our 1944 price list, but by fall of 1946, it was no longer available. You'll find it in only the first six colors.

Nappy, 8½" (center).
Here shown in medium green, these bowls were made from 1936 until the line was restyled in '69, so they come in all eleven colors.

Unlisted Salad Bowl (right). Although this salad bowl (3¾" deep by 9½" in diameter) was never listed on the company's price pamphlets, a trade paper from 1940 reported on the Homer Laughlin sales campaign that offered this bowl accompanied by the Kitchen Kraft spoon and fork for only $1.00 — another of the promotionals. The ad copy indicated that these bowls were offered in only yellow. They're very scarce even in that color, but a rare few have been reported in ivory, red, light green, and dark blue (see Plate 17).

Plate 17

This is a very rare example of the unlisted salad bowl, shown here in dark blue — it's just as rare in ivory, light green, and red.

Plate 18

Bulb Candle Holders. Both these and the tripod candle holders were part of the original line; this style was discontinued sometime between 1944 and 1946. They were made in the six early colors and are relatively easy to find. We've also heard from a collector who has these in Harlequin yellow.

Plate 19

Footed Salad Bowl (left).

According to our survey, these handsome bowls are scarce and becoming rare. They were made from the time Fiesta was introduced until 1946 in only the first six colors (this prize is Fiesta red, of course), and if one color is any harder to find than the others, it is probably ivory. Though they're listed on company material as being 12" in diameter, they're actually only 11¼". *Fruit Bowl (right).* These are hard to find, especially in red. They were made from 1937 until sometime between 1944 and 1946 in only the six original colors. They're shallow, only 3" deep, and 11¾" in diameter.

Plate 20

Tripod Candle Holders. These are regarded as very desirable additions to any collection. They've always been scarce and are even more so today. They were made in only the first six colors, since they were discontinued around 1942 or 1943. Though these normally are found with the wet (glazed) foot, occasionally you'll find an example with a dry, unglazed base. One set has been found in a most unusual deep aubergene.

Plate 21

Carafe. The carafe was part of the original line but was no longer listed by 1946. The stopper has a cork seal, and its wonderful Deco lines make it a favorite among collectors. These were made in the first six colors only, with ivory being the most difficult to find. The company lists its capacity as three pints.

Plate 22

Casserole. Considering that production of the covered casserole (as it was always referred to) was continuous from 1936, they're not especially easy to find. This one is shown in dark green, which along with the other colors of the '50s (rose, gray, and chartreuse) is very desirable, but the medium green example tops the charts.

Plate 23

Tricolator Bowl. This is simply the casserole bottom without the standard applied foot. It's a piece HLC didn't recall producing. It's marked Tricolator, a company that specialized in combining a piece such as this one with a warmer base, a metal frame, etc. It was common practice for a pottery company to make items such as this to fill a special order — not just for Tricolator, but for similar companies as well. You can also find coffeepots that were made for Tricolator by Hall, some of which bear the marks of both companies. These bowls have been reported in ivory, yellow, red, turquoise, green, dark blue, and Harlequin yellow. When found, they're normally open, though one collector tells us his was bought at an estate sale topped with the standard Fiesta casserole lid.

Plate 24
French Casserole.
Another of the eight special promotional items offered by HLC from 1939 to 1942, the French casserole is a relatively scarce item. Virtually all are yellow, though two bases and two complete units have been reported in dark blue, and a lid and base have been found in light green. Just before the last update, one was reported in ivory. The lid differs significantly enough from the one on the casserole in Plate 22 that you'll easily be able to tell which lid you have, should you find a spare. The French casserole lid measures 9" in diameter compared to 8" for the regular casserole lid, and the finial is ⅞" across the top compared to 1¼".

Plate 25
Promotional Casserole and Pie Plate. Though not marked, for many years collectors suspected that these casseroles had been made by Homer Laughlin, since they kept turning up in colors identical to several of HLC's standard glazes. When we inquired, however, company representatives denied they ever produced them, and so for years we had no choice but to exclude them from the Fiesta lineup. But a few years ago, evidence surfaced to the contrary. A company representative discovered on an old order sheet showing their #600 Gift Assortment of Colored Ware — and there it was, our mystery casserole! Then this set was found, still sealed in its original unopened carton which is stamped Fiesta on the side not shown. Note the colors are exactly as described in the promotional campaign we talk about on pages 10 and 11. The casserole is 3" deep and measures 8" in diameter. See Plate 282 in the Go Alongs chapter for another view. Most of them are red, turquoise, yellow, light green, and mauve blue, though dark blue, Harlequin yellow, and spruce green have also been found. (We listed maroon in our last edition, but two of our survey dealers doubt it exists — if you have one in maroon, let us know.) The Fiesta Kitchen Kraft pie plate is 9¾"; it's shown again later in the Fiesta Kitchen Kraft section. It has been reported in mauve blue, Harlequin yellow, and spruce, suggesting there may have been Harlequin promotional campaigns as well.

Plate 26

Coffeepot, Teacups, and Saucers. The coffeepot can be found in all of Fiesta's colors except medium green. It was in the original line but was not made after mid-1956. You'll find some interesting variations among teacups; these are discussed in more detail in Plate 28. Though cups are rarely ever marked (neither are mustards, demitasse cups, juice tumblers, and salt and peppers), a few have been reported bearing the HLCo USA ink stamp in blue-black or gold. These may have been some that were earmarked for export to Canada.

Plate 27

This stunning photo is a real attention-grabber! Unless you're one of those collectors who has to have every piece in every color (or you personally know someone who is), here are more coffeepots than you've probably ever seen in one group before or ever will again — one in each of the ten colors. Note the absence of medium green.

Plate 28

Here are three distinct styles of teacups — those with the inside rings (right) are the oldest. They also have a hand-turned foot. Only a few have been found in medium green which would seem to indicate that it was sometime around 1959 when the inside rings disappeared and the foot became part of the casting, no longer requiring expensive hand trimming. The teacup on the left represents the second style. Note that the third style (center back), though produced in the color assortment available through the '60s, has the "C" handle of Fiesta Ironstone — evidently manufactured near the time of the restyling. It's very rare to find a marked

cup. (If your cup has a molded-in mark, it's new; see Plate 26 for more information.) There is yet another style, but most of us have never seen it — probably never will. HLC believes it dates back to the inception of the line when the foot of items such as cups, creamers, sugar bowls, etc., was thrown separately and then attached to the body. But the collector that reported this variation has them in the six early colors (turquoise included), so we know they were produced for several months. He describes the cups as having a flat area inside at bottom about the size of a quarter, very similar, he says, to the unusual sugar bowl we show in Plate 35. The saucer that goes with this cup is flatter than normal, so they don't stack well with the regular style, and they have a series of several rings around the rim of the bottom and foot.

Plate 29

Demitasse Pot, Cups, and Saucers.
If you've never been sure of the meaning of the terms demitasse and A.D., they simply refer to small cups of strong black coffee meant to be slowly sipped and lingered over after a lovely dinner. Designed to serve after-dinner coffee with elegance and flair, demitasse pots and cups were included in the original line. The pot was discontinued before 1944; you'll find it in the six original colors only, with turquoise examples being especially hard to find. The cups and saucers were supposedly made in just ten colors — no medium green, since they were discontinued in '56, three years before the color was introduced — but four sets in medium green

were discovered just before the last edition. For you skeptics, we show the green lineup in Plate 30. Of the ten standard colors, the '50 colors are hardest to find and sell at a premium. A collector has reported finding one in brick red. Virtually never marked, a rare few have been found with the HLCo USA mark. (See Plate 26.)

Plate 30
Here's that medium green demitasse cup and saucer! Four sets have been in the same family since the '50s — and they're not even collectors! These are definitely medium green, not a heavy application of light green. If we've learned one thing about Fiesta over the past thirty years, it's that there are no absolutes. Just about anything is possible. Of the four, one saucer is marked Fiesta, two are unmarked, and the other has written under the glaze the following code: 1/3 (over) C-FY-FG. There is also a medium green demitasse pot at the East Liverpool, Ohio, Ceramics Museum. Plates in the background are forest green, light green, medium green, and chartreuse. (Photo by Joel Wilson)

Plate 31
Comport. These were made from 1936 until sometime between 1944 and 1946. They're 12" in diameter and can be found in only the six original colors — this one is turquoise.

Plate 32
This breathtaking lineup contains an example of all six of the colors the demitasse pot was made in. Note the vent hole in the lid of the yellow example. These were put in by hand and evidently most of the time regarded as a dispensable option.

Plate 33
Sweets Comport. We found that the sweets comports, part of the original assortment, were discontinued between 1944 and 1946, making them available in only the six early colors. They're 3½" tall, and only about one out of four examples is marked with the ink stamp.

Plate 34
Creamer and Sugar Bowl. Shown here in red, this is the creamer (collectors call it the 'regular' creamer) that replaced the original stick-handled version in the fall of 1939 and continued in production until restyled for the Ironstone line. The sugar bowl remained basically the same from '36 on, though the bases of earlier creamers and sugar bowls are flared out as compared to those made in the late '40s in the original colors and those in the '50s colors, when a slight change in the molds resulted in a base with a rather stubby appearance. *Stick-Handled Creamer.* These were made from 1936 until late 1939 when they were replaced by the ring-handled style described above. They come in the six early colors and are hardest to find in turquoise (as shown).

Plate 35
The sugar bowl on the left is very likely the early model, when the base and the body were molded as two separate pieces; the other is the standard sugar bowl. There are three distinct differences between them: the early example has a raised base and the inside bottom is flat; the width of the lid flange is twice as wide as the standard version; and the mark is Fiesta, HLC, USA. Because the style on the right could be molded in one piece, they were less expensive to manufacture.

Plate 36
Creamer and Sugar Bowl, Individual; Figure-8 Tray.
This set is from the 1939 – 1943 sales campaign. Nearly all sets are found with the sugar and creamer in yellow on a dark blue tray; however, occasionally you'll find a red creamer and once in awhile a turquoise tray. (This one is in my collection; it's marked Fiesta with an inkstamp, and I bought it during the very early days of our collecting in that wonderful shop in Newell where I bought two 12" vases for $7.00 each.) A yellow tray was reported years ago. Can anyone verify its existence? Though very few have been reported, creamers and at least one sugar bowl were found in turquoise, and a creamer was found in dark blue — well before the new line was introduced in 1986. A 1944 McClurg's catalog page that was reproduced on the cover of *The Fiesta Collector's Quarterly* (Winter 1998) features the dark blue figure-8 tray with a Harlequin sugar bowl and creamer!

Plate 37
Egg Cup. These were not part of the original line; they were added in mid-'36. They were discontinued between January and September of 1956 and are available in ten colors (no medium green). Collectors report that chartreuse and gray are the hardest to find.

Plate 38

Marmalade and Mustard Jars. Marmalades (the yellow one) and mustards (here shown in red) were two of the items mentioned in Rhead's August 1939 magazine article quoted in the chapter entitled The Story of Fiesta. He wrote that these were new to the line at that time. They were discontinued between 1944 and 1946, so they're found in the first six colors only. Marked mustards are extremely rare; the few that are carry the HLCo USA stamp in gold or blue-black ink. See Plate 39.

Plate 39

Disk Juice Pitcher, Juice Tumblers. Of all the promotional items, this set is the only one that is fairly easy to find. Nearly every pitcher you'll see will be yellow (collectors report a high incidence of the use of Harlequin yellow, a slightly brighter shade than Fiesta yellow), but once in awhile you may find one in red. The red pitchers, according to a recent report by a couple who discovered some of the original coupons, were offered as a promotion by the Dayton Spice Mills, the Old Reliable Coffee Company. "Yours for only three coupons and $1.19," one says, "six tumblers in lovely colors" (it lists turquoise, green, yellow, blue, ivory, and red) "and a superbly shaped red Fiesta jug. High quality both in material and texture...designed and executed with artistic skill of the first order." Though juice tumblers were discontinued before the '50s, rose tumblers are not uncommon. (See Plate 42 for comments.) The pitcher holds 30 ounces and is 5¾" tall; the tumblers vary in size notoriously (so do the mugs), they range in height from 3⅜" to 3½" and from 2⅜" to 2½" in diameter and vary in thickness as well. The juice tumbler that one of our readers has in his collection with the HLCo USA mark may well be the rarest of the "never marked" items. (The others are the demitasse cup, mustard, teacup, and salt and peppers shakers, listed in order of decreasing scarcity.)

Plate 40
A sales promotion offered in 1952 is represented here — the very rare gray juice pitcher along with a tumbler in each of these colors: dark green, Harlequin yellow, and chartreuse. These are seldom found. One collector's theory, and it may well be fact, is that this set was dipped to go with Rhythm. The dates coincide, and one tumbler in maroon (the fourth Rhythm color) has been reported, lending more credence to the theory. It seems to be the consensus of opinion that since the new gray juice pitcher hit the market, collectors are less in awe of the old one.

Plate 41
This juice set was glazed in the Jubilee colors — another sales promotion. The gray tumbler is especially interesting to collectors, since is exactly like the standard Fiesta gray from the '50s.

Plate 42
Though you might expect that the rose and gray tumblers (the pair to the right) were from the '50s, since those colors were standard '50s fare, you must remember that these tumblers were discontinued well before then. Instead, the gray is actually Jubilee's mist gray and the rose a standard Harlequin color of the late '30s, borrowed to add a seventh color to the seven-piece juice set. The pair to the left are glazed in Jubilee's shell pink and cream beige.

Plate 43
This juice pitcher in turquoise, shown alongside its larger counterpart, is a one-of-a-kind example, a legend among Fiesta collectors everywhere. (In the '50s, you could have had four or five new cars with the money this sold for a few years back!)

Plate 44
Disk Water Pitcher, Water Tumblers. Not original but added to the line in 1939, the disk water pitcher continued to be made until the end of production. It's very scarce in medium green and chartreuse and rather hard to find in the '50s colors. The tumblers were discontinued between '44 and '46, having been made since the onset of production, so they're found in the original six colors only, with turquoise perhaps being a little scarce. The pitcher holds two quarts, the tumblers ten ounces.

Plate 45
Relish Tray. Five individual sections fit into the base of the relish tray. Its round center is often mistaken for a coaster, and though we thought for years that the company never produced them with that use in mind (coasters were never listed on price brochures) at least once they did! The *Fiesta Collector's Quarterly* once reproduced a 1940s ad that offered a 13-piece beverage set: pitcher, six tumblers, and six coasters! Color make-up is important in determining the value of a relish tray. Red and dark blue are the most desirable base colors, and the more sections present in these colors, the higher the price. *2-Pint Jug.* The 2-pint jug (shown here in gray) was part of the original assortment. It was made until mid-'56, so it comes in all colors but medium green. *Ice Pitcher.* Made from 1936 until sometime between 1944 and 1946 in the original colors only, the ice pitcher is a little hard to find in ivory, but it's red and turquoise that top the price scale. Though its looks seem to suggest otherwise, it does not take a lid.

Plate 46
There are variations on the relish tray inserts, the most obvious is in the thickness of the walls. If you order one of these by mail, be sure to specify which you prefer, as they don't mix well and won't fit together properly. The thicker inserts are molded, so they usually carry the cast-indented mark — an integral part of the mold itself. The thinner ones were pressed by machine (a quicker and more economical method of production) and are usually not marked, though you will find some that are ink stamped. No doubt the thick ones are a little older, but this will have no bearing on value, at least to most collectors.

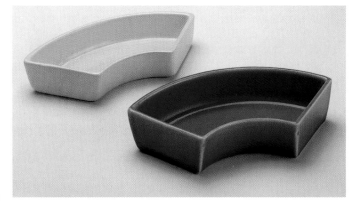

Plate 47

Cake Plate. The 10" cake plate is completely flat and very, very rare. We've never found it mentioned in any of the company's literature, but since it has only been found in the original five colors, it has to be an early piece. (Is there a turquoise example out there? We had one reported years ago, but advanced collectors are skeptical.) They're not marked, but one was reported bearing an original "Cake Kraft" label, and another bore the label shown in Plate 49.

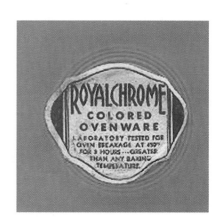

Plate 49

This is the label that was found on one of the cake plates — you may remember it from a very exciting eBay sale.

Plate 48

Handled Chop Plate. This is how the chop plate was marketed in the '39 – '43 selling campaign (so we're showing it here instead of in the Go-Alongs chapter). It was offered along with seven other items/sets at $1.00 or less each. The rattan-wrapped handles were of course manufactured by another company and shipped to HLC where they were fitted to these plates. They have been found in sizes to fit the 7", 9", and 10" plates (this size also fits the relish tray) as well as the 13" and 15" chop plates.

Plate 50

Compartment Plate, 12".
These were made from 1936 until mid-'37. They're not mentioned on the May 1937 price list and have never been reported in turquoise. They measure 11½" (actual measurement for a 12" plate). *Compartment Plate, 10½".* Not quite as scarce, this size replaced the larger one in mid-'37. It was dropped in 1956, three years before the advent of medium green. These measure very close to the listed size. *Chop Plate, 15".* Both chop plates were in the original assortment. This one

was discontinued early in 1956, so it is found in all colors except medium green. Actual measurement is 14¼". *Chop Plate, 13".* This size continued to be made until the restyling and can be found in all eleven colors, though it's rare in medium green. We had a photo of a stack of twelve to show you, belonging to a collector who has (choke) twelve of just about everything in medium green. We've searched everywhere for it, but it's been as impossible for us to find as that many medium green chop plates would be. (Sorry!) *Plates, 10", 9", 7", 6".* Plates have always been in good supply, however the 10" size is becoming harder to find. The number of rings within the foot area on the back of any Fiesta plate will vary; these identified the particular jigging machine that made it and were used for quality control purposes. Occasionally you may notice when you stack your plates that not all are the same depth. If there was a purpose for this variation, we're not aware of it. From the 10" down to the 6" size (they actually measure 10⅜", 9½", 7½", and 6½"), they're available in all eleven colors. Harlequin spruce green 10" and 6" plates have been found; the 6" plate is marked Fiesta.

Plate 51

Deep Plate.
The deep plate was an August 1936 item that continued in production until the restyling — it's 8¾" in diameter and found in all eleven colors. Most of us would call it a soup or salad bowl, though it is fairly shallow.

Plate 52
Recently discovered at an estate sale in Minnesota, this unlisted plate measures 11½". It's not from the new line, we're showing you the back — note the glazed foot ring, the saggar pin marks and the old trademark. The appearance from the front is line-for-line, ring-for-ring Fiesta, and the color is a perfect match for the vintage yellow.

Plate 56

Sauce Boat.

The sauce boat (gravy boat) was produced from 1937 until 1973 in all of Fiesta's colors, with red and the colors of the '50s most difficult to find. *Platter.* The 12½" was first listed in July 1938 and remained in production through the Ironstone phase. Though it was listed in the vintage line as 12" and in Ironstone as 13", collectors tell us the actual size never changed. It's easy to find in all eleven colors. *Utility Tray.* Added to the line in mid-'36, the utility tray (referred to as "celery tray" on Western price lists) was dropped from the line sometime between '44 and '46, so you'll find them in only the first six colors with red perhaps a bit hard to find. *Syrup.* Syrups rate very high with collectors. You'll find them in only the first six colors, and they're scarce in ivory. The

lids are plastic and some will fade with age; those in dark blue are especially bad as they tend to fade out to purple. Though it's a little hard to believe, considering the careful attention he paid to detail throughout the line, the syrup is the only piece of Fiesta that Rhead didn't design. The mold was bought from the DripCut Company, who made the tops for HLC as well. Other potteries, Vernon Kiln for one, also used this mold, and you'll find the same style in glass. (See the Miscellaneous chapter.) Decades ago, a tea company filled syrup bases with tea leaves, added a cork stopper and their label, and unwittingly contributed to the frustration of today's collectors who have have only a bottom. (See the chapter entitled Commercial Adaptations and Ephemera for a photo of one.) *Salt and Pepper Shakers.* These were made during the entire production period and can be found in all the Fiesta colors. Aside from the larger Kitchen Kraft shakers, this is the only style made in the Fiesta line. You may find a good imitation with holes on the side, but they are not genuine. Remember that Fiesta was widely copied, not only the bright glazes but often the band of rings as well. Though almost all shakers have the center hole, you'll find a few without. Virtually all are unmarked; only a very few have been reported with the "HLCo USA" marking, generally believed to indicate ware that was exported to Canada.

Plate 57

Sauce Boat Stand.

The sauce boat in this photo is from the original line, and may be found in all eleven colors. But the stand (underplate) didn't become available until the Ironstone line was introduced in 1969. Collectors pay dearly for one in Mango Red (shown here), since it makes a very desirable addition to any Fiesta collection. It measures 9" x 6½".

Plate 58

Teapot, Medium.

This size was added to the line in 1937 and was available throughout the entire production period. You'll find it in all eleven colors, though it's rare in medium green. *Teapot, Large.* This was in the original assortment. It was made only until sometime between '44 and '46, so it's found in just the first six colors. You will find some lids that have no vent holes.

Plate 59
Here's another knock-your-socks off shot, this time it's the large teapots in all the wonderful primary colors of the original assortment. (Photo by Craig Macaluso, Metairie, LA)

Plate 60
Tom and Jerry Mug.
These are sometimes referred to as coffee mugs; they were reported in Rhead's article (mid'-36) as being new to the line and continued in production until the end. They were made in all eleven colors, though ivory examples are scarce. Note the trademark ring handle. You'll find these will vary in thickness of the walls as well as height, as is evident in this photo. The example in Plate 61 is in maroon — one of a set of fifteen found with a matching punch bowl (the footed salad bowl, of course). It belonged to the widow of a former HLC manager who in addition to this unique Tom and Jerry set also owned a very large collection of Harlequin in maroon. This set was made to order match her Harlequin dinnerware.

Plate 61
Very Rare Maroon Tom and Jerry Mug.

Plate 62

Flower Vase, 8".

All three sizes of the flower vase were introduced in mid-'36 according to Rhead's magazine article we referenced back in the chapter entitled The Story of Fiesta. They're all very scarce and highly valued by collectors. This size continued longest in production — it was dropped between '44 and '46. *Flower Vase, 10".* This size was made only from mid-'36 until fall of 1942. One was recently found in ivory with red rings. *Flower Vase, 12".* This size was discontinued along with the 10" vase by the fall of 1942. All of these vases are available in only the first six colors. I can still remember finding a pair of 12" dark blue vases in an antique store in East Liverpool when we were doing our first research; we paid $7.00 for each them. *Bud Vase.* Part of the original line, the bud vase was discontinued between '44 and '46. It's fairly easy to find and was made in the first six colors. An unusual example in black was reported well before the new line debuted, and another was found in the brown-mottled orange shown later in the Experimentals, Samples, Trials, and Inventions chapter. It's 6¼" tall. Normally these all have a dry foot (no glaze on the foot ring), but we heard from a collector who has one entirely glazed over on the bottom.

Plate 63

Cream Soup.

This is a very rare, very desirable item — the most valuable of any medium green piece; in fact, in the entire Fiesta line it surpassed only by the covered onion soup in turquoise!

Plate 64

Over the past few years, we've had many newcomers who have asked for some help in sorting out all those greens. We've tried to show them side by side for the past several editions, without doing much toward clearing things up. This photo appeared in the Eighth Edition — exactly what went wrong, I'll never know, but the text and the photo didn't match up, and I apologize to you all who were more than a little dazed by the misinformation. Here is the correct order (left to right): chartreuse, light green, medium green, and dark green. If you are still confused, just look at our medium green cover!

Plate 65

We thought you'd enjoy seeing this full-page shot of some nice medium green items. This color is scarce and is considered very desirable by collectors today. Prices continue to increase for even the smallest items. Some pieces of Fiesta are very rare in medium green, for instance: the cream soup (see Plate 63), 6" bowl, 4¾" fruit, disk pitcher, casserole, and medium teapot. And, of course, since it was not introduced until '59 and many pieces had been discontinued by then, some items are simply not available in this color. Even to the most experienced eye, the difference between a heavy application of light green and an average coverage in medium green is sometimes a bit tricky to discern. Hopefully our wonderful new medium green cover on this edition will dispel the confusion once and for all.

Kitchen Kraft

Since the early 1930s, the Homer Laughlin China Company had been well known as manufacturers of a wide variety of ceramic kitchenwares. In 1939 they introduced a bake-and-serve line called Fiesta Kitchen Kraft as an extension of their already popular genuine Fiesta ware. This they offered in four original Fiesta colors — red, yellow, green, and blue. The following pieces (compiled from the April 1941 price list) were available:

Covered jars: small, medium, and large	Covered jug, large
Mixing bowls: 10", 8", and 6"	Spoon, fork, and cake server
Covered casseroles: 8½", 7½", and individual	Refrigerator set, 4-piece
Pie plate, 10"	Cake plate, 11"
Salt and pepper shakers, large	Plates: 6" and 9"

These were chosen from the standard assortment of kitchenware items which had been the basis of the many Kitchen Kraft and OvenServe decaled lines of years previous; none were created especially for Fiesta Kitchen Kraft. This line was in production for a relatively short period — perhaps being discontinued sometime during WWII prior to 1945.

In addition to the items listed above, there are at least three more to add. These may have been offered in the original assortment and discontinued by the 1941 listing. They are the oval platter in a chrome holder (which was shipped as a unit from HLC), a 9" pie plate, and a variation in size of the covered jug. The difference is so slight, even side by side it could go unnoticed. Collectors report as many of one size as the other. If you really want to label yours large or small, check the circumference. The larger one measures 21½" while the smaller one is 20".

The 6" and 9" plates listed on the 1941 illustrated brochure were used as underplates for the casseroles. When we visited the morgue at HLC, we saw examples of these. What we remembered was that they were of a thinner gauge with a moderately wide, slightly flared rim and seemed to have been taken from one of their other lines, since the style was not typically Kitchen Kraft. There are probably more questions raised about these underplates by collectors today than concerning any other item. In the last edition, we showed what seemed to be the elusive 6" underplate for the first time, not realizing then that it was the small Carnival plate. It looked perfectly correct: the double rings under the rim of the casserole complemented the double rings at the rim of the plate very well. The fact that there were three other reports of collectors buying the individual casserole with this plate seemed to reinforce the possibility that these actually were the elusive underplates we'd all been looking for so long. But now we're convinced otherwise. For one thing, no 9" Carnival plates have been reported to us — surely matching plates would have been used for both sizes. I searched through all our old research material to see if we had a photograph of the plates we saw in the morgue. And we did! They're like the ones on the Fiesta Kitchen Kraft brochure and exactly like the underplates in the decaled KK lines — all of which are Nautilus. Of the collectors I discussed this with, most agree that the correct underplate would be Nautilus (because of the two reasons I just mentioned), but since anyone has yet to see one in the Fiesta Kitchen Kraft colors, the consensus is that for some reason they were never actually marketed. Perhaps someday someone will have better answers, but after twenty-five years of research and study, we don't!

Over the years, collectors have reported finding the stacking refrigerator set, mixing bowls, 8½" casserole, salt and pepper shakers, pie plate, and other items in the ivory glaze. Just recently a large covered ivory jar as well as two more stacking refrigerator sets have been found. Ivory pieces are so rare that even a veteran collector who's spent twenty years concentrating on the more unusual items says that he has yet to see some of the items that have been reported to us. Collectors are split on the issue

of whether the glaze is truly ivory or more of a cream color (some describe them as ranging from a butterscotch ivory to a very light ivory); whatever your viewpoint, this was never listed as a standard Kitchen Kraft color, but at some point, an ivory line must have been produced, either separately or in conjunction with Fiesta Kitchen Kraft. No information exists to answer this question, at least that we're aware of. There is a white Kitchen Kraft line as well that's more often encountered than ivory. Of the four standard colors, dark blue is most in demand. Along with red, it represents the high side of the price range.

Plate 66

Mixing Bowls. The mixing bowls measure 10", 8", and 6" and have proven rather difficult to find. Note the original sticker on the large one (it's reproduced on page 38). They've been found in ivory as well as Harlequin, Jubilee, and Rhythm colors. They may or may not be marked. The 6" bowl was once used as an advertising piece for Wm. Jameson, Inc., N.Y., producers of Shorewood, 90 Proof Maryland Straight Rye Whiskey, the finest name in rye.

Plate 67

Cake Plate. These may or may not be marked — once in awhile you'll find one bearing a gold ink stamped "Fiesta HLC." The only hint of decoration is the narrow band around the edge formed by one indented ring. They are much easier to find than the regular, very rare Fiesta cake plate. *Pie Plates.* These come in two sizes: 10" and 9". Actually, they measure 10¼" and 9¾". (Read the chapter Dating Codes and English Measurements if this confuses you.) These  lack rings both inside and out and are usually not marked, though occasionally they will carry the gold mark. The 10" size has been reported in the maroon and spruce green of the Harlequin line. In the chapter called Go-Alongs, you'll see the metal frame that was sometimes shipped along with the pie plates directly from the factory. It is very unusual to find the small size in the Fiesta KK colors; it is more often found in ivory decorated with decals.

Plate 68

Casseroles. These come in three sizes: 8½", 7½", and individual. All are scarce. In Plate 69 you'll see the lid in greater detail.

Plate 69

Casserole Variations.

This 8½" casserole has a base with variations from the standard mold in that the lip is recessed, and this one has no mark. A variation on the individual casserole was reported as well: the two rings under the rim of the bowl are placed higher, and the knob on the lid is more recessed. It has the usual embossed mark.

Plate 70

Covered Jars.

To determine the size of your covered jar, measure the circumference. The large jar measures 27½", the medium 22", and the small one 17½". Lid detail is evident in Plate 71.

Plate 71

Here you'll see the lid in better detail. These are becoming hard to find in mint condition.

Plate 72

Covered Jug.

There are two sizes of these jugs, but the differences are subtle. The circumference of the larger is 21½"; the smaller jug measures 20".

Plate 73

Platter. This is the 13" oval platter, shown here in Harlequin spruce green, not a standard Kitchen Kraft color. They're very, very rare in this color. A few have been found in Harlequin yellow, and one has been reported in mauve blue. Even in the regular four colors, they're scarce, and they're not usually marked. The metal holder is an HLC issue, though, of course, not all of these platters were sold in a frame.

Plate 74

Servers: Spoon, Cake Lifter, Fork.
These are hard to find, especially in mint condition. Their handles are embossed with the same flowers as one of the OvenServe lines. One spoon has been found in ivory, not to be confused with the white spoons regularly found in the OvenServe lines. If you find one of these marked "CS" on the back, it is from a line of limited edition collectibles called Ovenserve Style Utensils, made for a private company, China Specialties, Inc. These were made in colors to match both old and new — old turquoise, old ivory, medium green, and lilac. Other colors may follow. These were not made by Homer Laughlin. *Salt and Pepper Shakers.* Look familiar? These are larger versions of their Fiesta dinnerware counterparts, although by no means are they as plentiful. These have been found in Harlequin yellow as well, but such a find is very unusual.

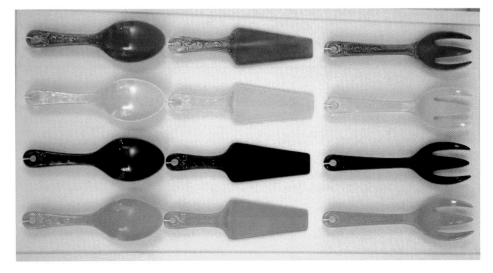

Plate 75
Here's how the completed set looks — something you certainly don't see everyday! A spoon has been reported in dark green and a cake lifter in turquoise, both extremely rare.

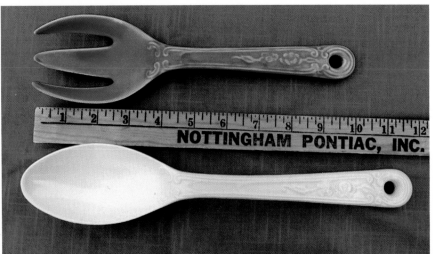

Plate 76
Spoon Variation.
Here's another version of the serving spoon — very rare indeed. It's slightly more narrow than the standard style and 11½" long. As far as we know, there are very few of these in ivory and white, one with decals, and another in turquoise which the owner says came from the Well's estate. He also tells us that he has seen a brochure from Homer Laughlin that shows a light green example. We've heard only rumors of a fork and pie server in a size that corresponds; they may not exist at all. We would enjoy hearing from anyone who has information on these items.

Plate 77
Stack Set (Refrigerator Jars). The covered refrigerator stack set consists of three units and a flat lid and is usually made up of all four Kitchen Kraft colors. See the most unusual example in Plate 78!

Plate 78
A very, very rare stack set — all four pieces in ivory!

Plate 80

How's this for a pristine example? This spoon not only has the elusive paper label in mint condition, it's also marked on the back: HLCo USA. In this condition and with the label, expect to pay at least double the suggested book value — add even more for the ink stamp — if you're ever lucky enough to find one like this! On top of all these attributes, one of our advisors in this survey is convinced that yellow is the hard color to find these in.

Plate 79

Ironstone

In 1969 Fiesta was restyled. Changes were made to some of the molds, and the size of the line was drastically reduced. A company flyer illustrated with photos of the entire Fiesta Ironstone assortment — nineteen items in all — and dated July 1, 1969, indicates that the line hit the market several months sooner than we once thought.

There were many factors that of necessity brought about this change. Labor and production costs had risen sharply. Efforts to hold these expenses down influenced the selection of colors. Fiesta red was retained but now called mango red. To complement the red, two additional colors were selected, antique gold and turf green, both of which were in use at that time for several other lines of dinnerware HLC was producing. These three colors fired at or about the same temperature, a significant cost-saving measure in contrast to the separate firings required for the older Fiesta colors. (It was pointed out to us as we toured the factory that since each of the old colors were fired at various temperatures, orders were running ahead of production for Fiesta as well as other lines.) These pieces were offered in antique gold only: covered casserole, tea server (teapot), water jug (disk pitcher), coffee server, and 10¼" salad bowl. To further economize, all markings were eliminated. (You will very seldom find a piece of Ironstone with the Fiesta stamp; the few that are marked were probably made during the transition from the original line to Ironstone.)

The restyled pieces had a more contemporary feeling — bowls were flared, and applied handles were only partial rings. The covered casserole had molded, closed handles, and the handles had been eliminated entirely from the sugar bowl. The covered coffee server made a return appearance after an absence of several years. Four additional items quickly supplemented the original nineteen for a total of twenty-three. The oval platter that was listed as 12" in the original line was now listed as 13". (In reality, the actual measurement was always 12½".) New items included the soup/cereal, the sauce boat stand, and the 10" salad bowl.

Finally in November 1972, all production of Fiesta/mango red was discontinued because many of the original technicians who developed this color and maintained control over the complicated manufacturing and firing processes had retired, and modern mass-production methods were unsuited to produced it successfully. On January 1, 1973, the famous line of Fiesta dinnerware was discontinued altogether.

Because Ironstone was made for a relatively short time, it is not easy to find. Red mugs and the sauce boat stand in any color are regarded as good pieces. Red is the most difficult color to find; green is scarce in some pieces, and gold, being the only color the complete assortment was made in, is the most available. You may find cups with the Ironstone handle in Fiesta yellow, medium green, and turquoise. (For a complete listing of available items, see Suggested Values in the back of the book.)

Plate 81

Amberstone

Amberstone was introduced in 1967, three years before the Fiesta line was restyled; yet the illustration on an old order blank shows that the sugar and creamer, cup, teapot, soup/cereal, casserole, and coffee server were from the same molds that were later used for Fiesta Ironstone. Only on the pieces that had relatively flat areas large enough to permit decoration do you find the black, machine-stamped underglaze pattern. The remainder were simply solid brown. Some of the hollow ware pieces are found with the familiar Fiesta cast-indented trademark.

Sold under the trade name of Genuine Sheffield dinnerware, it was produced by HLC exclusively for supermarket promotions; and several large grocery store chains featured Amberstone as a premium. (For a listing of items offered, see Suggested Values in back of book.)

Plate 82

Plate 83

Plate 84

Plate 85

Plate 86

Plate 87

Plate 88

Additional Amberstone Shapes.
The marmalade is shown in Plate 86 and the mustard (alongside salt and pepper shakers for size comparison) in Plate 85. Note the Ironstone pieces: casserole, flared fruit bowl, salad bowl (in Plate 89), mug, and sauce boat stand. We'd reported in previous editions that the elusive mug had a Fiesta ring handle, based on line drawings in a brochure the company gave us years ago. In Plate 87 you can see that we were in error. There's an oddity in Plate 88, an Amberstone cup with an old Fiesta handle; we've also had a report of a Nautilus cup in Amberstone brown. The sauce boat is sometimes marked Fiesta; and an unusual 13" chop plate has been found without the decal.

Plate 89
This is the Amberstone salad bowl — very few have been found.
Photo by Harvey Linn, Jr.

 *Casualstone*

In 1970 Homer Laughlin produced a second line of dinnerware to be sold exclusively through supermarket promotions. This dinnerware was called Casualstone and was presented under the trade name Coventry. The antique gold of the Fiesta Ironstone was decorated with an intricate gold machine-stamped design which, like Amberstone, appeared on only the shallow items. An old order blank shows that it was less expensive than the Amberstone of three years previous, possibly because a color already in production was used. (For a listing of available items, see Suggested Values in back of book.)

Plate 90

46

Casuals

There were two designs produced in the beautiful Fiesta Casuals; and although they are both relatively difficult to find, often when they are found the set will be complete, or nearly so. They were introduced in June 1962; and as sales were only moderately active, they were discontinued around 1968. The Plaid Stamp Company featured both lines in their illustrated catalogs during these years.

The Hawaiian 12-Point Daisy design featured a ½" turquoise band at the rim and turquoise daisies with brown centers on a white background. The other pattern was Yellow Carnation which featured the yellow flowers with a touch of brown on a white background. A yellow rim band completed the design. In each line, only the dinner plates, salad plates, saucers, and oval platters were decorated; the cups, fruit dishes, nappies, sugar bowls, and creamers were simply glazed in the matching Fiesta color. The designs were hand sprayed and overglazed using a lead mask with the cut-out motif. A complete service consisted of six place settings: dinner plate, salad plate, cup and saucer, and 5½" fruit. A platter, 8½" nappy, and the sugar and creamer were also included. (For a listing of available items, see Suggested Values in back of book.)

GENUINE

fiesta

**H. L. Co. USA
CASUAL**

Plate 91
Hawaiian 12-Point Daisy Design.

Plate 92
Yellow Carnation Design. The correct cups to use with these lines are those without the inside rings!

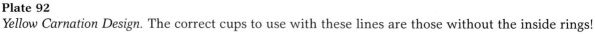 ## Striped

This line was obviously produced sometime before the fall of 1937, since the covered onion soup bowls were discontinued at that time. This dinnerware is very rare, and by far the vast majority is done with red stripes. The coffeepot in blue is very unusual. In addition to the items in our photos, a large comport, 10" vase, footed salad bowl, and bulb and tripod candleholders have also been reported. The stripes are well done and generally show no wear. You may find some plates with stripes that are over the glaze — one at the rim and a wider one inside the band of rings; these are usually very worn and have little value.

Plate 93
Coffeepot.

Plate 94
Covered Onion Soup Bowl.

Plate 95
Assorted Grouping.

 *Decals*

Here and on the following pages are examples of Fiesta with decals. You'll find many other examples as well. They may have been decorated by HLC, but more than likely the work was done by smaller decorating companies — there were several in the immediate vicinity.

Plate 96
Turkey Plates. We are sure that these were decorated by Homer Laughlin. Shown are the 9" plate with a maroon band, a 13" chop plate with the yellow band, and Kitchen Kraft cake plate that is trimmed in gold. The 15" chop plate has also been reported with the turkey decal, as has a Rhythm platter. All are very rare.

Plate 97
Butterfly Tidbit Tray.
With the addition of the center handle, the chop plate
is converted to a tidbit. Eight gold butterflies and gold
stripes complete the look.

Plate 98
Relish Tray.
Relish trays seem to have been a favorite item to decal,
as we have seen several; this one is especially attractive.

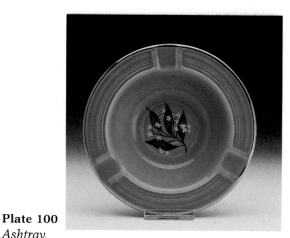

Plate 100
Ashtray.
Shown in the blue of Skytone with the Stardust
pattern. Blue lines were popular during the
'40s and '50s.

Plate 99
Demitasse Cup and Saucer.
Items with this decal
are becoming an area
of collecting interest all
their own, regardless
of which company's
mark they carry — it
was used not only to
decorate some of HLC's
lines but other companies'
as well. Much of this ware
was decorated by Royal China,
who often added their mark to that
of the pottery company. HLC's Georgian
line has been found with this decal, so have items marked
W.S. George, and there are others. In past editions we have
featured cake sets made up of the 15" Fiesta chop plate and
six matching dessert plates — one set in ivory, a second in
yellow. This decal has not been limited to dinnerware;
you'll often see lamps, vases, and other assorted pieces with
variations of this theme. The gold work on this piece is not
typical, usually the background is left undecorated; sometimes rim stripes or wide gold bands are added.

Plate 101
Sweets Comport Plate.

Plate 102
Juice Set in Original Box.
Anytime you find anything in the original carton it's a special treat! Not only is this the hard-to-find Jubilee color assortment, but each piece is decaled as well.

Plate 103
Tom and Jerry Set.
This is the large footed salad bowl and the Tom and Jerry mugs — a set that is hard to find compete. HLC made another set as well, but on shapes other than Fiesta. Values for the set shown here are listed in the Fiesta line-up; a picture of the second set we mentioned is shown in the Miscellaneous Chapter.

Plate 104
Calendar Plates.
HLC issued calendar plates for a number of years, using whatever blanks were available. In 1945 and 1955, they just happened to use Fiesta. The 9" plate in the center is the rare size; it may be found for either year. The 1954 plate has been found in ivory only; the 1955 may be green, yellow, or ivory.

51

Lustre

Every now and then over the past twenty-five years a piece or two of Fiesta with allover lustre decoration has been reported. Several small firms in the vicinity of HCL specialized in decorating ware from the area's several potteries and china companies — no doubt one (or more) of them are responsible for these pieces. We have file photos of a 2-pint jug and an egg cup that both sport silver lustre treatments. Other collectors told us about a dinnerware set they had acquired that they were able to trace back to 1948. It was in cobalt with gold bands and consisted of 7" plates, dinner plates, 4" fruits, teacups, and teapot.

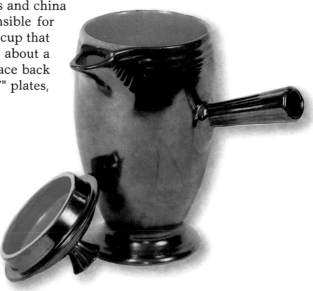

Plate 105
Demitasse Pot.
This was originally Fiesta red — as you can see inside — but it's now glazed in a copper-bronze lustre, and we know of another with silver over its original green.

Plate 106
Relish Tray.
The tray itself was once ivory, the inserts dark blue — now the entire tray is glazed in silver. All but one piece is impressed with the Fiesta trademark.

Plate 107
2-Pint Jug.
Silver lustre again, this time over turquoise.

52

New Fiesta — Post86

After a 13-year absence, Fiesta was reintroduced to the market on February 28, 1986. Its Art Deco style, which had looked somewhat dated in 1973 when the Fiesta Ironstone line was discontinued, had again become the rage in home decoration. Only a short time before this, several lines of solid color dinnerware had been introduced by competitors (including Moderna by Mikasa and a line-for-line interpretation of Fiesta by Rego China made for the restaurant trade). Sample items were produced and dipped in a number of colors to gauge consumer preferences at a Chicago trade show in December 1985. Gray and yellow were also tested in addition to the five winning colors of cobalt blue (darker and denser than the original), rose (a true pink), white, apricot (a pale tannish peach), and black. Interest was deemed great enough to begin production. In order to appeal to the restaurant trade, HLC made a last-minute decision to go with a vitrified body (as opposed to the semi-vitrified body used for the original Fiesta).While vitrified china is denser and will not absorb moisture, it also has to be fired at a higher temperature and shrinks more during firing. Because of this, new molds had to be designed for the dinner plates to keep them at 10½". The higher firing also caused some shapes to have a tendency to deform or sag. Thus the Ironstone-style casserole, sugar bowl, coffee server, and flat teapot lid had to be redesigned. The original brochure (see Plate 110) had photographs of the semi-vitrified samples and showed a casserole with handles in the Ironstone style. But this particular item was never produced in the new line; instead it was restyled into the covered casserole shown in Plate 111. The coffee server was replaced by the restyled version. (See Plate 114 for both styles — the restyle is in the foreground.) Today the original (old style) coffee server has a market value of approximately $200.00. Note the differences in the finials. The original has the Ironstone-type knob, while the restyle has the more familiar flared, fluted knob from the old Fiesta line. This fluted knob eventually became standard on virtually every item in the line that took a lid. The sugar bowl was replaced with one made from the old marmalade mold (without the notch for the spoon) in the first few months of production. See the 1987 brochure which shows the actual shapes of the new Fiesta casserole, sugar bowl, coffee server, and teapot lid in Plate 111.

Note: The term now accepted within the collecting community is Post86. This encompasses all Fiesta items produced after February 1986. We use "Post86" and "new Fiesta" interchangeably throughout our text.

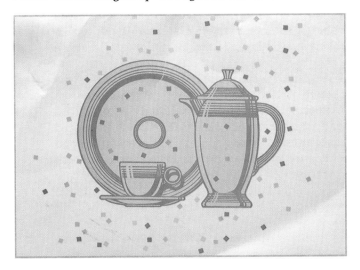

Plate 108
Less than three hundred of these invitations were sent out for the exhibition that unveiled the new Fiesta line. They were from the Governor of the state of West Virginia Arch A. Moore, Jr. Imagine the thrill of receiving one!

THE HOMER LAUGHLIN CHINA COMPANY: A FIESTA OF AMERICAN DINNERWARE is the Department of Culture and History's celebration of a major West Virginia industry.
A leader in design and production in the nation for more than a hundred years, the company's achievements stem from 1870 when the Laughlin brothers, Homer and Shakespeare, dared to produce American dinnerware fine enough to challenge English imports.
The culmination of the latest in design and technology, Homer Laughlin Company's Fiesta provided brightness and flair in a Depression-weary world, and was affordable to everyone. Energetically sought by collectors today, its color, design and uniqueness make Fiesta collectible at any price.

Governor Arch A. Moore, Jr.

invites you to share in the opening festivities of

"The Homer Laughlin China Company: A Fiesta of American Dinnerware"

a major exhibition presented by the
Department of Culture and History
Saturday, March 9, 1985
8:00 p.m.

The Cultural Center
State Capitol Complex
Charleston, West Virginia

Reception immediately following ribbon-cutting

R.S.V.P.   Entertainment

Plate 109

Post86 Fiesta Colors

Over the years, ten new colors have been added to the 1986 assortment of white, black, rose, apricot, and cobalt blue. Nine are included in the following listing, along with the year of their introduction.

Yellow (very pale and creamy)..1987
Turquoise (darker, with more of a green cast than the old color) 1988
Periwinkle blue (pastel gray-blue)..1989
Sea Mist green (pale mint or Jade-ite green 1991
Lilac (a rich, deep lavender tone, a limited two-year color) ....1994 – 95
Persimmon (a reddish coral shade) 1996
Chartreuse (brighter than the old, a limited two-year color)...........1997 – 99
Pearl gray (only slightly lighter than vintage gray) 1999
Juniper (a deep teal green, a limited two-year color)...................1999 – 2001

The entire assortment of pieces which were in the line at the respective times were produced in the colors listed above. The tenth color, sapphire (a bright blue, slightly lighter and more brilliant than the 1930s cobalt) was very limited. It was produced exclusively for Bloomingdale's during the winter of 1996 in a narrow selection of pieces. Unlike the lilac, chartreuse, and juniper which were produced for two full years, sapphire was limited to 180 firing days, and sapphire was only available in the following items: five-piece place settings, 13½" oval platter, 32-ounce serving bowl, large disk pitcher, 6½-ounce tumbler, medium flower vase, wall clock, handled serving tray, and the newly restyled carafe. In addition, the jumbo 18-ounce cup and saucer from the Fiesta-Mates line were also dipped in sapphire. To collectors' consternation, no sugar and creamer or salt and pepper were ever produced in sapphire.

There is one more color, raspberry, which was officially produced in only one item, the presentation bowl pictured in Plate 125. Five hundred of these were produced by HLC in December of 1998 to celebrate the 500 millionth piece of Fiesta that had been manufactured since 1936. The bowls were donated to three charity auctions to benefit education scholarship funds in the Newell/East Liverpool area in June and August of 1999. And while the bowls at these charity auctions went for $5,000.00 +, it should be remembered that many purchasers were not collectors of Fiesta but wealthy benefactors with ties to the town, the local college, or the Aaron and Wells families, and prices realized at these particular auctions did not necessarily reflect the values of the bowls themselves, but were in actuality donations to the towns' scholarship funds. Subsequent sales between private individuals that have taken place at lower amounts do not reflect a decline in the value of the raspberry presentation bowl but an elimination of the dollar value of the substantial charitable donation layer found on the ones sold at the charity auction.

Homer Laughlin discontinued apricot in December 1997, and we already see apricot trading for a small premium over currently produced colors, even though it was made in large amounts over the course of eleven years. HLC tells us that black is on non-stock status, meaning it will only be produced to order several times a year and will require a longer lead time for orders, rather than being produced and carried in stock. They also say that black may be discontinued at any time in the near future and that it is only available in a limited number of items. Items once made but no longer available in black include the napkin rings, clock, medium vase, coffee server, handled carafe, bud vase, round (bulb) candle holders, after dinner cup and saucer, pyramid (tripod) candle holders, and the small disk pitcher. Newer items added after 1996 such as the 2-cup teapot and pedestal bowl were never officially made in black or apricot.

In 1987 Homer Laughlin decided to try a Christmas line featuring Fiesta. White Fiesta was decorated with a green holly decal and red piping at the edge. The line was not a huge success for most retailers and was produced for the 1987 Christmas season only. The decoration was redesigned to include a larger sprig of holly that incorporated a red ribbon, and it was reintroduced to the market in 1989. The newly redesigned Holiday Fiesta has been more successful than the original design and is currently available from Homer Laughlin. The original 1987 Holiday Fiesta is shown in Plate 129; the redesign is in Plate 128.

Post86 Fiesta Shapes

Many new items and shapes have been added to the line since 1986, some of them designed for the restaurant trade. The original 1986 assortment of pieces as well as some (not all) subsequent additions are shown on the company flyer on page 60. To help identify the new colors, we've also shown the flyer front (page 59).

The following items, along with their official item code number, are the full Post86 Fiesta assortment as of summer of 2000.

Item No.	Description	Item No.	Description
0463	Plate, B&B, 6⅛"	0766	Tripod Bowl
0464	Plate, Salad, 7¼"	0476	Cup, A.D., Stick, 3-oz.
0465	Plate, Luncheon, 9"	0452	Cup, 7¾-oz.
0466	Plate, Dinner, 10½"	0453	Mug, 10¼-oz.
0467	Chop Plate, 11¾"	0149	Jumbo Cup, 18-oz. (*)
0460	Snack Plate with well, 10½"	0098	Chili Bowl, no handle, 18-oz. (*)
0456	Platter, 9⅝"		(Jumbo Cup without a handle)
0457	Platter, 11⅝"	0424	Pedestal Mug, 18-oz.
0458	Platter, 13⅝"	0446	Tumbler, 6½-oz.
0468	Round Serving Tray, 11"	0497	S&P Set
0753	Hostess Tray, 12¼"	0821	Sugar and Cream on Tray Set
0505	Pizza Tray, 15"	0479	Sugar Packet Holder (*)
0765	Pedestal Bowl, 9⅞", 64-oz.	0492	Individual Cream, 7-oz.
0460	Bowl, Small, 5⅝", 14¼-oz.	0469	Napkin Rings, 4-Piece Set
0461	Bowl, Medium, 6⅞", 19-oz.	0486	Sauce Boat, 18½-oz.
0471	Bowl, Large, Serving, 8¼", 40-oz.	0488	Round Candlestick Holder, 3⅝"
0455	Bowl, Extra Large, Serving, 2-qt.	0487	Deep Dish Pie Baker, 10¼"
0421	Small Mixing Bowl, 7½", 44-oz.	0490	Bud Vase, 6"
0422	Medium Mixing Bowl, 8½", 60-oz.	0491	Medium Vase, 9⅝"
0482	Large Mixing Bowl, 9½", 70-oz. (same as covered casserole base)	0484	Disc Pitcher, Large, 67¼-oz.
		0485	Disc Pitcher, Small, 28-oz.
0495	Covered Casserole, 70-oz.	0475	Mini Disc Pitcher, 5-oz.
0462	Rim Pasta Bowl, 12", 21-oz.	0448	Carafe with Handle, 60-oz.
0451	Rim Soup, 9", 13¼-oz.	0493	Covered Coffee, 36-oz.
0459	Fruit, 5⅜", 6¼-oz.	0496	Covered Teapot, 44-oz.
0472	Stacking Cereal Bowl, 6½", 11-oz.	0764	Teapot, 2-Cup
0450	Bouillon, 6¾-oz.	0499	Relish Tray, 9½-oz.
0470	Saucer, 5⅞"	0756	Range Top Salt and Pepper, Handled
0477	Saucer, A.D., 4⅞"	0473	China Face Wall Clock
0293	Jumbo Saucer, 6¾" (*)	0409	12" Oval Serving Bowl

Each of these items are pictured individually on the official Homer Laughlin Fiesta Page on the Internet at http://www.hlchina.com/fiestaitems.htm, should you have access to the web and wish to see them in detail.

In addition, a boxed child's set called My First Fiesta® is available and consists of the following:
1 Teapot, Yellow (2-cup, same as 0764)
2 Teacups, Rose and Periwinkle (demi cups with a ring rather than stick handle)
2 Saucers, Rose and Periwinkle (same as adult size A.D. saucer 0477)
1 Creamer, Turquoise
Sugar Bowl, Turquoise
2 – 6" Plates, Yellow (same as bread and butter plate 0463)

A number of items were borrowed from the restaurant line and dipped in Fiesta colors to fulfill the needs of the food service industry. These were named Fiesta Mates. They will lack the concentric rings or other elements of typical Fiesta styling and will be marked with the Homer Laughlin backstamp rather than the Fiesta mark shown below. They include the Tower mug, the Denver mug, Seville 3½-oz. ramekin, 10" oval baker, skillet server, Irish coffee mug, 18-oz. Colonial teapot, and 5-oz. jug creamer. Items in the list on page 55 (sugar packet holder, jumbo cup and saucer, chili bowl) marked with an asterisk (*) are items from the Fiesta Mates line which have been incorporated into the official Fiesta assortment since late 1999.

Other Fiesta items will no doubt be designed and introduced as retailers request them. All of the above pieces are marked Fiesta (including cups) with the exception of the four Fiesta Mates indicated with the asterisk. The cast-indented mark is very similar to the old; the ink-stamped items are marked with a newer version that is shown here. Notice that all letters are upper case — contrast this with the original Fiesta script marks on page 15.

GENUINE

FIESTA

H•L•Co

U.S.A.

～～～～～

New or Old? — Vintage or Post86?

Because there was so much variation in the old vintage turquoise glaze and because the new pearl gray is so close to the vintage gray, these two colors (and to a lesser extent, sapphire and new cobalt) are the ones most likely to cause any confusion to a collector of the old. Only those pieces that are still being made from the old, original molds will carry the old-style in-mold mark (such as the disk water and juice pitchers, medium and bud vases, pyramid and bulb candle holders and sauce boat). In response to collector's concerns about the similarity of the old and new gray glaze colors, concurrent with the introduction of pearl gray in 1999, Homer Laughlin as added a raised "H" to the underside of those items that shared the old-style molds with the old-style mark to distinguish them from vintage ware. This was added to the mold and thus is found on all colors of these items made in 1999 and later. They may, however, be obscured by a heavy application of glaze. In addition, turquoise, cobalt, and sapphire were produced for a number of years prior to the "H" being added, so newer collectors may need to compare some items (such as the new medium vase to a supposed vintage medium vase) to verify the age of such an expensive piece before purchase. All the new items will be slightly smaller and feel relatively heavier than the old, due to the vitrified clay body used since 1986. (Vitrification relates to the temperature of firing — new Fiesta is fired hotter, thus the clay particles tend to fuse together and become more glasslike. Less air is captured in the clay body, making each item slightly heavier, smaller, and more durable. Because it is more dense, it does not absorb moisture or bacteria, thus making it suitable for restaurant use.)

If you can't compare colors and sizes when shopping, remember that saggar pin marks and a fully glazed foot always indicate old Fiesta. (Homer Laughlin just doesn't use saggar pins anymore.) To clarify, old Fiesta plates, for instance, always had a fully glazed foot (the part of the plate that touched the table), and in the firing process, the old plates had to be propped up on three little pins called saggars so they would not fuse themselves to the kiln shelf when the glaze melted during firing. This left the three little scars (or saggar pin marks) on the underside of the plates and under the rims of the vintage bowls we are all so familiar with. New Fiesta pieces all have a dry or wiped foot; there is no glaze covering the area that touches the table. Old tripod candlesticks almost always had a fully glazed foot and three saggar pin scars on the underside; new ones will always have a dry, wiped foot. Even compared to those items which in the vintage line had a wiped foot (the bulb candlesticks, tall and bud vases, pitchers, and sauce boats, for instance), the new ones display a raw clay that has a bit more shine and is brighter white than the clay used to make the old line. In addition, old items were dipped in the glaze by hand, whereas the glaze on the new Fiesta is sprayed on. It is often possible to see the speckled spray pattern on new items, especially under the handles of the pitchers, etc., or under the foot of items like the candle holders, sauce boats, or bud vases.

Specially Decorated Fiesta

You may find various decorations on Fiesta (produced not only by Homer Laughlin but after-marketing firms as well). Specially decorated and crested Fiesta such as the Cookies for Santa snack set and the Bunnies child's place setting pictured in Plate 139 will continue to be designed and brought to market by Homer Laughlin. In addition, you may find exclusive designs done by after-market decorating firms (such as the pieces pictured in Plate 143) as well as several lines done especially for China Specialities, including versions of Sunporch and Mexicana, a new release, both on white Fiesta. (See Plates 144 and 145.)

Licensed Fiesta Accessories

Homer Laughlin licensed several companies to use the name "Genuine Fiesta Accessories." These were initially limited to the items shown in Plate 132, a rather restrained offering of table linens and a metal diner-type napkin dispenser. Since 1997, however, they have licensed many, many firms to produce a plethora of items from glass, acrylic, cloth, wood, resin, plastic, metal, enamelware, wax, and paper, as well as numerous electrical appliances — even a steam iron. (See Plate 133.) Some ceramic items (like the small hurricane lamp and picture frames) are from China; they were not made at HLC. Several items are made of a dense, heavy synthetic resin that might appear to the inexperienced collector to be ceramic (for instance, the miniature items or the picnic tablecloth weights). The variety of these items is mind boggling, and we won't even attempt to survey the scope of them all at this writing. Some were specially designed to coordinate with Fiesta's design elements (for example, the enamel cookware); some share only the colors of Fiesta (like the electric waffle iron); and some have only the Fiesta name emblazoned on the side (like the black and chrome '50s-style steam iron). Many of the accessory items have been very well received while others haven't. As of this writing, a number of them are now being discontinued by some major retailers and are available at liquidation stores. If these appeal to you, buy them — especially when they can be found at liquidations at a fraction of their original price. They will no doubt be of interest to collectors at some point in the future as curiosities. It is unlikely that some of the more unpopular or impractical items will be made again.

Editor's note: We are very grateful to Joel Wilson (China Specialties, Inc., and the *Fiesta Collector's Quarterly*) for supplying us with this up-to-date information as well as many photographs. Because of the lapse between the time we release our book to the publishers and when it actually hits the market, changes to the line may have occurred in the interim.

The *Fiesta Collector's Quarterly* is a newsletter published by China Specialties for collectors of old and new Fiesta and features regular updates on color and item additions to the new Fiesta line. A sample copy and subscription form are available free upon receipt of a self-addressed, stamped, long envelope. The address for the newsletter is Fiesta Collector's Quarterly, P.O. Box 471, Valley City, OH 44280. China Specialities is an Ohio company catering to the interests of collectors of a number of locally produced dinnerware lines of the 1930s and 1940s. They also publish the *Hall China and Tea Company China Collector Club Newsletter* and commission and distribute dated, limited edition shapes never originally produced in such patterns as Autumn Leaf, Red Poppy, Orange Poppy, Silhouette, and Blue Bouquet. They are also the exclusive source for Hot Oven China rolling pins. In addition, several of the specially decorated Fiesta collector items shown in this section were made exclusively for China Specialties.

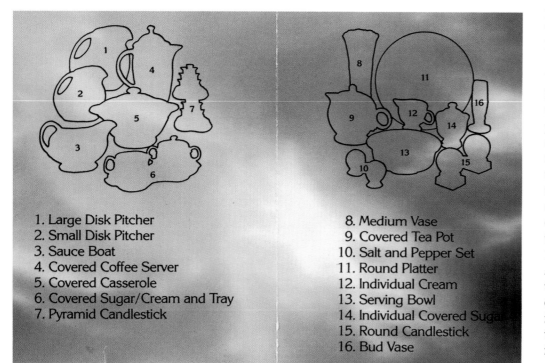

1. Large Disk Pitcher
2. Small Disk Pitcher
3. Sauce Boat
4. Covered Coffee Server
5. Covered Casserole
6. Covered Sugar/Cream and Tray
7. Pyramid Candlestick

8. Medium Vase
9. Covered Tea Pot
10. Salt and Pepper Set
11. Round Platter
12. Individual Cream
13. Serving Bowl
14. Individual Covered Sugar
15. Round Candlestick
16. Bud Vase

Plate 110
The original advertising brochure from the February 1986 introduction party at the West Virginia Cultural Center in Charleston. These publicity photographs were of sample items made from semi-vitreous clay that never made it into regular production. (Note the old-style teapot lid, Ironstone-style sugar bowl, casserole, and coffee server, and compare them to those shown in the 1987 brochure, Plate 111.) After these pictures were taken, the company made a decision to use a fully vitrified body in order to make the line more appealing to the food industry.

Reproduced by permission of the Homer Laughlin China Company.

Plate 111
This is an advertising brochure from 1987 that shows actual items being produced from the vitreous clay. Note that the original coffeepot lid is now being used on the teapot (the dome shape deformed less than the original flat lid), and the casserole and coffee server as well as the sugar bowl have been changed from the examples in the previous brochure.

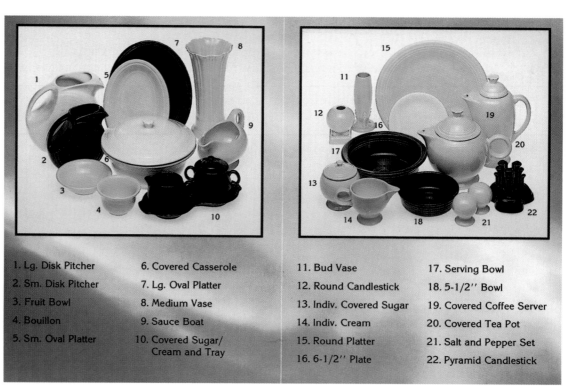

1. Lg. Disk Pitcher
2. Sm. Disk Pitcher
3. Fruit Bowl
4. Bouillon
5. Sm. Oval Platter

6. Covered Casserole
7. Lg. Oval Platter
8. Medium Vase
9. Sauce Boat
10. Covered Sugar/Cream and Tray

11. Bud Vase
12. Round Candlestick
13. Indiv. Covered Sugar
14. Indiv. Cream
15. Round Platter
16. 6-1/2" Plate

17. Serving Bowl
18. 5-1/2" Bowl
19. Covered Coffee Server
20. Covered Tea Pot
21. Salt and Pepper Set
22. Pyramid Candlestick

Reproduced by permission of the Homer Laughlin China Company.

Plate 112
Front of company flyer, ca 1996.

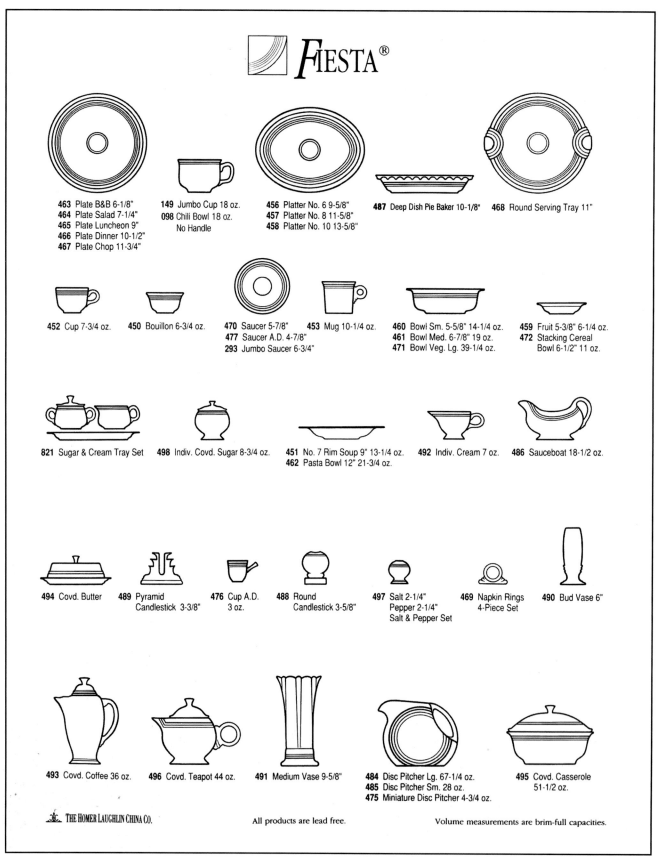

FIESTA®

463 Plate B&B 6-1/8"
464 Plate Salad 7-1/4"
465 Plate Luncheon 9"
466 Plate Dinner 10-1/2"
467 Plate Chop 11-3/4"

149 Jumbo Cup 18 oz.
098 Chili Bowl 18 oz.
No Handle

456 Platter No. 6 9-5/8"
457 Platter No. 8 11-5/8"
458 Platter No. 10 13-5/8"

487 Deep Dish Pie Baker 10-1/8"

468 Round Serving Tray 11"

452 Cup 7-3/4 oz.

450 Bouillon 6-3/4 oz.

470 Saucer 5-7/8"
477 Saucer A.D. 4-7/8"
293 Jumbo Saucer 6-3/4"

453 Mug 10-1/4 oz.

460 Bowl Sm. 5-5/8" 14-1/4 oz.
461 Bowl Med. 6-7/8" 19 oz.
471 Bowl Veg. Lg. 39-1/4 oz.

459 Fruit 5-3/8" 6-1/4 oz.
472 Stacking Cereal
Bowl 6-1/2" 11 oz.

821 Sugar & Cream Tray Set

498 Indiv. Covd. Sugar 8-3/4 oz.

451 No. 7 Rim Soup 9" 13-1/4 oz.
462 Pasta Bowl 12" 21-3/4 oz.

492 Indiv. Cream 7 oz.

486 Sauceboat 18-1/2 oz.

494 Covd. Butter

489 Pyramid
Candlestick 3-3/8"

476 Cup A.D.
3 oz.

488 Round
Candlestick 3-5/8"

497 Salt 2-1/4"
Pepper 2-1/4"
Salt & Pepper Set

469 Napkin Rings
4-Piece Set

490 Bud Vase 6"

493 Covd. Coffee 36 oz.

496 Covd. Teapot 44 oz.

491 Medium Vase 9-5/8"

484 Disc Pitcher Lg. 67-1/4 oz.
485 Disc Pitcher Sm. 28 oz.
475 Miniature Disc Pitcher 4-3/4 oz.

495 Covd. Casserole
51-1/2 oz.

THE HOMER LAUGHLIN CHINA CO.

All products are lead free.

Volume measurements are brim-full capacities.

Plate 113
Back of company flyer, ca 1996.

Plate 114
The coffeepot in the background was the original design, but when the decision was made to switch to a fully vitrified body, it warped so severely, few lids would fit, resulting in an unacceptable scrap rate. This style was made through a couple of production runs in the early months of 1986 before it was changed to the one in the foreground. Collectors value the original style coffeepot at $200.00+, if the lid fits reasonably well. (Note: Our picture, though well composed and photographed, tends to make the restyled pot artificially large in comparison to the one in the background — in reality, the opposite is true.)

Plate 115
Compare the lids on these teapots. Their intention had been to use a flat teapot lid like the original, but due to the tendency of the vitrified clay to warp, the original style coffeepot lid was substituted, as you can see on the white example. Later, once all the existing coffeepot lids were used up, a fluted finial was adapted to this lid. The teapot opening remained large until about 1989 when it was modified to a smaller opening with a flange. The teapot still looks the same as the pink one once the lid is on, but the lid now has an inner groove, and a raised flange was added to the base, resulting in a tighter and more satisfactory fit.

Plate 116
The new cobalt is much darker than both the original 1936 cobalt or the limited edition sapphire. Just how dark is evident in the juice pitcher at the left of the picture. The oval platter is black and the bulb candlesticks white. Both old and new bulb candlesticks have a dry foot. Remember to look for the shine and the mark, and try to learn to recognize the new colors. The large pasta bowl (center back) is in periwinkle; the gravy boat is rose. In 1986 when it was introduced, rose was the lighter, baby pink shown here. Over the past several years, HLC has been slowly making it a deeper and richer tone; it's now almost a hot pink, which becomes especially obvious if you try to add to a set purchased ten years ago.

Plate 117

A warm sunny Southwestern atmosphere is created here by apricot (casserole, chop plate, disk pitcher, etc.) new turquoise (medium flower vase, butter dish, platter), new yellow (tripod candle holders, cup, and saucer), and sea mist green (coffee mug). If you have trouble deciding whether your cobalt and turquoise tripods are old or new, take a look at their bases. If they are fully glazed underneath, they're most certainly old.

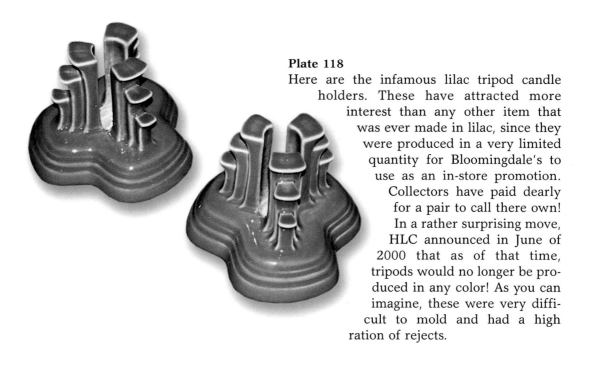

Plate 118

Here are the infamous lilac tripod candle holders. These have attracted more interest than any other item that was ever made in lilac, since they were produced in a very limited quantity for Bloomingdale's to use as an in-store promotion. Collectors have paid dearly for a pair to call there own! In a rather surprising move, HLC announced in June of 2000 that as of that time, tripods would no longer be produced in any color! As you can imagine, these were very difficult to mold and had a high ration of rejects.

Plate 119

Plate 120

Lilac Fiesta has proven to be (thus far, at least) the medium green of the new line, several lovely pieces are shown in these two photographs. The bulb candle holders and bud vases were made exclusively for China Specialties, the after dinner cup and saucer for both Bloomingdale's and China Specialties. As Homer Laughlin traditionally gives only a six-month exclusive on items such as these, some may have been made for other retailers as well during the two-year production period.

Plate 121
This photo features items in persimmon and the limited edition color that was produced in winter of 1996, sapphire. Unlike the limited edition, lilac, which was made for two full years, sapphire was limited to 180 firing days in an extremely narrow number of items.

Plate 122
These are exciting examples of the two-year limited color, chartreuse, which was retired at the end of 1999. Only twenty-four coffee servers were made for a charity auction to benefit the East Liverpool Alumni Association. They are, no doubt, the rarest and most expensive items in the new chartreuse. (This particular example is numbered 4/24 — 1998.) It is difficult to place a value on items like this, as so few have actually sold. Asking prices for them, however, are generally $1,000.00 and up. The demitasse cups and saucers sold for a limited time only through the Homer Laughlin Outlet Store. (Photo by Craig Macaluso, Metairie, LA)

Plate 123
HLC made three different pieces exclusively for the East Liverpool (Ohio) High School Alumni Association, the chartreuse coffee server in the previous photo and these two vases: Millennium I in black for the 1999 auction and Millennium III in juniper for the year 2000 auction. These colors were not included in the standard line of production for those particular molds. Only 24 of each item were produced. (Photo by Harvey Linn, Jr.)

Plate 124
Here are the two newest colors in the line. Pearl gray, which is a permanent addition, and the new, limited-edition two-year color, juniper, which will be made for 2000 and 2001 only. During 1999 in anticipation of the millennium, Homer Laughlin produced three different vases. Millennium I (far right) was an exclusive for Bloomingdale's and was limited to 1,000 of each color. Millennium II, which resembles a double-spouted disk pitcher, was an exclusive for Macy's. Millennium III (which resembles the 1930s 12" red vase shown in the morgue photograph in this book) was available in all colors except black and apricot, and it was available to all retailers. All three were discontinued at the end of 1999. (Photo by Harvey Linn, Jr.)

Plate 125
The presentation bowl is shown in raspberry, a special glaze specifically formulated for this piece. Only five hundred were produced in December 1998 to commemorate the 500 millionth piece of Fiesta produced since its inception. In 1999 and for that year only, this bowl was made in the regular lineup of colors then available. It is shown here turned over, of course, in order to display it's striking design lines and the logo.

Plate 126
The newest limited edition color is juniper, which is to be produced for 2000 and 2001 only. A deep teal blue-green, it is shown here in the medium vase. Next to it is a piece that will never be made in chartreuse with the exception of this sample, a 7½" vase. This smaller vase is a planned addition to the line at some point in the future, but chartreuse was discontinued in December 1999, and as of summer 2000, the 7½" vase has yet to be introduced.

Plate 127
Two more sample items that may be introduced at a future point. The persimmon spoon rest is a very good example of a successful adaptation of traditional Fiesta design elements to an entirely new object. The chartreuse 7½" vase is the same on as shown in Plate 126. (Can we hope for a 12" vase in the future to complete the trio?) The rose oval tray is 12" long and can be used for a bread tray, or, because it is flat, as a serving tray under the coffeepot and a couple of mugs.

Plate 128

The original line (sans the ribbon, below) was produced for the 1987 Christmas season only and was not a huge success, even with collectors. The revised line, left, currently offered by Homer Laughlin, has a larger decal and features a red ribbon in addition to the holly and berry motif. (Much better!) You will also find several other Christmas themes, including Christmas trees in various Fiesta colors at the rim of white Fiesta plates and one with snowmen, done as exclusives for various retailers.

Plate 129

Plate 130

Homer Laughlin produced 60th anniversary commemorative items for Fiesta's 60th birthday in 1996. The disk pitcher in Plate 131 is part of a five-piece beverage set that included four tumblers (marked with the 60th anniversary backstamp on their bases). These sets were produced in lilac as well as six other colors: turquoise, cobalt, periwinkle, rose, persimmon, and sapphire. Rose sets were very limited (possibly to less than three hundred, although there is no way to be exact). These sets normally retailed at about $50.00, although sale prices were nearer $30.00. The sapphire five-piece beverage set is pictured in Plate 130 along with a pair of mugs emblazoned with "Genuine Fiesta, 60th Anniversary, 1936 – 1996, still proudly made in the U.S.A. by the Homer Laughlin China Company." The round serving tray is a newly designed item, but one we feel Rhead would approve of (note that this is the earliest version...subsequent versions of this tray feature smooth-edged handles). The anniversary clock on the right features the special logo instead of the dancing senorita at the 12 o'clock position.

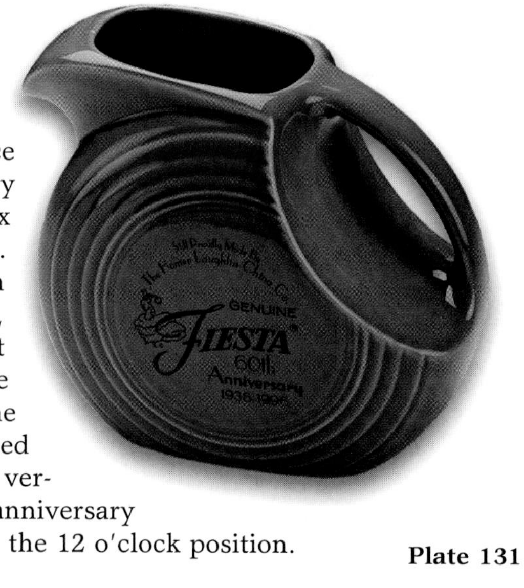

Plate 131

Plate 132

Here are some of the earlier licensed Fiesta products (made by manufacturers other than Homer Laughlin). The metal diner-type napkin dispenser is one of the more enduring designs and has been available in all colors except lilac. The paper napkins are printed with a Fiesta plate design in assorted pastels. Also shown is a fabric tablecloth produced by Dakotah for a limited time, 1994 to 1995. These fabric accessories were available in a scatter print as well as an allover plate design. In addition to tablecloths, you may find chair pads, curtains, place mats, and napkins by the same company. All items were available in the "original color" version (eagerly sought by collectors) as well as a pastel-colored print that coordinates well with the Post86 Fiesta lineup.

Reproduced by permission of the Homer Laughlin China Company.

Plate 133

An official promotion card showing Fiesta licensed accessories made by other manufacturers (those are HLC-produced genuine Fiesta mugs on the mug rack and a handled Fiesta serving tray). Included are enamel cookware and colanders, resin magnets and cheese picks, picture frames and wax candles. The plaid fabric items are by Audrey, and these (in various combinations of Fiesta colors) replaced the earlier Fiesta print by Dakotah shown in Plate 132.

Plate 134

Homer Laughlin has also introduced coordinating plastic-handled flatware. The solid-color plastic handles feature a partial ring design, and each piece is marked Fiesta on the back on the stainless steel tang. Besides the place settings: dinner and salad forks, tea and soup spoons, and dinner knives, there are serving pieces, including a pie lifter, slotted and regular tablespoons, and a cold meat fork. It was made in all the colors listed for the dinnerware except sapphire. (Lilac was made in place-setting items only — no serving pieces.) In addition, true red and emerald green were made as accessories for the Holiday Fiesta. (To keep yours looking new, use the air dry cycle on your dishwasher and avoid lemon dish soap.)

Plate 135

The Fiesta lamp (shown with its original shade) was produced in 1993 as a J.C. Penney exclusive. It met with little success and was offered for one season only. To the right is the clock. Introduced as Penney's exclusive in 1993, it was discontinued for a brief period, then brought back to the general line. It may be found in all colors except lilac.

Plate 136

Assortment of items from the Fiesta Mates line. This line lacks the typical Fiesta styling; these pieces were taken from the regular restaurant line and dipped in Fiesta glazes. From left: sugar packet holder, fry pan server, 18-oz. jumbo cup and saucer, 4-oz. ramekin, 18-oz. jumbo bowl, 5-oz. creamer, Tower and Denver mugs, and the 10" oval baker.

Plate 137
Homer Laughlin has also produced Fiesta place setting and serving pieces for Warner Brothers stores which feature a different Looney Tunes character for each color (it's very popular with collectors). White features Tweety Bird, periwinkle blue Bugs Bunny, turquoise Daffy Duck, and so forth. To the right is an exclusive for Macy's Department stores, featuring white Fiesta to which Homer Laughlin has added four concentric rings in periwinkle, sea mist green, yellow, and persimmon.

Plate 138
Since 1997 Homer Laughlin has produced a yearly Fiesta Christmas ornament shaped like a miniature Fiesta plate. In addition to the two 1997 ornaments you see here (both fronts and backs are shown), there is also one that features the same holly and red ribbon decoration found on the Holiday Fiesta line. These are produced in solid colors like this one (in persimmon), adorned with the Fiesta Senorita in 24k gold. Chartreuse was the color of the 1998 ornament; other colors will represent succeeding years.

Plate 139
Special novelty gift gets of Fiesta available in 1999 at the HLC outlet store: Cookies for Santa (welled snack plate and cup), and Some Bunny's Been Eating Out of My Fiesta, a child's place setting with an Easter theme, consisting of a 9" plate, 12-oz. cereal bowl, and tumbler.

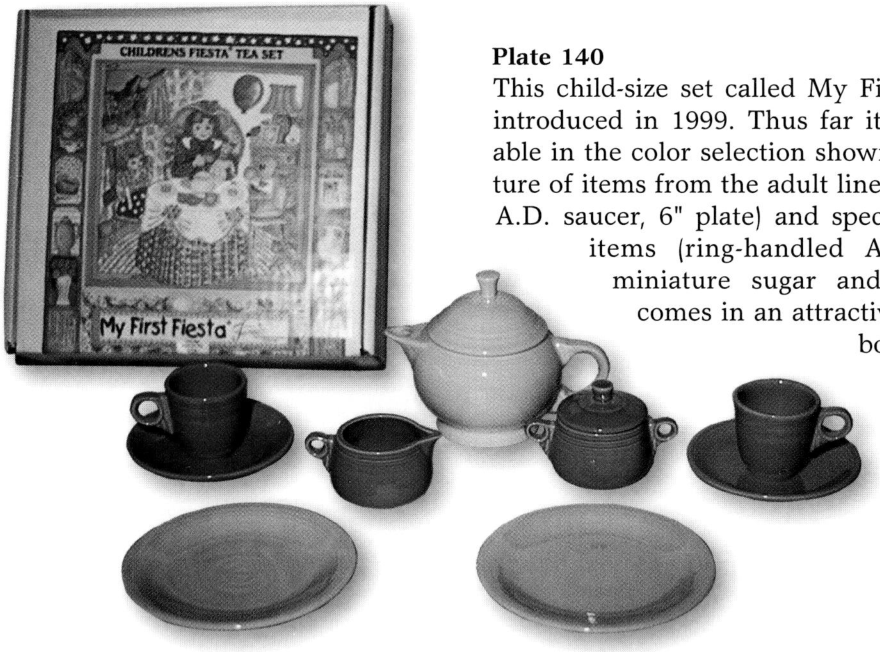

Plate 140
This child-size set called My First Fiesta was introduced in 1999. Thus far it is only available in the color selection shown here. A mixture of items from the adult line (2-cup teapot, A.D. saucer, 6" plate) and specially designed items (ring-handled A.D. cup and miniature sugar and creamer), it comes in an attractively decorated box.

Plate 141
Fiesta 2000. Homer Laughlin recently added a new shape to its retail dinnerware line. (Bear in mind that Fiesta is one of the most popular consumer dinnerware lines on the market today, but HLC's entire retail lineup to this point consists of Fiesta and only Fiesta; all other production is geared to the food service industry. HLC realizes they must develop other retail dinnerware lines to justify supporting their retail sales operation overhead if and when Fiesta's relative popularity in the retail marketplace declines.) This new line has a contemporary, vaguely Oriental feel, with abstract embossed designs reminiscent of bamboo leaves in a 1¼" band at the outer rim. It is dipped in a number of the more popular Fiesta glazes, including cobalt, persimmon, pearl gray, and juniper. Only because retail store buyers felt it would be more easily marketed to the public if it carried the Fiesta name, it was dubbed "Fiesta 2000." But it is not part of the Fiesta line. Fiesta 2000 is totally separate and is related to Post86 Fiesta in the same tangential way Tango was to the Fiesta ware of the 1930s or Rhythm in the 1950s and in the future will no doubt be viewed in much the same way as those lines are by today's Fiesta collectors.

Specialty Custom-designed Fiesta
Plates 142 through 146 feature wonderful items designed for *Fiesta Collector's Quarterly*, a club and newsletter for Fiesta collectors. Some were available only to members and subscribers, while the Sunporch and Mexicana could be purchased at an antique mall near the HLC plant in East Liverpool as well. Other examples are shown in Plate 147, where you'll see juice pitchers made especially for the Homer Laughlin China Collector's Association, an organization for collectors of all types of Homer Laughlin wares.

Yearly, 1995 through 1999, the Fiesta Club of America (now disbanded) issued handled serving trays with their logo to their members. 1995 was in lilac, 1996 in persimmon, 1997 in sapphire, 1998 was chartreuse, and 1999 was black.

Plate 142

For the *Fiesta Collector's Quarterly*, Homer Laughlin has designed a special Fiesta shelf display sign, similar to department store advertising pieces you often see in other china lines. Available to subscribers only, it is produced in a different color each year. The 1995 color was persimmon, in 1996 turquoise, in 1997 apricot, in 1998 chartreuse, and in 1999 it was rose. The colors for 2000 and 2001 will be pearl gray and yellow respectively.

Plate 143

The black pitcher is an example of a 60th anniversary of Fiesta commemorative (limited to 600 pieces) that was made exclusively for subscribers of the *FCQ*. The decal was re-created for them from original vintage advertising brochure artwork and is permanently fired on. These may be found with a subscriber's name and a serial number inscribed in gold under the base, also permanently fired on. The calendar plate was made on special order as well. The coffee server and tripod candle holder are from a pattern called Moon Over Miami, which features a pink flamingo design fired onto black Fiesta. You may find many examples of Fiesta that have been custom crested with names or special motifs for restaurants and hotels, such as this cobalt mug crested for Tamarack Resort in West Virginia.

Plate 144
A big hit with collectors, here's the Sunporch decoration on white Fiesta from 1998. The decal design was modified somewhat from the original Sunporch so as to leave no doubt in anyone's mind that the dinnerware pictured on the table actually is Fiesta! All the items in this line were limited to five hundred pieces and were available only to *FCQ* members and through an antique mall near the HLC plant in East Liverpool.

Plate 145
This is the new version of Mexicana, available for the first time in 2000. The decal is fired on white Fiesta and features cobalt lines and accents. It duplicates a concept from an original 1930s set featuring Mexicana Century cups with cobalt interiors and saucers in that saucers and undertrays in the new line are solid cobalt. Like Sunporch, all items in this line were limited to five hundred pieces and were available only to club members/subscribers and at the antique mall near the HLC plant in East Liverpool.

Plate 146

Also just for China Specialties, HLC produced a limited edition commemorative Fiesta 50th Anniversary Collector's Mug set. Less than six hundred sets were made, each consisting of ten white mugs decorated with the Fiesta Dancing Senorita trademark in a Fiesta color (red, yellow, dark blue, turquoise, light green, forest green, rose, chartreuse, gray, and medium green). Later, HLC brought out a collector/dealer sign, a 12" white chop plate with the Fiesta logo on mango red. A relative few were produced in yellow and apricot with the mango red decoration. The plate on the left was made by HLC for their dealers — it shows their new logo.

Plate 147

For the Homer Laughlin China Collector's Association, HLC has produced two juice pitchers. The theme for the decorations are landmarks of Art Deco design. The 1999 pitcher is in pearl gray with a scene of the Chrysler Building (which opened in 1930), and the 2000 pitcher is white with the fabulous Dick Tracy motif. (The Dick Tracy comic strip debuted in October 1931.) The Homer Laughlin China Collectors Association (HLCCA) is a member-run, non-profit, 501(c)(3) organization for collectors of all types of Homer Laughlin wares, especially Fiesta. Membership information may be found on page 6. (Photo by Craig Macaluso, Metairie, LA)

Plate 148

This line, reflecting a retro space pattern, was made for the American Museum of Natural History in New York City to commemorate the opening of the Rose Center for Earth and Space. It features colorful Deco planets on cobalt. These items were produced: T&J mug, 9" salad plate, bud vase, serving tray, disc pitcher, and clock. (Photo by Harvey Linn, Jr.)

In Memory of Jonathan O. Parry
Art Director of HLC since 1984

Jonathan O. Parry joined Homer Laughlin's art department in 1975 and was promoted to art director in 1984. He was intimately involved with bringing the Fiesta line back to the consumer marketplace in 1986 and with design and color choices since that time.

Jonathan lost his battle with cancer on April 28, 2000, at the age of 51. Our condolences and sympathies are extended to his son, his mother, and his co-workers. His unique contributions to the Fiesta world continue to live on in our collections. (Reprinted with permission from *Fiesta Collector's Quarterly*, Summer 2000.)

Harlequin

Dinnerware

Harlequin was produced by Homer Laughlin in an effort to serve all markets and to fit every budget. It was a less expensive dinnerware and was sold without trademark through the F. W. Woolworth Company exclusively. The following is an excerpt from one of the company's original illustrated brochures:

> The new Harlequin Pottery offers a gift to table gaiety. It brings the magic of bright, exciting color to the table, dresses the festive board with pleasantness and personality, makes of every meal a cheerful and companionable occasion.
>
> The new ware comes in four lovely colors . . . Yellow, Green, Red, and Blue . . . and offers the hostess endless possibilities for creating interesting and appealing color effects on her table. All the colors are brilliant and eye-catching . . . designed to go together effectively in any combination the hostess may desire. To set a table with Harlequin is an adventure in decoration. Plates are of one color, cups of another, saucers and platters of another . . . you can give free range to your artistic instincts.
>
> And it is very easy to build up a comprehensive set of Harlequin in whatever items and colors you desire, because it may be bought by the piece at extremely reasonable prices.
>
> Sold Exclusively by
> F. W. WOOLWORTH CO. STORES

Although it was first listed on company records as early as 1936, Harlequin was not actively introduced to the public until 1938.

It was designed by Fredrick Rhead, and like Fiesta the style was pure Art Deco. Rhead again used the band of rings device as its only ornamentation, but this time chose to space the rings well away from the rim. Flat pieces were round and concave with the center areas left plain. Hollow ware pieces were cone shaped; bowls were flared. Handles were applied with small ornaments at their bases and, with few exceptions, were extremely angular.

Over the years the color assortment grew to include all of Fiesta's lovely colors with the exceptions of

Plate 148
Company Brochure, 1979.

ivory and dark blue. The original colors (those mentioned in the brochure we just quoted), however, were developed just for Harlequin. Harlequin yellow was a lighter and brighter tint than Fiesta yellow; the green was a spruce green, and the blue tended toward a mauve shade. It is interesting to note that the color the company referred to as "red" is actually maroon. To avoid confusion, today's collectors reserve "red" for the orange-red color of Fiesta red.

It seems logical here to conclude that because Harlequin was not extensively promoted until 1938 that it would have been then or soon after that the line was expanded and new colors added. The new colors of the '40s were red (orange-red like Fiesta's — called tangerine by the company), rose (though records show a color called salmon that preceded rose, if indeed these are two individual shades, the difference is so slight it is of no significance to today's collectors), turquoise, and light green. (There are some pieces whose production dates we can't pinpoint beyond the fact that they were not part of the original line but were listed as discontinued by 1952. Many of these are rarely if ever found in light green. This leads us to believe that light green may not have been added until the mid-'40s.)

Gray, chartreuse, and forest (dark) green were new in the '50s. Harlequin yellow, turquoise, and rose continued to be produced. By 1959 the color assortment was reduced to four colors again — red (coinciding with the resumed production of Fiesta red), turquoise, Harlequin yellow, and the last new color, medium green.

The original line consisted of these items: 10", 9", 7", and 6" plates; 8" soup plate; 9" nappy; salt and pepper shakers; covered casserole; teacup and saucer; creamer, regular; sugar bowl; 11" platter; 5½" fruit; double egg cup; and 4½" tumbler.

These pieces were soon added to the original line: cream soup cup, sauce boat, after dinner cup and saucer, novelty creamer, 13" platter, teapot, syrup*, service water jug, 36s bowl, basketweave ashtray, regular ashtray, 36s oatmeal, individual salad bowl, 22-ounce jug, 4½" tumbler, ashtray saucer*, basketweave nut dish, relish tray with inserts*, individual egg cup*, individual creamer*, candle holders*, marmalade*, butter dish, large cup (tankard), and 9" baker. Of the assortment, those items marked with an asterisk (indicating them to be rare or non-existent in light green) were probably the first to be discontinued. Knowing that the Fiesta line suffered a severe pruning during 1944 – 45, it would certainly follow that the same fate would befall Harlequin.

The material available to us for study dated May 1952 indicates that even more pieces had by then been dropped: the 9" baker, the covered butter dish, the individual creamer, and the tankard.

Harlequin proved to be quite popular and sold very well into the late '50s when sales began to diminish. Records show that the final piece was actually manufactured in 1964.

In 1939 the Hamilton Ross Co. offered a Harlequin look-alike which they called Sevilla. It came in assorted solid colors, eight in all, with the same angular handles, similar style and decoration. The round platter was distinctive. It featured closed handles formed by the band of rings device which was allowed to sweep gradually outward to just past mid-point; no doubt you have seen an occasional piece.

In 1979 Homer Laughlin announced that they had been approached and would comply with a request from the F.W. Woolworth Company to reissue the Harlequin line, one of that company's all time bestsellers, as part of their 100th Anniversary celebration. The Harlequin Ironstone dinnerware they produced was a very limited line and is easily recognized. It was made in two original colors: yellow and turquoise; a medium green that was slightly different than the original; and a new shade, coral. The sugar bowl was restyled with closed handles and a solid finial. A round platter (the original was oval) in coral was included in the 45-piece set which was comprised of only plates, salad plates, cereal/soups, cups and saucers, yellow sugar, turquoise creamer, and a round green vegetable bowl. The plates were backstamped Homer Laughlin (the old ones are not marked), and even the pieces made from authentic molds are easy to distinguish from the old Harlequin. Because many of the lovely colors of the original line and virtually none of its unique accessory pieces were reproduced, this late line has never been a threat to the investments of the many collectors who love Harlequin dinnerware. We have talked with several dealers who actually felt the reissue stimulated interest in the old line.

A letter from the company dated April 1983 advised that Woolworth's as well as a few other dealers throughout the country were carrying the new Harlequin. It stated that a few round platters and vegetable bowls had been made in yellow by mistake, and that some of these were backstamped "through error in the Dipping Department." (These are shown in Plate 149 along with a white, a nonstandard color, plate backstamped 1980 and a coral saucer, which should have been unmarked, backstamped 1982.) Production continued for no more than a couple of years; and compared to the old line, sales were much more limited.

Plate 149
Items glazed/backstamped in error.

Plate 150
Ashtray Saucer.
Though very rare, a few of the ashtray saucers have been reported in ivory — not a standard Harlequin color, though we know of an ivory tumbler as well.

Plate 151
Basketweave Ashtray (left front).
None of the ashtrays were in the original assortment, but all were added very early — possibly even before 1940. The basketweave version may be found in all twelve colors including medium green.
Ashtray Saucer (top).
This is an unusual item, made to serve a dual purpose. These are hard to find; and because none have been reported in the '50s colors (gray, chartreuse, and forest green for this line), medium green, or light green, they were probably discontinued in the mid-'40s. Advanced collectors question the existence of rose — let us know if you have one.
Regular Ashtray (right).
So dubbed by collectors to make a distinction between the three styles, this one comes in the first eight colors only; it's scarce in light green.

Note: In the early 1980s, HLC produced a line called Table Fair in ivory with rusty brown speckles. The salad and dinner plates were made from Harlequin molds. A second line utilizing the speckled glaze was decorated with a textured rim band and a blooming strawberry plant in the center well.

Plate 152

36s Oatmeal Bowl (far left).

Shown here in light green, the 36s oatmeal measures 6½" in diameter. They're scarce in spruce green and maroon. See the chapter entitled Dating Codes and English Measurements for an explanation of the term "36s."

Nappy (center back).

The nappy, shown in spruce green, was part of the original line and can be found in all colors, although it is rare in medium green. It's 9" in diameter.

Individual Salad Bowl (right back).

The individual salad is not so hard to find in the '50s colors; it's scarce in red, maroon, spruce green, and medium green.

36s Bowl (far right).

Shown in a very rare color, medium green, the 36s bowl was evidently made not much later than 1959 when this color was added to the line. It's scarce in maroon and spruce.

Fruit Bowl, 5½" (center front).

This bowl has also been found in a slightly larger version (6" diameter) in maroon, blue, spruce green, and yellow.

Plate 153

Cream Soup Bowl.

This piece can be found in all colors; like its Fiesta counterpart, it's very rare in medium green and commands a hefty price when one comes up for sale.

Plate 154

Oval Baker.

Discontinued before the '50s colors were introduced, the oval baker is found in the first eight colors only. (Remember, though rose was a '50s color in Fiesta, it was introduced to the Harlequin line soon after 1938.) This bowl measures 9" in length.

Plate 155

Mixing Bowls.

These are the Kitchen Kraft bowls — the original owner bought them from the factory by mail order for $2.05 plus postage ($1.00 for the 10", 65¢ for the 8", and 40¢ for the 6"). They are unmarked. The set was also available with the smallest bowl in red for an additional 20¢.

Plate 156
Butter Dish, ½-lb.
Originally a Jade/Century piece, this butter dish was later glazed in Harlequin and Riviera colors and sold with both lines. They have been found in these colors: cobalt blue, rose, mauve blue, spruce green, light green, maroon, turquoise, red, ivory, and Fiesta and Harlequin yellows.

Plate 157
Candle Holders.
These are not at all easy to find in any color, in fact, we once thought they were non-existent in light green, but we polled our readers and they came up with reports of five pair. At least four pair are in permanent collections at the moment. Whether one of the four was a purchase of the fifth, I have no way of knowing.

Plate 158
Casserole.
These are scarce in the '50s colors especially dark green — and they're extremely rare in medium green (shown here, one of two known).

Plate 159
High-Lip Creamer (top row).
The "high-lip" creamer is found in the four original colors only. Note the difference in the length of the lips on the two shown. The fact that they were trimmed by hand doesn't wholly explain the difference, since only these two variations have been reported. Evidently the style was deliberately changed at some point.
Individual Creamer (top right).
You'll find this tiny pitcher only in the first eight colors. They're really not at all difficult to find, but they are scarce in light green.
Regular Creamer (bottom row).
This item is available in all twelve colors.
Sugar Bowl.
One collector reports that upon comparing several sugar bowls in his collection, he suspects those with the inside rings were earlier and that these rings were eliminated sometime during the '40s.
Novelty Creamer.
As far as we know, only one of these exists in medium green, but you can expect to find them in all the other colors.

Plate 160
Novelty Creamer.
Until the eighth edition we always reported that the novelty creamer was non-existent in medium green, but this photo shows there's at least one — and collectors believe this is the only one! It's shown alongside another very rare item, a medium green service water pitcher.

Plate 161
Demitasse Coffee Cup and Saucer.
The little demitasses have become rare in the '50s colors — gray, chartreuse, and forest green — and they're extremely so in medium green. They don't appear on the 1959 listing when medium green was introduced, so they couldn't have been made in any large quantity in that color.

Plate 162
Large Cup.
This may be the tankard found listed in company material as being discontinued before 1952. As close as we can pinpoint the introduction of the '50s colors is fall 1951, which would leave this in production for only a few months and explain why it is so rare. But there are two factors that seem to discredit the tankard theory: for years, I had one in medium green, a 1959 color, in my own collection, and the body of this cup is the same shape as the Epicure cups from the mid-'50s. Only recently have the saucers been found — they're the same as the Rhythm saucers, but old store stock discovered in original cartons confirmed that they did double duty as saucers for these Harlequin cups.

Plate 163

Double Egg Cup.

This egg cup will hold an egg in both the top and bottom (not all at once!). The small end was to accommodate a boiled egg; the larger end was for a poached egg, the custom at that time being to dunk toast points into the soft poached egg yolk. They're found in all twelve colors, but only four have been reported in medium green.

Nut Dish.

The small basketweave nut dishes are found in the first eight colors; they're scarce in light green, though not as rare as we once believed.

Individual Egg Cup.

Though fairly common in yellow, spruce green, mauve blue, maroon, turquoise, rose, and red, they're very rare in light green.

Perfume Bottle.

These are not a standard part of the Harlequin line

but are of interest to Harlequin collectors since they were dipped in Harlequin glazes. They're hard to find; most of them are yellow, but light green has also been reported.

Marmalade.

Found in the first eight colors only, they're scarce in rose, and light green marmalades are very rare.

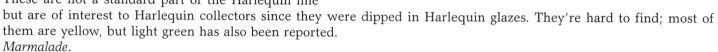

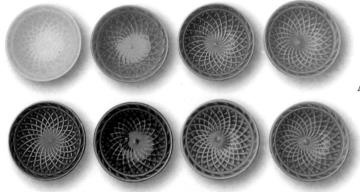

Plate 164

A complete set of Harlequin nut cups in all eight colors. (Photo by Craig Macaluso, Metairie, LA)

Plate 165

Japanese Imports.

The basketweave ashtray and nut dish were copied from these Japanese imports. We thought you'd enjoy seeing the originals. They carry the mark "Marutomo Ware Made in Japan."

Plate 166

Tumblers.

These were discontinued before the '50s colors were introduced, so they're found in only the first eight colors. Remember, though rose was strictly a '50s color in the Fiesta line, it was made in Harlequin from the late '30s until late in the '50s, so don't be surprised to find a rose example, even though we don't show one here. One has been reported in ivory, a non-standard Harlequin color.

Service Water Pitcher.

Look for the Fiesta-like band of rings near the base of this pitcher. This will help you identify the Harlequin pitcher from several look-alikes by other companies. These were produced in all twelve colors; they're very rare in medium green and scarce in gray and dark green. Several have now been reported in Fiesta yellow; we once saw one of these etched "Treasure Island, 1939."

Plate 167

Salt and Pepper Shakers.

These were made in all of Harlequin's colors; they're all easy to find except medium green.

Jug, 22-oz.

These are commonly found in the first eleven colors; they're extremely rare in medium green — only three have been reported.

Deep Plate.

These can be found in all twelve colors; they're 8" in diameter.

Sauce Boat.

These are fairly easy to find in any of the twelve Harlequin colors, though they're scarce in medium green.

Plate 168

Plates, 10", 9", 7", 6".

The 10" dinner plate is becoming very hard to find; the 9" and 7" have been reported in ivory, not a standard Harlequin color.

Platters, 10", 13".

These are generally easy to find in all twelve colors, though they're both rare in medium green.

Plate 169

This piece has long been a mystery that finally may be solved with this edition. We've always thought the rings looked like Harlequin, and since many collectors refer to it as the "Harlequin pie plate," we'll put it in this section. Collectors have long believed that it was an HLC product, but company representatives wouldn't verify that for us when we questioned them about it years ago. Through further research, however, information has come to light that strongly suggests that it is. You can recognize this plate by the three rings on the outside of the wall and the four on the inside. (Collectors report a similar plate by another company that has four rings on both the outside and the inside walls and makes a dull flat sound when tapped rather than the ring made by the Homer Laughlin plate.) These have been found in cobalt, Fiesta green, and yellow. My source tells me that this plate as well as a second style was mentioned in Rhead's journal. The second style is a custard pie plate that is 9" in diameter, has no rings, and a rounded flange. It has a larger wet foot than the ringed pie plate or the KK pie plates, and it's not as deep as other pie plates produced by Homer Laughlin. When the pie server is placed in this one (and only this one), it rests perfectly flat on the flange as well as the bottom of the plate. Of the latter, two are known to exist in private collections, one cobalt and the other yellow. Neither of these pie plates has ever been found on company price lists.

Plate 170
Relish Tray.
These are rare! As strange as it seems, the true Harlequin relish tray base is found only in turquoise; these pie-wedge inserts are occasionally found in bases of another color, but those bases are actually Fiesta. The inserts are found in only six of the first eight colors — no light green or spruce. The color combination as shown is the most common, but other combinations have also been reported. Two examples with all rose inserts have been found.

Plate 171
Syrup.
Syrups are scarce and have been reported in only red, yellow, mauve blue, spruce green, turquoise, light green, and ivory (and just one in each of the last three colors — let us hear from you if you have one in these colors. A veteran collector of twenty-two years doubts they even exist. It's been years since these were reported to us, so we have no idea from whom the reports originate — but we had doubters that light green candle holders existed, too, now we know of five pairs.)

Plate 172
Teacups and Saucers.
These are relatively easy to find in all twelve colors. One has been found in a non-standard shade, Skytone blue.
Teapot.
Teapots were made in all twelve colors but are very rare in medium green.

Plate 173
Medium Green Harlequin.
Medium green Harlequin is even rarer than medium green Fiesta. The water pitcher is extremely rare; so is the teapot. No more than four or five of either are accounted for at this time. Only one novelty creamer is known to exist. (See Plate 160.)

Animals

During the late '30s and early '40s when miniatures such as these were enjoying a heyday, HLC produced this menagerie as a part of the Harlequin line. There are six, each were made in four colors: maroon, spruce green, mauve blue, and yellow. They were marketed primarily through Woolworth Company stores.

There are no original Harlequin Animals other than those pictured in Plate 174, although you may find some that are very similar. The duck has a twin, a perpetually hungry little gander — his head bent into a permanent feeding position; but he was made by the Brush Pottery Company. Although several collectors were almost sure their 2½" elephant belonged in the group, HLC disowned him. A donkey look-alike pulling a cart may make you wonder at first, but a closer examination will reveal an uncharacteristic lack of sharp detail, and some of these have been found to bear a "California" mark.

"Maverick" animals is a term adopted by collectors to indicate animals that have been glazed by someone outside the Homer Laughlin China Company. In rare cases, you may find one in a standard Harlequin color that has been completely covered with gold, or it may be simply gold trimmed. One company involved in decorating the animals was Kaulware of Chicago, who utilized an iridescent glaze and gold hand-painted trim. You will find salt and pepper shakers in a slightly smaller size, indicating that they were cast from molds made from the original animals (see Plate 176). The Maverick guard cats in Plate 178 are in white with colored trim.

Another company responsible for producing some of the Mavericks was founded by John Kass, who operated in the East Liverpool, Ohio, area. During the Depression after his retail business failed, Kass built a small pottery, employed members of his family, and began to make novelty items — salt and pepper shakers, small animal figures (Mavericks among them), and cups and saucers. A descendant of Kass's explained that it was a common practice in those days for area potters to "make each other's items, and no one took offense." All Kass's work was done painstakingly by hand from the casting to the final decoration. Business increased in the 1940s; the old buildings were replaced with modern structures, and more people were employed. "We made the Harlequin animals from the very beginning," she continues. "For some reason the ducks and penguins were made right up into the 1950s." The letter goes on to say that there were other companies in the area who also made these animals. You will find that some of these are considerably smaller than the Harlequin animals and made of a finer, more porcelain-like material. Though most will be white with gold trim, some may be in colors. We have a gold-trimmed cobalt cat; and, until you compare it with the genuine article, you can't be sure that it isn't authentic. It measures 2½" long compared to the one I have in maroon that is a good ¼" longer. These smaller animals are worth considerably less than Mavericks that are full size or nearly so.

Plate 174
Original Harlequin Animals in authentic glazes.

Plate 175
"Maverick Animals."

Plate 176
Salt and Pepper Shakers.
These penguins are a slightly smaller size, indicating that they were cast from molds made from the original animals.

Plate 177
Red Animals.
Though probably not a
production run, there are a few red cats being found; a red duck and penguin have been reported as well as a penguin in black. Be alert for painted frauds. Collectors tell us of finding red animals whose color, feel, and weight were perfect but the paint was chipping off.

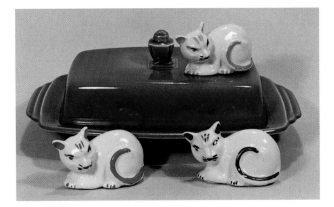

Plate 178
"Maverick Guard Cats."

Plate 179
Rare Animals.
Shown are turquoise, light green, and cobalt blue animals borrowed from HLC for their portrait photo. These are from their archives — don't expect to find them on the market, though a rare few have made it to the outside.

Riviera was introduced in 1938 and until sometime prior to 1950 was sold exclusively by the Murphy Company. In contrast to Fiesta and Harlequin, the line was quite limited. It was unmarked, lighter in weight, and therefore less expensive. Only rarely will you find a piece with the Homer Laughlin gold stamp. Of the three colored dinnerware lines, it has the rather dubious distinction of being the only one which was not originally created as such. Its forerunner was a line called Century — an ivory line with a vellum glaze. Century shapes were also decorated with a wide variety of decals and were the basis of many lines such as Mexicana and Hacienda. An enterprising designer (Rhead, no doubt) applied the popular colored glazes to these shapes, and Riviera was born. Even the shakers were from another line. They were originally designed as Tango, which accounts for the six-section design in contrast to the square Riviera shape.

Though all the company literature we've seen never included ivory as a standard Riviera color, it must have been, since it was the company themselves who marketed a 16-piece set of mauve blue, yellow, light green, and ivory during the war when red had been temporarily withdrawn. Collectors appreciate the effect of the ivory with the other colors and find there are interesting items that are available to them only in the ivory glaze.

Records for this line are especially scanty; but as accurately and completely as possible, here is a listing of the items in the line as it was first introduced. Sizes have been translated from the English measurements listed by the company to actual sizes to the nearest inch.

11" Dish (Platter)	13" Dish (Platter)	10" Plate	9" Plate
6" Plate	Teacup and Saucer	Fruit	9" Baker (Oval Vegetable Bowl)
Salt and Pepper Shakers	Covered Casserole	8" Deep Plate	8" Nappy
6" Oatmeal	Tumbler (with Handle)	Open Jug	Teapot
Sauce Boat	Creamer	(also found with lid)	Covered Sugar

We have also found 15" platters, a covered syrup pitcher, a juice pitcher, juice tumblers, and butter dishes in two sizes — a half-pound and a quarter-pound.

Plate 180
(Photo by Harvey Linn, Jr.)

Plate 181

Batter Sets.
The color combination of the set on the left was standard issue. Notice that it utilizes one of the rare cobalt pieces as well as the lid for the jug. These lids had been reported only in green and ivory until we received the photo of an all red set, shown in Plate 181. In Plate 182 is a very unusual set. Not only is the tray square (virtually all are rectangular) but it includes a covered sugar bowl as well — a seldom seen component. All four of these pieces carry the Wells peacock mark.

Plate 182

Plate 183
Bowls: Baker, Nappy, Fruit, Oatmeal.
Left to right: Baker, oval with straight sides, 9" long; Nappy, 7¼" diameter; Baker, oval with curved sides, 9" long. In front: Fruit, 5½"; Oatmeal, 6". The oatmeal is slightly deeper than the fruit bowl and is rather scarce.

Plate 184
Unusual Sugar Bowl and Creamer.
This is the green glaze trimmed in gold; these have also been reported in an unusual lime green (not chartreuse).

Plate 185
Cream Soup Bowl with Liner.
Don't expect to find these in the colored glazes — they're technically Century, but collectors enjoy adding them to their Riviera for contrast. Here the 8" plate (actual measurement 7¾") does double duty as the underliner.

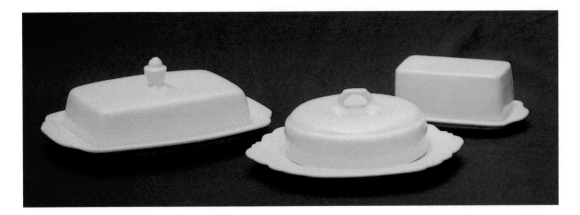

Plate 186
Butter Dishes in Ivory.
These three ivory butter dishes were utilized with the Century Vellum line as well as Riviera. None are marked. (Photo by Harvey Linn, Jr.)

Plate 187
Butter Dishes.
This green example still has the original Riviera sticker and price tag; for an example in such wonderful condition and with the very seldom-seen labels, you should expect to pay about double book price. These are rarely found in the cobalt and turquoise glazes — both are shown in the photo on the right.

Plate 188
Butter Dishes, Creamer and Sugar Bowl, Covered Jug.
Occasionally, the green jug, though still very hard to find, turns up complete with lid; red examples are scarce and very seldom are they found with a lid. Lids have never been found on mauve blue and yellow examples. The larger ½-lb. butter dish is more readily found than the smaller and is available in mauve blue, rose, spruce green, light green, turquoise, maroon, cobalt blue, red, ivory, and in both Fiesta and Harlequin yellow. For further information on the butter dish, see the section on Jade.

Plate 189
Covered Jugs.
All are hard to find and the mauve blue and yellow jugs that have been reported have all been without lids.

Plate 190
Casserole.
A very nice piece and one that may prove difficult to find; the large size of these casseroles along with their distinctive styling and wonderful colors make them spectacular additions to any Riviera collection.

Plate 191
Juice Pitcher.
Shown here in the very rare red color.

Plate 192
Juice Pitcher, Juice Tumblers.
The pitcher is scarce in any color but is standard in yellow. It's very rare in mauve blue, shown here, and red (see Plate 191). In the original sets, the tumblers were turquoise, mauve blue, red, yellow, light green, and ivory.

Plate 193

Compartment Plate, 9¾".

This unique item was reported to us just as we went to press with the Seventh Edition, and to date, we've never heard of a second one. It was a gift to a collector given by a friend with the comment, "This looks like that stuff you collect."

Plate 194

Deep Plate, Salt and Pepper Shakers, Syrup Pitcher, Handled Tumblers.

As you can see, there are six orange-like segments that make up the design of the salt and pepper shakers. These were borrowed from the Tango line, so you may find them in Tango's color too. Two pairs have been found in a true primary red glaze — origin unconfirmed. Here's the covered syrup in red again; it's a darling piece and very hard to find. Ivory tumblers are scarce and command high prices. Though not a Homer Laughlin product, you may find sets of glass tumblers (one style with a smooth surface, another with vertically paneled sides), each with a solid band of one of the Riviera colors at the rim. One set was bought at auction still in the original box marked "Juanita Beverage Set, Rosenthal and Ruben, Inc., Binghampton, NY, 1938." There were two each of the four colors (light green, mauve blue, yellow, and red) in four sizes: 3", 3½", 4", and 5¼". Matching swizzle sticks completed the 40-piece set. See Plate 274 for an illustration of the glassware.

Plate 195

Plates, 10", 9", 7", 6".

The 10" plates are very hard to find. The 7" plate is sometimes found in cobalt blue, and collectors also report this size in Fiesta yellow. (See Plate 323 for a Fiesta Ensemble ad showing both cobalt and Fiesta yellow 7" plates.) An 8" plate (7¾" actual measurement) has been reported in ivory.

Plate 196
Platters.
Shown: 11½", no handles; 11¼" with closed handles. You'll also find 13¼" and 12" platters with the closed handles, and one in ivory measuring 16" has been reported as well. There is a square platter with handles that measures 11½"; it's shown with the batter set in Plate 182.

Plate 197
Sauce Boat.
These have never been considered at all hard to find, but since sending out our last survey, we have had many comments made to us indicating that Riviera in general is becoming scarce.

Plate 198
Fast Stand Sauce Dish, Demitasse Cup and Saucer.
These two ivory items are from the Century line; none have ever been found in the other four colors, and both are hard to find. (Photo by Harvey Linn, Jr.)

Plate 199
Teapot, Teacups, and Saucers.
Teapots have been scarce for several years. Now that Riviera is getting harder to find, good serving pieces are all in short supply. Even the once common cups and saucers are difficult to acquire in mint condition.

Plate 200
Tidbit Tray, 4½" Jug, Utility Bowl, Salt and Pepper Shakers.
Here are more Century items. You will find the shakers in Riviera colors, and one two-tier tidbit tray has been reported in mauve blue. But the jug (a size between the batter pitcher and the syrup) and the utility bowl were never part of the Riviera line. One collector reports the earliest backstamp she has in her Century collection indicates a 1933 production date.

Carnival

Carnival was made exclusively for the Quaker Oats Company who gave it away to their customers, one piece packed in each box of Mother's Carnival Oats. While no records exist to verify the year in which it was first produced, we must assume it was in the late '30s or early '40s by reason of the color assortment. Harlequin yellow, turquoise (both of which were first used by HLC in 1938), light green, and Fiesta red were evidently the original colors. The only mention of Carnival in company files was dated 1952; it lists these glazes: dark green, turquoise, gray, and Harlequin yellow. You'll also occasionally find examples in cobalt, Fiesta yellow, and ivory. (Notice the cups on the front of the boxes shown below — all are different versions of the Mother's Oats boxes that featured a Carnival, each with cups that vary in color.) The 1952 record also itemized the pieces in production at that time; these are listed with suggested values in the back of the book. A company representative recalled that coupons were included in the boxes, redeemable for the larger pieces. Perhaps there were plates, bowls, and platters — to date, however, none have been found, leading collectors to believe it was a breakfast set shown in its entirety on the box.

Plates 201
Examples of Mother's Oats boxes featuring Carnival.

Epicure

Epicure is a '50s line — with the '50s streamline styling and bright pastel colors. Anyone who remembers what a great era that was for growing up can tell you about pink and gray. Argyle socks were pink and gray! If your sweater was pink, your skirt or corduroys were gray. Turquoise was popular in home decorating — even down to appliances. And these were the colors of Epicure: dawn pink, charcoal gray, turquoise blue, and snow white.

The designer was Don Schreckengost, who also designed Rhythm. We can find no information pinpointing production dates, but collectors tell us that virtually all of their Epicure is stamped 1955. The only exception ever reported was a set of plates in pink that were marked 1960. The line consisted of the following items:

Bowls: Cereal/Soup	Coffeepot, 10"
Fruit	Creamer
Nappy, 8"	Gravy Bowl
Nappy, 9"	Ladle, 5½"
Platter, Large Oval	Nut Dish
Salt and Pepper Shakers	Pickle (Small Oval Platter)
Sugar Bowl with Lid	Plates: Dessert, 6½"
Teacup and Saucer	Snack, 8½"
2-Tier Tidbit Tray	Dinner, 10"
Casseroles: Covered Vegetable, Individual	

The nut dish could pass for a butter pat; and one collector tells us that of the eleven in his collection, all are turquoise — and none in any other color has been reported. Another collector believes that they were made and promoted only as samples, since he has one in the original plastic wrapping, containing a price pamphlet as well. No one has ever reported an Epicure ashtray to us, but an Epicure-related website lists them.

Epicure is not easy to find, but many collectors view it as an exciting challenge. Dealers tell us that it sells well due to the influence of its famous designer and today's strong interest in the designs and colors of the '50s.

Plate 202
Tidbit, Creamer, Cereal/Soup, Sugar Bowl, Salt Shaker, Cup and Saucer, Individual Casserole. Very nearly the same size as the sugar bowl, the individual casserole (shown in charcoal gray) is very hard to find. Collectors tell us the cups and saucers are also very scarce, and one says he has a Fiesta cup in Epicure charcoal gray.

Plate 203
Coffeepot, Plates, Nappy, Gravy Bowl, Ladle, Covered Vegetable Casserole.
The pink nappy is the 9" size (it actually measures 8¾"); plates are 10" and 6½". The turquoise gravy boat holds a charcoal gray ladle.

 *Five Petal Daisy*

Here's another line for those of you who enjoy a challenge. The name isn't official, merely descriptive. The official company name for this shape is Marigold, and it was used as a basis for several decaled lines. This piece is back-stamped 1937, so it was made early in the days of HLC's campaign to promote this type of colored dinnerware. This is the deep plate in the company's standard light green glaze. In fact, the few pieces that have been reported are all in this color; a 9" plate is dated D37 N8.

Plate 204

Jubilee

Jubilee was presented by Homer Laughlin in 1948 in celebration of their 75th year of ceramic leadership. Shapes were simple and contemporary. It was offered in four colors: celadon green (blue-gray), shell pink, mist gray, and cream beige. Very soon after its introduction, HLC began to market many other lines of dinnerware employing its basic shapes.

Plate 205
Double Egg Cup; Coupe Soup, 8"; Demitasse Cup and Saucer; Plates, 6", 7", 9", 10"; Teacup and Saucer; Cereal/Soup Bowl, 6"; Fruit Bowl, 5½".

Plate 206
Platters, 11", 13"; Teapot; Coffeepot; Creamer and Sugar Bowl; Casserole; Nappy, 8½"; Salt and Pepper Shakers; Fast-Stand Sauce Boat; Chop Plate, 15".

Plate 207
Kitchen Kraft Bowl Set.
This set was glazed in the Jubilee colors and along with the Fiesta juice set shown in Plate 41 was part of a promotion to stimulate sales. All of these items are very rare, and because of that, it's taken us what seems like an unbelievably long time to arrive at correct conclusions. Fact: only one of these three bowls was ever produced in gray, and that is the 10" size. Colors do not vary from size to size; they are as shown — shell pink, 6"; celadon green, 8"; and mist gray — an exact match to Fiesta gray — 10". Because of the fact that Jubilee's mist gray and Fiesta's gray were one and the same, the 10" bowl has always been a very desirable piece to own and has always stirred up much interest. They're not as rare as we once thought — several have surfaced since the Eighth Edition; though I haven't kept records, I have heard from at least a dozen collectors who have one.

Pastel Nautilus

HLC's Nautilus was made from the '30s into the '50s. It was often decaled; it was fancy-trimmed without decals; it was combined with Fiesta's first four colors to make the four Harmony sets; and in 1940 (no other date marks have been reported) it was dipped in the pastel glazes of Serenade — pink, yellow, green, and blue — and offered to the public as Pastel Nautilus.

The line is scarce, to be sure, but very attractive; and if you have the patience to work at it, collecting a complete set would represent quite an accomplishment. For a complete listing of available items, see Suggested Values in the back of the book.

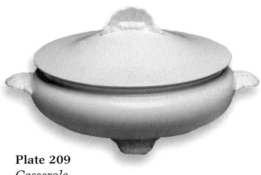

Plate 209
Casserole.

Plate 208
Bowls.
Clockwise: tab-handled soup, 6" cereal, 5" fruit, and cream soup.

Plate 210
9", 7", and 6" Plates; Teacup; Double Egg Cup; and Creamer.

Rhythm

Rhythm is a '50s line designed by Don Schreckengost, a designer who's streamline styling is attracting more and more attention as interest in dinnerware from this era continues to increase. Though we found very little information on this line at HLC, those with large collections report backstamps with dates indicating a span of production from 1950 to 1960. It was made in Harlequin yellow, chartreuse, gray, forest green, and burgundy (collectors call it maroon).

Though the spoon rest has been found in the colors of Harlequin and bearing a Harlequin paper label, Mr. Schreckengost confirmed the fact that he had originally designed it for Rhythm. It was a piece that HLC used in several lines. You'll sometimes find it with decals — Rhythm Rose and American Provincial are the most common.

For a complete listing of available items, see Suggested Values in the back of the book.

Plate 211
Casserole, Nappy, Soup, Fruit, Footed Cereal/Chowder.
The 5½" fruit is shown center front; to the right is the 5½" footed cereal. The nappy (forest green) measures 9"; the soup is 8¼". The casserole is very hard to find.

Plate 212
Plate, 8"; Sauce Boat, Soup/Cereal Bowls.
The 8" yellow plate and the brown soup/cereal are marked Rhythm though both are non-standard colors. The sauce boat shown here in cobalt has also been found in black, turquoise, and brown, made in these colors to go with other lines. It was a common practice to mix hollow ware shapes from one line with flatware shapes from another to create new patterns of dinnerware. Cavalier and Charm House were from the same period as Rhythm, and all three shapes were often blended. A few items from a line called Brittany have also been discovered glazed in Rhythm colors.

Plate 213
Calendar Plate.
The company issued a calendar plate for a number of years, using whatever blanks were available. This one is Rhythm.

Plate 214
Mixing Bowls.
These are the Kitchen Kraft bowls; this particular combination of color identifies them as Rhythm. They measure 10" (always chartreuse), 8" (yellow), and 6" (forest green), and they have a dry (wiped free of glaze) foot. They were part of a sales campaign, a ploy the company also used to promote Fiesta and Jubilee. The Eighth Edition shared the discovery of a maroon Fiesta juice tumbler, which seems to indicate that the theory held by collectors for many years was fact: the gray juice pitcher and tumblers in chartreuse, forest green, gray, and finally maroon were a Rhythm promotion.

Plate 215
Plates, Sauce Boat and Stand, Sugar Bowl, Snack Plate, Salt and Pepper Shakers.
Plates measure 10", 9", 7", and 6"; the 7" and 8" (see Plate 212) are scarce. Though once considered nonexistent, we have had reports of a few divided plates in maroon. They're very hard to find in any color.

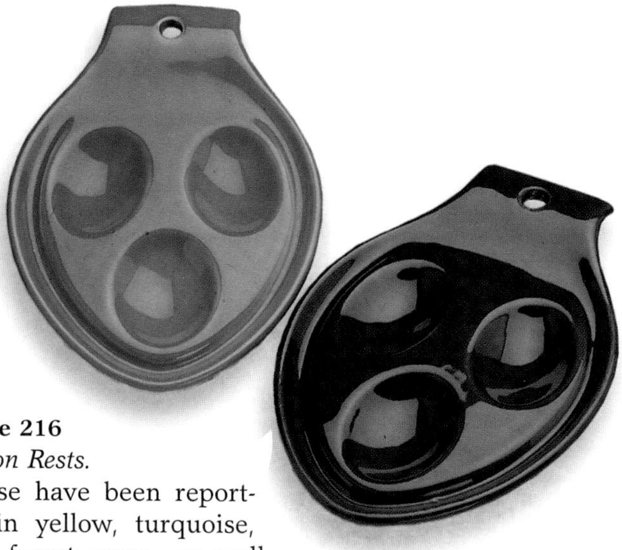

Plate 216
Spoon Rests.
These have been report-
ed in yellow, turquoise,
and forest green, as well
as a very rare example in medi-
um green and one in Fiesta Red. One of the
turquoise spoon rests was found with a Harlequin label still intact, so obviously these were
sold with that line as well. You'll also see them in
white with a decal decoration, but those are
much less valuable.

Plate 217
These 7" plates are decorated with decals of popular Disney characters.

Plate 218
Three-tier Tidbit, Platters, Cup and Saucer, Teapot.
These platters measure 13½" and 11½" long. We've had a report that a Rhythm plat-
ter has been found with the turkey decal. (See Plate 96.)

Plate 219
Demitasse Cups.
These utilize a standard HLC dinnerware shape called Brittany. They're shown along with a sugar bowl for scale.

Plate 220
The focus of this photograph is the salad bowl (shown with other pieces for scale). Collectors report that these are often acquired from among the remnants of original Rhythm sets. They've been found in forest green as well as turquoise. If you have information concerning these bowls, let us hear from you.

Plate 221
These flat soup bowls are Brittany shapes glazed in all the Rhythm colors. They're marked HLC and carry dates coinciding with Rhythm's production period.

Seller's Line

In the Eight Edition, we included a photo of a Seller's cup, not really knowing much about it. Since then we've heard from two collectors who were willing to share the information their research has revealed. These cups and saucers were produced for the M. Seller Co., a distributing firm with locations in the west. They may have just been salesmen's giveaways. Note the cross between Carnival (the body of the cup) and Harlequin (colors, saucer rings). Since this photo, one of the researchers has reported finding one in Harlequin yellow. Fiesta yellow is shown here. These are very rare.

Plate 222

Serenade

Serenade was a pastel dinnerware line that was produced for only three or four years from about 1939 (it was mentioned in the American Potter's brochure from the World's Fair) until the early '40s. It was offered in four lovely pastel shades — yellow, green, pink, and blue. Although not well accepted by the public when it was introduced, today's collectors find its soft delicate hues and dainty contours appealing. There is growing interest in this elusive pattern, but prices are still relatively moderate.

Lug soups and teapots are rare; so are 10" plates. You may also find deep plates, 7" plates, 5" fruits, and 9" nappies to be scarce. Sugar bowls are harder to find than creamers, and the lid for the casserole (the only Kitchen Kraft piece dipped in Serenade colors) is very rare — only five have ever been reported.

Plate 223
Chop Plate, 13"; Teapot; Creamer and Sugar Bowl; Cup and Saucer. (Photo by Shel Izen)

Plate 225
*Deep Plate; Nappy, 9";
Sauce Boat; Fruit
Bowl, 6"; Lug (Tab-
Handled) Soup Bowl.*

(Photo by Shel Izen)

Plate 224
Casserole, Kitchen Kraft.
For many years, the lid to this casserole
could not be found. Finally we're up to
five — two in yellow, one in blue, one in
ivory, and this one in green.

Plate 226
Casserole.
This is the standard Serenade casserole. (Photo
by Shel Izen)

Plate 227
Plates, 10", 9", 6"; Platter, 12½"; Pickle Dish; Salt and Pepper Shakers. (Photo by Shel Izen)

Skytone

This is a seldom-seen but very attractive line of dinnerware utilizing the shapes of Jubilee. It was sold through the '50s in both the plain blue and white seen here and with decals. What makes this line unusual is that the beautiful blue hue comes not from the glaze but from the clay used in its production. In addition to the pieces shown with the Jubilee line, you may also find a butter dish in the Amberstone shape with a blue lid and a white base.

Plate 228
Example of Skytone.

Suntone

Here's another colored line of dinnerware — the shapes are Jubilee, and it is from the same time period as Skytone. The clay used in its production was terra-cotta brown, the glaze itself was clear. According to company records, decaled Suntone was marketed as well. The Jubilee shapes proved very popular through the '50s, and the company utilized them for many attractive patterns, changing the name of the shape to Debutante when the lines were white-glazed.

Plate 229
Cup and Saucer.
A very interesting, very small cup and saucer, shown with the teacup and Jubilee demitasse cup for comparison. Was it from a child's set? We don't know. Does anyone?

Plate 230
Suntone Grouping.

Tango

Tango was introduced in the late 1930s, made for promotion through Newberry's and the McLellan Stores Company, New York City. For some reason, it was not a good seller — perhaps its rather Colonial design seemed a bit out of step alongside other styles of colored dinnerware. Standard colors were spruce green, mauve blue, yellow, and maroon; but, as you can see, a few pieces may also be found in Fiesta red.

The line was rather limited; all available items are shown right, although uncon-

Plate 231

firmed rumors occasionally circulate concerning the existence of an egg cup. Until the egg cup can be verified, we assume that the line consisted of a fruit bowl; deep plate; oval vegetable bowl; round nappy; casserole with lid; creamer and sugar bowl; cup and saucer; plates, 10", 9", 7", and 6"; platter; and salt and pepper shakers. The shakers should look very familiar to Riviera collectors. They were original with this line; but since their shape was compatible, they were borrowed for use with Riviera.

Though many collectors like the shapes and colors of the line, dealers tell us that because it's so hard to find, few actually attempt to collect it. Proving once again that value is a relative thing, those that collect recommended much higher prices in our survey than those who sell, because to them, the fact that it is so scarce makes it worth much more than suggested book prices — no doubt a sentiment shared by collectors of other minor lines as well.

Demitasse cups and saucers are available in all of Tango's colors (including red), on HLC's Republic shape.

The W.S. George Company made a line very similar to Tango, but their glazes are rather dull and the definition of the "petals" somewhat indistinct in comparison. You'll be able to recognize Tango by the raised line just inside the shaped rim.

Wells Art Glaze

This line was produced from 1930 until at least 1935 in the colors shown: rust, peach, green, and yellow. A burnt orange matt similar to Fiesta red has also been reported as well as turquoise matt and an unusual gray-blue matt (examples in Plate 234). It's a lovely design, and records list an extensive assortment. It's very scarce and to reassemble a set is a challenge to be sure, but one collectors don't mind rising to meet, and values continue to appreciate. Dealers tell us Arts and Crafts enthusiasts have discovered this line, accounting for some of the price increases.

Plate 232
Chop Plate, Covered Jug, Baker, Sugar Bowl with Lid, Teacup and Saucer, Demitasse Cup and Saucer, Handled Coffee Cup.
The handled chop plate is 10", the covered jug is 9", and the oval baker is 9" long. The cup on the far right is inscribed "Coffee" and is 4¾" tall.

Plate 233
Teapots.
Both teapots are scarce, and though we once thought the one on the left was very rare, several more have been found. The shape is from a standard HLC line called Empress. Most seem to be in yellow, though one was reported in turquoise, one in green (both marked Wells), and one in the celadon green of the Jubilee line. On the right is the traditional Wells Art Glaze teapot, you'll see it again in Plate 237.

Plate 234
Unusual gray-blue matt examples.

Plate 235
Cream Soup Bowl with Underliner.
These are seldom seen items; the underliner has a recessed ring.

Plate 236
Coffee Mug.
Here's a better view of the 4¾" coffee mug, a seldom seen piece.

Plate 237
Plates, Teapot, Teacup and Saucer, Creamer and Sugar Bowl.
Shown are the 9", 8", and 6" plates, and a square one that measures 8".

Plate 238
Covered Muffin.
These are wonderful items and very rare.
They fit on the 8" plate.

Plate 239
Batter Set.
The covered jug, covered syrup pitcher, and oval tray comprise this very rare set. You may also find these in white with floral decals.

Plate 240
Demitasse Pot, Individual Sugar and Creamer.
Note the differences in the handles on the sugar bowl shown here and the one in Plate 237.

When first introduced in the late '30s, Homer Laughlin's Mexican-style dinnerware lines were met with great enthusiasm. Speaking of Mexicana, which would prove to be one of their bestsellers, a trade-paper from May 1938, had this to say:

> When this Homer Laughlin pattern was first exhibited last (1937) July at the House Furnishing Show, it was an immediate smash hit. Its popularity has grown steadily ever since, and retailers have found it a constant and dependable source of profit. It started the vogue for the Mexican motif in crockery decoration which has since swept the country.
>
> And small wonder! For this Mexicana pattern is smart, colorful, and attractive. It embodies the old-world atmosphere of Mexico with the modern verve and personality which is so appealing to American housewives. Applied to the pleasing, beautifully designed Homer Laughlin shapes, it presents a bestseller of the first order.

Several other companies produced similarly decorated lines with a decided Mexican flavor — Paden City, Vernon Kilns, Crown, and Stetson to name but a few. Besides the Mexican lines shown in the color plates, HLC also made Arizona, decorated with a large green cactus, adobe house, yucca plant, and pottery jug; however, this line is seldom seen.

HLC's three principal Mexican decals are Mexicana (occasionally marked "Mexicana" with a gold backstamp), Hacienda, and Conchita. With rare exception, these lines are virtually always found on two shapes: Century and Swing. Century, based on the number of pieces that have turned up, was the much more successful line. (There are, however, rare items in Swing that may be nonexistent in Century.)

Neither Hacienda nor Conchita has been found with trim lines other than red, but Mexicana turns up comparatively often with blue trim — especially in Kitchen Kraft, Eggshell Nautilus, and Swing. In its first year of Century production, green and yellow trim lines were used as well. Yet here's an anomaly: the non-red trim on Century Mexicana 10" plates, 7" plates, cups, fruits, flat soups, and serving nappies, but on no other items — not even saucers, which seems especially strange. One collector found a mixed set of cobalt Fiesta (saucers, 6" plates, sugar bowl, and original creamer) with blue-line Mexicana (cups, 10" plates, and flat soups). The Mexicana cup looks great on the Fiesta saucer. Could it be this was another Harmony set that HLC didn't advertise in a national medium? Besides the primary-color trims we've mentioned, we've had a single report of some pieces with brown trim and some with no trim at all.

Conchita

Conchita is a line that utilizes Century shapes. A fairly extensive line of Kitchen Kraft was offered as well, though collectors tell us that it's not as plentiful as Kitchen Kraft with the Mexicana decal. Virtually all Conchita is trimmed in red.

Plate 241
Platter, 11½"; Creamer and Sugar Bowl; Cup and Saucer.
These tumblers were featured in the Fiesta Ensembles (see Plate 273). They look especially good with the Mexican lines. There were two sets — one comprised of the three directly in front of the platter. A second set consisted of the one to the far left, a larger tumbler with the Fiesta dancing girl, and a small juice glass with a guitar. These fired-on designs can be found on both plain and lightly paneled glasses. A third set along with a matching pitcher is shown in the chapter called Go-Alongs (Plate 270). Still another style has been reported. Paneled tumblers in two sizes with no top ring of color but two tiers of fired-on designs in the four primary colors: a bull and cactus scene on the front and pottery jars and a burro on the back. They're very rare and were likely made by the same company during the same time period.

Plate 242
Kitchen Kraft Server; Underplate; Individual Casserole.
Notice the original label on the underplate. This is the Nautilus shape, which is the shape collectors tell us was used with virtually every Kitchen Kraft line.

Plate 243
OvenServe Casserole, Kitchen Kraft Underplate, Cake Plate, Covered Jar, Covered Jug.
The casserole is marked Handy Andy on the base; and although it's hard to see in the photo, there is an embossed design at the rim of the lid as well as around the outside of the underplate above it. These two pieces were found together, complete with the metal base — a rare find. You'll find this casserole with other decals, one a wheat and flower motif.

Plate 244
Kitchen Kraft Jars, Small, Medium, and Large; Salt and Pepper Shakers.
The shakers are turned to show the decals on both sides.

Hacienda

This is a rather extensive line and is probably second only to Mexicana in availability. Both patterns are on Century shapes with few exceptions. Unlike Mexicana, however, you'll find no matching Kitchen Kraft line for Hacienda. The only exceptions ever reported were nested mixing bowls (6½" x 3¾", 8¼" x 4½", and 10¾" x 5¾"), evidently a special order for a Birmingham, Alabama, furniture store.

Plate 245
Butter Dish, ½-lb.; Teapot; Cream Soup Bowl.
All of these items are relatively hard to find. Because of the consistency with which these butter dishes have been used in Century-based lines, we originally assumed their shape to be Century. The butter bottom even looks like Century because of its striped tab-like extensions; but if you'll look at the La Hacienda pattern on the Jade shape shown in Plate 428, you'll see that they're actually Jade instead. The Hacienda teapot turns up more often than its matching casserole. The reverse is true of Century Mexicana, and only the casserole has been reported in Century Conchita.

Plate 246
Covered Jug.
Because this piece is complete with the lid, it's twice as nice. This is a rare item.

Plate 247
Dinner Bell, Butter Dish.
The bell has the Hacienda decal, but it's very doubtful that it was produced by HLC. The round butter dish is hard to find; this piece we guarantee to be Century.

Plate 248
Plate, 10"; Fruit Bowl, 5"; Cup and Saucer; Creamer and Sugar Bowl.

Plate 249
Casserole.
This is the regular Century casserole. It's a large, very attractive item, and extremely hard to find.

Plate 250
This is a better view of the lovely and very elusive Nautilus casserole shown at the bottom of the page.

Plate 251
Swing Demitasse Cups and Saucers; Teacup and Saucer.
These are the only demitasse cups and saucers we've ever heard of with Mexican decals. Here are two, Mexicana and Hacienda, shown for size comparison on either side of a Swing Conchita teacup and saucer.

Plate 252
Nautilus Deep Plate; Platter, 13"; Plate, 9"; Casserole; Creamer and Sugar Bowl; Sauce Boat; Teacup and Saucer.
Hacienda on the Nautilus shape is rare, and the line is doubly unusual in that the color is white, not ivory.

Plate 253
Swing Creamer and Sugar Bowl; Utility Tray; Casserole with Lid; Luncheon and Bread and Butter Plates; Fruit Bowl; Cup and Saucer; Platter, 11½"; Covered Sauce Bowl with Saucer; Salt and Pepper Shakers.
This is another rare example of the Hacienda decal applied to an HLC shape other than Century. This is Swing, and again the background color is white. Mexicana and Conchita also appear on Swing.

 Mexicana

Of the tree major patterns, this one is the most extensive. Trim lines may be red or blue (to a lesser extent), but green, yellow, and even brown trims are also found, though rarely. Mexicana found on shapes other than Century is very unusual.

Plate 254
Liberty Mexicana.
Here's a very rare item — Mexicana on the Liberty shape. Although the decal is the same, the colors vary from the usual.

Plate 255
Platter, 13½"; Sugar Bowl and Creamer; Baker, 9"; Lug Soup Bowl.

Plate 256
Kitchen Kraft Cake Plate; Covered Jug; Stacking Refrigerator Units and Lid; Salt and Pepper Shakers.

Plate 257
Teapot; Cup and Saucer; Deep 1-Pint Bowl.

Plate 258
Covered Casserole.

Plate 259
Batter Set.
Decaled Century lines from the early '30s (such as English Garden or Columbine) often include batter sets, but here's one from a mid-to-late '30s line, Mexicana. Adding to the intrigue is the fact that the larger jug is dated "D-35" (April 1935), a full two years before HLC put this decal into general use! The smaller syrup jug is not dated but we assume from the creamier color of its glaze, that it's a later production. The two jugs were not found together, but nevertheless make a nice pair.

Plate 260
Virginia Rose — this time as a very rare variation of the Mexicana line.
Shown are the 9½" and 6" plates, teacup and saucer, and the 5" fruit bowl.

Plate 261
Nautilus Eggshell.
Pieces shown here are dated 1937. Note the blue-line trim and the stark white background. This line is very, very rare. Shown are the 13" platter, 9" and 7" plates, 5" fruit, creamer and sugar bowl, and the teacup and saucer.

Max-i-cana

We've never found an official name for this pattern anywhere in the company's files, but it's been dubbed "Max-i-cana" by collectors. The siesta-taking Mexican snoozing under his sombrero amid jugs, jars, and cacti decorate the shape known as Yellowstone in Plate 263 and looks just as much at home on ivory Fiesta in Plate 262.

Plate 262
Fiesta Max-i-cana Platter; Cup and Saucer; 4¾" Fruit.

Plate 263
Yellowstone Max-i-cana Platter; Sauce Boat Liner; Sauce Boat; Egg Cup; Rolled-Edge Egg Cup; Casserole; ½-lb. Butter Dish; Creamer and Sugar Bowl.
The platter measures 13½"; directly in front of it, the sauce bowl liner is 8½" long. A teapot has never been reported.

Mexicali

Yellow Harlequin Mexicali.
Until the seventh edition, Virginia Rose was the only shape we knew that was decorated with the Mexicali decal. These pictures show a set of yellow Harlequin Mexicali. This must have been a very exciting acquisition. Not a single other piece has ever surfaced that we know of, but the owner was lucky enough to buy the set intact. Century has also been found with this decal.

Plate 264

Plate 265

Plate 266
11½" Platter; Creamer and Sugar Bowl.
Swing is the shape shown here with the 11½" platter decorated in the Mexicali pattern. The creamer and sugar bowl are in the Conchita design. All pieces are marked "Eggshell," a term used to indicate HLC's lightweight semiporcelain.

117

Plate 267
Virginia Rose.
Shown here with the Mexicali decal. You'll have to look long and hard for an example of this line or the two shown previously. All are extremely rare.

Plate 268
Here's a very similar but unknown pattern on Century.

 Ranchera

Plate 269
Nautilus Shape.
This final south-of-the-border dinnerware line utilizes the Nautilus shape again, this time with a decal we've never seen before. We have no knowledge of its official name, but the collector who is sharing this find with us suggests we call it "Ranchera."

With the unprecedented popularity of the brightly colored dinnerware lines made by Homer Laughlin and its contemporaries, many types of housewares were designed to enhance the festive look they evoked, and today's collectors search for these wonderful items to extend the scope of their interests. They've coined the term "Go-Alongs" to refer to the metal parts (frames, handles, etc.), woodenware, flatware, and linens made during the years when this type of home decor was in vogue. It is not uncommon to find items that carry the name "Fiesta." We've seen a Fiesta-labeled tablecloth (a damask plaid that we've shown in past editions), a Fiesta Ware Mohawk Brandy bottle (simply a black jug, not made by HLC), and a Fiesta Outing Kit (two plastic aqua and pink thermos bottles and accessories in a thermal carrying case). Just remember that HLC's patent was for dinnerware production only — they made nothing else.

Glassware and Place Accessories

Many go-alongs have a strong South of the Border look. Colors are vivid, primary tones, and the dancing senorita or the guitar-strumming Mexican gent are prevalent motifs. The water set in Plate 270 is decorated with both — the pitcher is 9½" tall, the tumblers range from 4¾" (8-ounce) to 3¾" (the center one holds 8 ounces while the one on the right holds only 4 ounces). Collectors report that

Plate 270

the larger tumbler is most common, and shot glasses in this pattern have been found as well. In Plate 271 are tumblers we've never shown before, and in Plate 272 you'll see wooden napkin rings, placecard holders, cord-wrapped enameled tumblers, and a set of coasters in a wireware frame. Plate 273 displays a wonderful set of glassware in the original box that is stamped "40 Pc Genuine Fiesta Ensemble." It contains twenty-four tumblers in three sizes and four colors, eight clear glass ashtrays and eight swizzle sticks, each tipped in the four colors. These were included in one of the Fiesta Ensembles (see Plate 323) that were boxed and shipped at the factory along with a service of matching Catalin/Bakelite cutlery with handles in matching colors. Examples of these go-alongs are shown in Plate 275. Note also the salt and pepper shakers that accompanied some of the ensemble sets. The tumblers in Plate 274 illustrate another style of coordinating glassware. This style was paired up with the Juanita Ensemble, which consisted of a service for

Plate 271

Plate 272

eight in the Riviera pattern, matching cutlery, these tumblers in four sizes, glass ashtrays, and swizzle sticks. While the glassware pictured here is paneled, there is another style that is not. Shown are red (5¼"), light green (4"), yellow (3½"), and mauve blue (3"). There are other lines of glassware that are compatible with the '50s colors of both Fiesta and Rhythm: water

Plate 273

and juice tumblers with narrow bands of color in gray, dark green, chartreuse, and burgundy. In Plate 276 you'll see the glassware from a dessert service for eight that contained 7" Fiesta plates, two each in red, cobalt, yellow, and green, and these tumblers and sherbets. Though the glass is of good quality, the red is only fired on. The current owner was able to trace this set back to the '40s when an HLC employee gave it to a friend as a wedding gift. Rattan holders have been dyed to match genuine Fiesta tumblers in Plate 277.

Plate 274

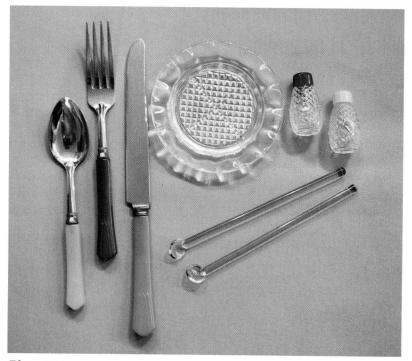

Plate 275
(Photo by Fred Mutchler)

Plate 277

Plate 276

Quickut Cutlery

Quickut Cutlery. The Fiesta Ensemble (see Plates 323 – 327) offered by the company in the early years of production included a set of flatware with Catalin (plastic) handles, color coordinated to match the dinnerware. Several other patterns of Catalin-handled cutlery were on the market during this period — an especially intriguing set is shown here (note the name on the box). Collectors love to use this type of flatware to re-create the ensemble look. Prices vary greatly — if you buy it a piece at a time, you should be able to buy at much lower prices proportionately than if you purchase a place setting, especially if salad forks or tablespoons are included. Boxed sets that contain service for eight or more with several extra serving pieces go at a premium. The matching Chef's set is extremely rare — this boxed, unused set is the only one known in such wonderful original condition.

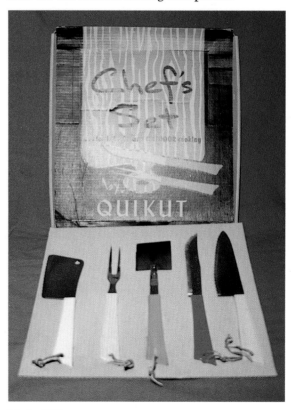

Plate 278

Plate 279
(Photo by Desert Productions)

Metal Fittings

The cream soup bowl, marmalade, and cake plate with metal fittings (Plate 280), the #609 double tidbit with folding stand (Plate 281), the #610 salad service set (Plate 283), the #608 8" casserole and frame (Plate 282), and the condiment set (salt, pepper, and mustard, illustrated in the drawing) were part of Homer Laughlin's #600 Gift Assortment of Colored

Plate 280

Ware. Because the colors listed on the company order sheet that shows this assortment are red, green, blue, and yellow, we assume that it was offered in the early days of production. There is another frame that will hold both the marmalade and the mustard, and you may find a metal rotating base that turns the six-part Fiesta relish tray into a lazy-susan.

Note that the tidbit tray in Plate 285 has a ring handle; you'll also find examples with the triangular terminal that was used on the Amberstone tray. Both are generally accepted as original. There may even have been other styles. When you buy, though, make sure the fittings are not new. Drilling plates and adding hardware is a relatively simple matter!

You'll find rattan-wrapped handles similar to the one on the mixing bowl (now ice bucket) in Plate 284 in sizes to fit

Plate 281

Plate 282

Plate 283

Plate 284

Plate 285

the 7", 9", and 10" plates (this size also fits the relish tray), as well as both of the chop plates. All are exact matches to the metal handle offered in combination with the chop plate in the 1939 – 43 selling campaign, so we'd almost bet these were routed through HLC! The ash stand in Plate 287 is a fantastic futuristic style right out of the '50s — so is the Fiesta deep plate in chartreuse.

The beverage carrier in Plate 286 is wireware; you'll see another style in Plate 293 (this one has been reproduced). Were they marketed by HLC? Not that we know of. But there were evidently promotions offered by the company for which there are no documentation, so who is to say!

Riviera and Harlequin with metal enhancements are shown in Plates 288 through 291. Notice that the fittings on

Plate 287

the two nut bowls and the two-tier tidbit are obviously the work of the same company. The tidbit is usually found only in ivory, but one has been reported in green, complete with a green glass knob. The decaled Harlequin tumbler has been outfitted with a footed base and handle for a soda-fountain look. (Other metal enhancements are shown in Plate 293 as well — a 5½" dripolator insert converts the teapot to a coffeepot,

Plate 286

123

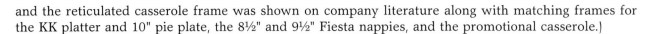

and the reticulated casserole frame was shown on company literature along with matching frames for the KK platter and 10" pie plate, the 8½" and 9½" Fiesta nappies, and the promotional casserole.)

Plate 288

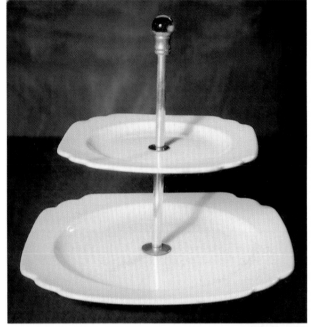

Plate 289

Plate 290

Plate 291

124

Woodenware

The woodenware items in Plates 292 through 295 are all examples of Fiestawood. It was made by the G.H. Specialty Co., Milwaukee, Wisconsin. Note its characteristic band of rings. The 10" glass insert for the large server in Plate 293 is from a line called Intaglio, made by Indiana Glass during the 1930s. The mushroom-shaped center section in the party tray is for hors d'oeuvres; it's pierced to hold toothpicks and can be removed. You'll find other Fiestawood items as well. Plates 295 and 296 illustrate woodenware by other companies — another hors d'oeuvres tray with a snoozing Mexican punctuating the banded border and a fruit-decorated lazy-susan base that holds a 15" Fiesta chop plate. We've also seen nappies in holders very similar to this one. (See page 123 for description of the metal items in Plate 293.)

Plate 292

Plate 294

Plate 293

Plate 295

Plate 296

Decaled Tin Kitchenware

Plate 297

Notice the Fiesta-like dinnerware shown in the decals on the items in Plates 297 through 299. Collectors tell us that these pieces are sometimes found on yellow in addition to the white background shown here, and a matching three-tier vegetable bin and a kitchen stool have been found as well. The bread box in Plate 300 has a Mexicana-like decal — the only piece with this design that we know of. Owens-Illinois Can Co. made a line of tinware called Fiesta (what else) that was decorated in "Roman stripes in red, blue, and green on yellow." This set consisted of canisters, a bread box, a dustpan, a garbage pan, a 14½" wastebasket, and a kitchen stool. Yet another line is shown in Plate 306 with the Fiesta cabinet. In our files we have a photo of a 12" turquoise chop plate to which has been added a tinware cake-safe top. The lid is enameled in a matching turquoise, and it's topped with a wooden knob.

Plate 298

Plate 299

Plate 300

Enameled Tinware

Here is the Fiesta Popcorn Set marketed during the '40s. This set was bought at an Arizona auction still in the original carton marked "Snack Set #90, US Mfg Corp, Decatur, IL." Note the genuine Fiesta salt shaker and creamer, no doubt for the melted butter. The auctioneer said there had been a wooden spoon that had disappeared from the box. Though we have no way of knowing for sure, the presence of the two pieces of Fiesta suggests this set may have been marketed by HLC themselves. The bowls turn up every once in a while, but this set — complete, unused, and in the original box — may well be the only one around. You may find a very similar set made for Jolly Time Popcorn — without the Fiesta-like rings. The bowls in the cloverleaf wireware stand are the same as the popcorn bowls in Plate 301.

Plate 301
(Photo by Desert Productions)

Plate 302

Miscellaneous

Plate 303
Hankscraft Egg Cooker.
In the early 1940s, the Hankscraft Company marketed their electric egg cooker in service sets that included the cooker as shown, "four vari-colored Fiesta egg cups (red, yellow, blue, and green), ivory (pottery) poaching dish, Fiesta salt and pepper shakers, and maple plywood tray." They called this set the Fiesta Egg Service and sold it for $9.50 to $13.70, depending upon whose catalog you happened to be using. The set as shown has not been listed in any of these catalogs but is the one more often found. Obviously, these egg cups are not Fiesta. They're made of the same vitrified material as the cooker itself (which is identical to the one pictured with the Fiesta set mentioned above) and are smaller than genuine Fiesta egg cups. The colors are fired on, and in addition to the red example shown here, the cooker has also been found in green and yellow. Remember, this was a Hankscraft product — not made by Homer Laughlin, not genuine Fiesta!

A similar idea found in a gift-giving ad from a Christmas 1937 *American Home* magazine featured a Westinghouse sandwich grill on a tray large enough to accommodate it, a small cutting board, and several pieces of Fiesta: the utility tray with what appears in the photograph to be the center relish tray insert nestled in one end, a stack of small plates, salt and pepper shakers, a mustard, and a marmalade.

Plate 304
Buzza Cardozo Fiestacraft Paper.
Fiesta colors and a Mexican theme make this wrapping paper a fun go-along. It's copyrighted 1938.

Plate 305
Serviset by Sutherland.
Found in its original cellophane wrap, this set contains a paper table cover and four paper napkins. It was made in Kalamazoo, Michigan, and copyrighted 1949.

Plate 306

Kitchen Cabinet and Accessories.
We've heard of some strange things, but none has ever topped the kitchen cabinet shown here. Note the red, green, cobalt, and yellow trim. The Hoosier-type cabinet has a porcelain work surface, flour sifter,

NO-U-28-F-FIESTA

Plate 307

and utensil and bread drawers. Attached side cabinets house storage shelves. Each piece is marked with code numbers and "Fiesta." Detective work by the current owner located the manufacturer, the Marsh Furniture Company of Hig Point, North Carolina, who is still in business today. Their sales manager said it was common at the time for Marsh to special order a variation of their cabinets for large customers such as Montgomery Ward or J.C. Penney. With the introduction of Fiesta by HLC in 1936, he assumed the special order may have been a marketing tie-in by one of their retailers or even possibly for a store display. All tinware accessory items pictured are stamped Tindeco, once a major tin products company in Baltimore. Plate 307 shows the code numbers stenciled on the back of the cabinet.

Plate 308
Do-it-yourself Decals.
These were readily available in 5- and 10¢ stores, and collectors have reported finding sheets of them such as the one shown here. The back of the sheet reads "Designs by Betty Best, Festivalware, Set #5001." They were produced in 1945 by the American Decalcomania Co. of Chicago and New York. You may find tiles that have been commercially decorated with these decals, and shelf paper by Betty Brite that also features Fiesta dishes.

Plate 309
Japan Tea Set.
This set will be as close as you'll get to a vintage Fiesta children's tea set, but this one never saw the light of day at HLC. It's marked "Made in Japan." We show the teapot, creamer, and sugar bowl, but also included in the service for six were plates, cups, and saucers.

Commercial Adaptations and Ephemera

The commercial use of Fiesta in advertising and television has become so commonplace that we've become almost blaisè about it. You see it alongside featured recipes, in store ads, and on product containers, cookbook covers, greeting cards, etc. It's always fun to recognize Homer Laughlin dinnerware in the kitchens of many TV sitcom homes, and though more often than not it's Fiesta you see; occasionally the other HLC lines show up as well.

If you enjoy collecting vintage ephemera, try to find the October 10, 1936, issue of *The Saturday Evening Post*. Inside is a beautiful two-page Armstrong floor covering ad with a vintage kitchen-dining room fairly blooming with Fiesta. Another ad featuring Fiesta appeared in *Better Homes and Gardens*, December 1936. *Household Magazine*, September 1937, has a full page of quick and easy luncheon recipes. The picture shows an uncovered Fiesta casserole full of onion soup and three uncovered onion soup bowls sitting around it.

Company Price Lists

Plate 310

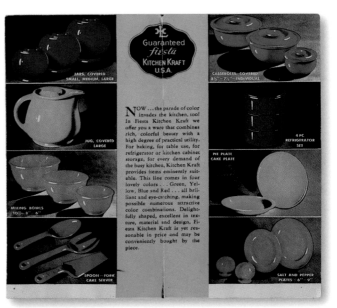

Plate 311

Advertising materials — especially HLC's own — make interesting and desirable additions to our collections, and they're certainly worthwhile investments as well! The company's price lists contain a wealth of information. They've been our main source of study, and as new ones are found to fill in the gaps, we may yet learn more. Because most of them are dated, we have been able to learn when items were introduced or dropped, what colors were in production during a given year, and occasionally we would pick up a tidbit of information that would help in answering one of our many questions. Fiesta price lists, though by no means easy to find, come up for sale much more often those that represent the company's other lines.

Plate 312

Plate 313

Plate 314

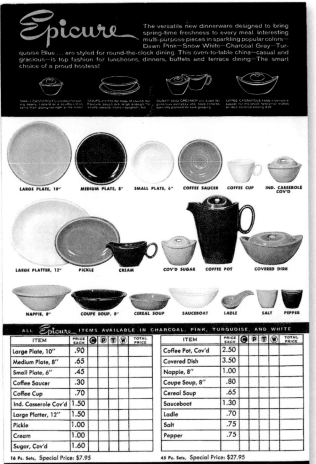

Epicure

The versatile new dinnerware designed to bring spring-time freshness to every meal. Interesting multi-purpose pieces in sparkling popular colors—Dawn Pink—Snow White—Charcoal Gray—Turquoise Blue . . . are styled for round-the-clock dining. This oven-to-table china—casual and gracious—is top fashion for luncheons, dinners, buffets and terrace dining—The smart choice of a proud hostess!

LARGE PLATE, 10" MEDIUM PLATE, 8" SMALL PLATE, 6" COFFEE SAUCER COFFEE CUP IND. CASSEROLE COV'D

LARGE PLATTER, 12" PICKLE CREAM COV'D SUGAR COFFEE POT COVERED DISH

NAPPIE, 8" COUPE SOUP, 8" CEREAL SOUP SAUCEBOAT LADLE SALT PEPPER

ALL Epicure ITEMS AVAILABLE IN CHARCOAL, PINK, TURQUOISE, AND WHITE

ITEM	PRICE EACH	C	P	T	W	TOTAL PRICE
Large Plate, 10"	.90					
Medium Plate, 8"	.65					
Small Plate, 6"	.45					
Coffee Saucer	.30					
Coffee Cup	.70					
Ind. Casserole Cov'd	1.50					
Large Platter, 12"	1.50					
Pickle	1.00					
Cream	1.00					
Sugar, Cov'd	1.60					

16 Pc. Sets, Special Price: $7.95

ITEM	PRICE EACH	C	P	T	W	TOTAL PRICE
Coffee Pot, Cov'd	2.50					
Covered Dish	3.50					
Nappie, 8"	1.00					
Coupe Soup, 8"	.80					
Cereal Soup	.65					
Sauceboat	1.30					
Ladle	.70					
Salt	.75					
Pepper	.75					

45 Pc. Sets, Special Price: $27.95

THE HOMER LAUGHLIN CHINA CO., NEWELL, W. VA.
• WORLD'S LARGEST MANUFACTURERS OF DINNERWARE •

Plate 315

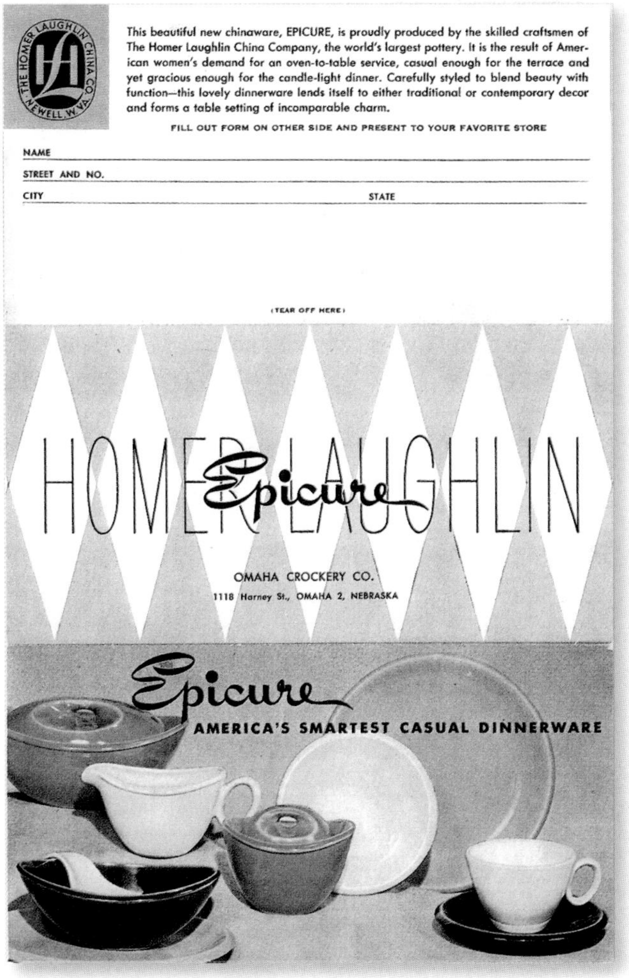
THE HOMER LAUGHLIN CHINA CO. NEWELL, W. VA.
This beautiful new chinaware, EPICURE, is proudly produced by the skilled craftsmen of The Homer Laughlin China Company, the world's largest pottery. It is the result of American women's demand for an oven-to-table service, casual enough for the terrace and yet gracious enough for the candle-light dinner. Carefully styled to blend beauty with function—this lovely dinnerware lends itself to either traditional or contemporary decor and forms a table setting of incomparable charm.
FILL OUT FORM ON OTHER SIDE AND PRESENT TO YOUR FAVORITE STORE
NAME
STREET AND NO.
CITY
STATE
(TEAR OFF HERE)
HOMER LAUGHLIN
Epicure
OMAHA CROCKERY CO.
1118 Harney St., OMAHA 2, NEBRASKA
Epicure
AMERICA'S SMARTEST CASUAL DINNERWARE

Plate 316

Fiesta Store Display

Plate 317

This cardboard store display captures and conveys the festive appeal of Fiesta dinnerware. This particular one never left the HLC pottery, but a few collectors report being lucky enough to have found one elsewhere. There were actually two of the small side sections; one is missing from this example. You can judge its size from the mixing bowls on either side. One of these complete and still in its original box, setup instructions included, has been found! The box is embossed "1 Set Fiesta Display, Omaha Grocery Co., Omaha Nebr. To Breeding Hdwe Co. Winterset Iowa."

Original Packaging Material

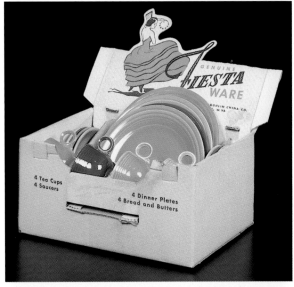

Plate 318

Plate 319

Examples such as these are very popular with collectors — especially those with the dancing girl logo. Imagine finding the four-place dinner service still mint in the box. The sugar bowl and creamer, left, are special enough on their own, they're medium green! But factor in the original packaging and they're fantastic. Medium green teacups (packed two per carton) have been found in a box similar to the photo above.

Plate 320

Plate 321

The left photo contains the box for the 45 Piece Service for Eight that the 1978 reissue of Harlequin dinnerware came in as well as a carton for a 16 Piece Set of Riviera in green, mauve blue, yellow, and ivory. The box is stamped "Recycle for the War" which is probably the reason red was not included! Amberstone items in their original wrapper are shown below. Many of these pieces were accompanied by a "Bonus Certificate" good for a "Free Sheffield Deluxe Amberstone Tray with attractive golden handle" (redeemable for 10 bonus certificates). (Photos by Harvey Linn, Jr.)

Plate 322

Fiesta Ensemble Ads

Plate 323
(Photo by Desert Productions)

Described in an earlier chapter, these ensembles were offered in only four basic colors along with coordinating glassware tumblers and accessories. There were two styles of tumblers that we know of, those with the fired-on Mexican motif and those with a band of color at the rim (either with paneled or plain sides). You'll see both in these ads and again in the Go-Alongs chapter. The cobalt 7" Riviera plates pictured in the ensemble in Plate 323 affirm our suspicions that they were indeed dipped to go with an ensemble set. Note the terms: $2.00 down and $2.00 per month — how's that for an easy payment plan! This particular Fiesta ensemble ad ran in a Sear's Christmas catalog (Special Edition, Dec. 1939). Also shown (Plates 324 – 326) are three full-page newspaper ads — one for the Juanita ensemble (all Riviera, though the name is mentioned nowhere in the ad), one for an ensemble featuring genuine Fiesta, and one that is a pleasant mix of both Fiesta and Riviera. Newspaper ads are very rare (as one

Plate 324

Plate 326

collector observed: "even harder to find than a turquoise onion soup bowl"), and they're valued very highly. Both sides are shown (Plates 327 – 328) of an insert flyer that was probably included in a box of Fiesta to introduce merchants to the ensemble promotions. Its colors are pristine, the folds are original, and the sepia-tone graphics and copy on the

Plate 325

back have never been seen before. Its owner believes this to be the only example of an ad of this type found thus far. One other ensemble reported to us included ninety pieces of Fiesta (no Riviera at all) that was given away by a lumber store to the winner of a 25-word essay contest. (Photos by Fred Mutchler)

Plate 327

Plate 328

137

Commercialized Fiesta Ware

The ashtray, right, seems to have been a popular item for advertising use. This one reads "Compliments of Sears, Roebuck & Co." In the center left photo you'll see an ivory 9" Kitchen Kraft pie plate that was a grocery store giveaway more than fifty years ago. (Alongside it is an example in a non-standard KK glaze — Harlequin spruce green.) For several years, the Lazarus Department issued Fiesta items to commemorate their anniversaries — mugs for the 86th year, a fruit bowl for their 87th, a plate for their 88th, an egg cup for their 89th, and a tumbler for their 90th. The syrup bottom (bottom right photo) is still full of the Dutchess brand tea that was sold in it many years ago; one has also been found in ivory. Just reported for this edition — a turquoise syrup complete with the top with this label: "SS Pierce Co. Boston, Epicure Cal. Orange Blossom Honey."

Plate 329

Plate 330

Plate 331
(Photo by Craig Macaluso, Metairie, LA)

Plate 332

Plate 333

Plate 334

Plate 335

Can Labels, Cereal Boxes, and Seed Packets

As more and more collectors begin searching for related material to add to their ever-growing collections, paper items like these are becoming very popular.

Plate 336
Can Label.
(Photo by Harvey Linn, Jr.)

Plate 337
Seed Pack.
This seed package features a pair of red and yellow Harlequin salt and pepper shakers.
(Photo by Harvey Linn, Jr.)

Plate 338
Can Label.
(Photo by Harvey Linn, Jr.)

Plate 339
Rolled Oats Box.
(Photo by Harvey Linn, Jr.)

Plate 340
Soup Can Label.
(Photo by Harvey Linn, Jr.)

Punch-Outs

Plate 341
These were distributed by the National Dairy Council during the 1950s. Originally there were eight in the series, but they were reissued in the '60s, and four more were added for a total of twelve.

Miscellaneous

Plate 342
Flour Sack.
This is no doubt the strangest item ever reported to us — a Fiesta Flour sack, made of printed cotton — the type that housewives used to make aprons and dresses out of in the '40s. The dancing girl is identical to HLC's down to the wavy lines that surround her, and (talk about spooky) the style of print in "Fiesta" matches the new Fiesta mark — and even better matches the title of this book! It was bought at a farm sale in Nebraska in 1998, and I've never heard of another one, so passing it off as a hoax seems premature. HLC had no information on it. Does anyone?

Plate 343
Ice Cream Parlor Decoration.
This heavy cardboard wall decoration piled high with cake and an ice cream sundae measures 8½" x 6". (Photo courtesy Harvey Linn, Jr.)

Plate 344
Restaurant Soup Menu.
Genuine Turtle soup? How exotic is that! Here's a great Heinz metal and cardboard advertising piece with double appeal due to the great Fiesta graphics. It measures 25" x 12", and it's from the early 1940s. (Photo by Desert Productions)

Advertising Mugs

Collectors have reported a variety of advertising mugs — one decorated with a caricature of Lucille Ball signed "Love, Lucy," from the Desilu Studios sounds especially unique. The Jackson Custom China Co. of Falls Creek, Pennsylvania, once made mugs similar to the Tom and Jerry. We've heard of them in brown with a cream interior and (hold on to your hats) maroon! How'd you like a set of those for your morning coffee! These were evidently not made on any large scale, but in case you should see some of them around, don't be taken in. The same company also produced a child's set consisting of a divided plate, a 6" bowl, and the Tom and Jerry, all in white decorated with a blue stenciled Donald Duck and friends.

T and Js in Fiesta colors with advertising are rare, though it isn't uncommon to find examples with color on the inside only (and some will be found without the advertising). These were produced during the late '60s into the early '70s; interior colors are turquoise, yellow, rose, amberstone, or turf green.

Plate 345
White, not ivory, is the color of these mugs.

Buick Mugs, Ashtrays, and Coasters

Plate 346
Coasters.
These accompanied the mugs shown in Plate 348 and are very hard to find.

Plate 347
Ashtray.
Inscription reads, "1963 Buick Management Meeting, Dec. 11-12." It is 8¾" in diameter and has six cigarette rests.

Plate 348
Series of Six Mugs.
These were distributed at annual meetings of Buick Management and their Retirement Club members, 1964 through 1969. Represented on the mugs are a 1924 Model 48 Buick, a 1904 Model B Buick, a 1936 Buick Special, a 1941 Buick Roadmaster, a 1908 Model 10 Buick, and a 1916 Model D Buick. Plate 346 illustrates the coasters that accompanied them; these are hard to find.

New Fiesta Commerorative Mug

Plate 349
This is the vintage-style mug; it was presented by the State of West Virginia to commemorate the introduction of the newly redesigned Fiesta Ware line.

As any collector of colored dinnerware knows, there are many lines with characteristics very similar to Homer Laughlin's. Not just Fiesta, but in fact nearly any of HLC's solid-color patterns has a look-alike. Potteries made a practice of reproducing each other's colors and designs, especially those that had proven to be successful on the market. For instance, Bauer's Monterey (1934) is very similar to Fiesta in both color and design. The cake stand shown in Plate 353 is a good example of that line. The band of rings, weight, and feel of this piece might cause even a seasoned collector to have second thoughts. In addition to the turquoise shown, Monterey also came in maroon, yellow, green, orange-red, medium blue, and ivory. Bauer's earlier line called Ring (1932), though with chunkier, heavier lines, was also produced in the bright solid glazes.

Serenade's counterpart was Lu-Ray by Taylor, Smith & Taylor. Pastel colors and simple lines were characteristic of both. Rhythm had a twin in Universal's Ballerina line. W.S. George made Rainbow, which is very easily confused with HLC's Tango line. And many other companies, among them Vernon Kilns, Franciscan, Metlox, Coors, and French Saxon China, produced solid-color dinnerware as well.

Plate 350

Teapots.

This photo contains a wonderful array of shapes and colors. These teapots represent lines that were Fiesta's contemporaries; they were produced by various manufacturers, all located in Ohio. The green pot is Taylor, Smith & Taylor's Vistosa, a line styled with pastry-crimped rims and handles daintily trimmed with tiny blossoms. Vistosa was made in Fiesta-like red, cobalt blue, yellow, and light green. Caliente (the cobalt teapot) was made by Paden City; its streamlined styling featured hollow ware whose bases were designed with four petal-like feet, and its colors were identical to Vistosa's. The large red teapot (top right) is Valencia by Shawnee, and the smaller red pot (bottom right) is part of Knowles' Yorktown line.

Even the Mexican decaled lines had competition. Stetson made Mexicalis, Paden City had Patio, Mt. Clemons produced Old Mexico, and Tia Juana was a line by the Knowles Company. So it is obvious that it takes a certain amount of study and caution to become a knowledgeable collector. To become familiar with the lines mentioned above, we recommend *The Collector's Encyclopedia of American Dinnerware* by Jo Cunningham. If you are a beginning collector intending to limit your buying to a particular line of Homer Laughlin's colored dinnerware, use this book as your guideline. It would be rare (though not entirely impossible) to find an authentic, previously undiscovered item that by now we have not shown, thanks to the faithfulness of our readers in reporting such finds, so be extremely suspicious.

Marks can be confusing as well. In the late 1970s, Franciscan marketed a line called Kaleidoscope, but according to Deleen Enge in the book *Franciscan: Plain and Fancy*, the serving pieces that went with the line were called Fiesta. Pitchers with a "Fiesta" ink stamp and the familiar large F (Franciscan) trademark have been found in white, yellow, cobalt, and gray-blue, but according to Enge, the color assortment also included cocoa, tangerine, dark green, and a color they called Sandman.

In Plate 351, right, is a line by Mikasa called Moderna, designed by Larry Laslo. This line was carried by some of the larger mail-order firms in 1985 and 1986. It was available in several colors; each piece is marked Mikasa. White "Fiesta" has been featured in restaurants located in Rockefeller Center by Restaurant Associates who commissioned Rego China of Whitestone, Queens, to make the ware for them. Nineteen pieces were designed; although none of the original molds were used, the style is unmistakable.

In the fall of 1998, Wal-Mart carried a knock-off line very similar to Fiesta — plates, bowls, and mugs — using the graduated concentric ring design. The mugs were larger than genuine Fiesta and had a "C" handle, rather than the ring. This line came in turquoise, yellow, periwinkle, and persimmon. By summer 2000 lilac and seamist green had been added, along with a line of "Mates" in two different patterns. Differences are obvious, though, and it isn't hard to distinguish between it and genuine Fiesta. Much of it is marked "Gibson, Thailand." And that seems to have been only one of many lines produced in recent years that draw either from the colors of the new Fiesta or the styling, some copy both. Nearly any housewares catalog or discount department store offer at least one copycat line.

Plate 351

Plate 352

Fiesta-like Cup.

The collector who reported this Fiesta fraud chose this cup from among several that were probably genuine, because it seemed to be in better shape than some of the others. When he got home with it, he noticed that it was slightly smaller and lighter and that there were abnormalities in the shape of the bowl and the handle. On closer examination he found that it was faintly marked "England."

Plate 353

Other HLC Look-alikes.
The bud vase, with an obviously inferior glaze, is just enough smaller to indicate that it has been cast from a mold made from an original. The little disk pitcher really is not from a child's set of Fiesta, even though its color and design suggest that it might well be. The cobalt pitcher looks very much like the Harlequin novelty creamer, but it has no band of rings. The donkey may look like its Harlequin double but sometimes pulls a cart marked "California." In the background is the Bauer cake stand mentioned earlier.

Plate 354

Plate 355

In past editions, we've called these our "mystery bowls," and collectors' opinions were split — were they or were they not Fiesta? We may still be less than 100% sure, but we feel like we are very close to the truth of the matter — thanks to an unrelenting researcher on a mission to identify the set her mother left her. Her mother "received them in the '30s as a premium from Jewel Tea" (first clue). She goes on: "At a show, a dealer had the same shapes in red (outside) and white (inside) and said they were Hall, though not marked." In a second letter dated April 2000 she relates that by now she has found decaled bowls marked Hall made from the same molds as her bowl set (second clue!), which led her to compare the rings on her bowls to those on a piece of Hall's Five-Band. They matched exactly. (Refer to *The Collector's Encyclopedia of Hall China* by Margaret and Kenn Whitmyer, page 127, to see illustrations of Five-Band.) Here's what she says about color (clue #3): "The green and yellow do not match those colors in my Fiesta collection. The cobalt and red do. The green matches a Hull teapot I have." Refer again to the Whitmyer book, page 169.

Plate 356

Illustrated here is Hall's Rainbow Bowl Set; it's in the same colors as our mystery set, down to the color progression: red (8¾"), cobalt blue (7¾"), yellow (6¾"), and green (5½"). The text explains that this set was produced for Jewel Tea in the '40s. In addition to all this information (thanks, Mary), here's Homer Laughlin's thoughts. When questioned only recently about these bowls, the HLC representative didn't think they were HLC at all. You, of course, are still entitled to your opinion. Some things remain a mystery forever!

Many years ago on one of our visits to HLC, we were allowed a rare treat — a visit to the dark secretive room hidden behind a locked and barred door in the uppermost niche of the office building that somehow down through the years earned the name "the morgue." Dark and dingy it might have been, but to a collector of HLC dinnerware, it was filled with excitement! We were allowed to dig through boxes and shelves where we found fantastic experimentals, beautiful trial glazes, and unfamiliar modifications of standard forms. On our second visit some years later, we returned with a professional photographer through whose photos we are able to share the fun with all of you.

One item we especially liked on our first trip through the morgue was a vase that was out on loan when we made our return visit. We've yet to have the opportunity to photograph it ourselves, but we'll try to describe it for you. It was glazed in ivory with a 6" upright disk body that looked like the joined front halves of two juice pitchers without their ice guards — actually much like the new Millennium II Vase but with more pronounced spouts. There was a stack of Fiesta plates in unbelievable trial glazes — a pink beige, a spatter effect in dark brown on orange, a smoky delphinium blue, a dark red grape that might possibly be the rose ebony referred to in Rhead's article (see Plate 371), a dark russet, a deep mustard yellow, and our favorite — black with four chromium bands.

Other goodies that were out on loan during our second visit were two different styles of Harlequin candle holders that we had cataloged before. One pair was large and flat, 5½" in diameter with a 2½" tall candle cup in the center. The others were shaped like the large half of an inverted cone, 4¼" across the bottom, and 3" tall. Both styles were lovely but not quite as nice as our regular Harlequin candle holders. One of the most exciting Harlequin pieces we saw was a demitasse cup and saucer in a beautiful high-gloss black. Trial glaze plates included light chocolate, deep gray, delphinium blue, vanilla, caramel, black, and a luscious lavender.

We hope you have found this peek inside the morgue to be as much fun as it was for us to bring it to you. If you have the opportunity to visit Newell, be sure to stop at the company's musuem. Many of the treasures are now on display there.

The morgue as it appeared on our first visit.

Experimentals, Samples, Trials, and Inventions

In addition to the experimentals from the morgue, a few more rare or one-of-a-kind items have been found outside the factory. Those that were made from a specifically designed mold we'll call experimentals. Occasionally the experimental molds were used to produce a very short sample run; generally those pieces were unmarked and more often than not glazed in ivory. A few of these have escaped the confines of the factory and have been snatched up by a sprinkling of collectors richly blessed by the Fiesta deity! Many collectors enjoy looking for trial glazes, pieces (often plates) in experimental colors, usually earmarked on the back with code letters in black marker. Inventions were unconventional items that were built at the whim of an imaginative employee from handles, bowls, stems, etc., never meant to be co-joined.

Plate 357
6" Tray.
This was probably never a production piece; more than likely it was one that made its way out of the morgue at some point. It ended up in the Newell, West Virginia, area where it was found several years ago. There's a very similar tray in Plate 360; both are marked Fiesta. The original owner had used this one under the syrup pitcher, saying that it fit perfectly.

Plate 358
Sherbets.
Unproduced though clearly marked in the mold, this pair of sherbets was made in swirling pastels. Was someone trying to imitate Niloak's Mission, using the blue Skytone clay, terra cotta from the Suntone line, and their standard white?

Plate 359
Riviera Experimental.
This piece is 1½" x 2" and has the typical lines of Riviera as well as the standard mauve blue glaze. A toothpick holder? A salt dip? (Photo by Harvey Linn, Jr.)

Plate 360

Left to right: Divided Relish, Carafe, Vase, Syrup, 5" Tray, Divided Relish, Coffee Mug.

The divided relish is molded in one piece; it measures 11" in diameter and has the look of Fiesta. The carafe, 10" tall and glazed in Fiesta green, was actually produced for a buffet-ware line they called Kenilworth which was marketed by Marshall Fields during the mid-'50s. These have been found in turquoise, snow white, and dawn pink as well, and they carry the Kenilworth mark. A gold-tone metal neck sleeve with an angular handle and a cork-lined plastic stopper supplemented the pottery bottle. The Kenilworth line also utilized Rhythm and Cavalier shapes. With the increased interest in dinnerware lines from the '50s, examples of this line sometimes sell through Internet auctions at substantial prices; it's one to watch! In the center of the photo is a magnificent red Fiesta 12" vase over which wars would certainly be waged if it were up for grabs, which, of course, it is not, but notice the similarity to the new Millennium III vase! The piece to the right of the vase looks very familiar except for its size. It's 6½" tall, and its proportions exactly match the Fiesta syrup's. Directly in front of it is the only marked piece we saw in the morgue. Most experimentals were merely marked with a number or not at all. This one, however, was embossed "Fiesta" in the mold. It's 5" across and has the band of rings on the flange. The green relish section on the right was designed so that four would fit a large oval wooden tray. The coffee mug in yellow is 3" high and except for the short tapered base is exactly like the standard mug.

Plate 361

Footed Console Bowl, ¼-lb. Butter Dish.

The tall 6" Riviera candle holders we had fallen in love with on our first visit to the morgue were on loan, but the footed console bowl was there for our photography session. It's huge — 3½" x 8½" x 13½" long! Although the butter dish on the right is just the size to hold a quarter-pound stick of today's butter, this style was passed up in favor of the shorter quarter-pound version and the one-half pound size. This one was never marketed; it's 7½" long.

Plate 362
Harlequin Experimentals: Nappy, Sauce Cup, Deep Dish, Bowl.
The nappy is 4" across and is shaped like the small Fiesta fruits. Next, is a sauce cup, perhaps, made from the demitasse cup mold. The deep dish in mauve blue is 2½" x 7" — it has the Harlequin rings inside. On the far right, the yellow bowl measures 2½" x 5½" in diameter.

Plate 363
Jugs.
Shown is our regular two-pint jug alongside another that holds just one pint. This is the only one we've heard of and really have no information whatsoever on it.

Plate 364
Creamer and Sugar Bowl on Figure-8 Tray.
No doubt sample items, the sugar and creamer rest on a standard figure-8 tray. This set and another creamer have been found in ivory, and the sugar bowl was shown in previous editions in a near-Wells Art Glaze brown.

Plate 365
French Casserole Variation.
This is a footed version of the more familiar yellow one, and one of a kind, as far as we know.

Plate 366
10" Comport.
This is a scaled-down model of our standard 12" fruit comport. There are at least three collectors who have been lucky enough to find one of these.

Plate 367
Fiesta Experimental: Individual Teapot.
This is one of several unmarked ivory pieces made as samples only — they were never produced in quantity. The teapot is 6" high, and the lid is interchangeable with the standard demitasse pot. Only three have been reported. It was never marketed due to the onset of the war. In fact, many already existing HLC lines had to be cut back due to restrictions on materials.

Plate 368
Footed Mixing Bowl.
This measures 9¾" tall by 6" in diameter; the high foot that has been added nicely transforms a utilitarian mixing bowl into an elegant serving piece.

Plate 369
Spaghetti Bowl.
This piece has all the earmarks of being a sample item — it's become known as the "spaghetti bowl," but we really don't know what it was specifically designed for. It's shown in a relish base for size comparison. Under the flange on the outside is the familiar band of rings. It's 1⅜" deep and 10⅞" in diameter. It's unmarked, but almost certainly Fiesta.

Plate 370
Unusual Bowl.
This bowl is marked Fiesta in the mold. It measures 2½" x 11½", more shallow than the standard fruit bowl by ½".

Plate 371
Trial Glaze Fiesta Plates.
Rare, early 9" test plates, both numbered 3403 underglaze. They are made of a frail, more porous type of clay, and the glaze may be a variant of the rose ebony glaze. (Photo Craig Macaluso, Metairie, LA)

Plate 372
Riviera Syrup in Unusual Glaze.

Plate 373
Trial Glaze Fiesta Grouping.
These trial pieces, sixteen in all, were probably made during the reintroduction of Fiesta red in the late 1950s, since the teacups have no interior rings and the feet are not flared. A five-digit numbering system has been used, and this seems to affirm this assumption, since most earlier trial pieces have four-digit codes under the glaze. It's very rare to find such a large number of test pieces in one grouping with code numbers that fall as closely together as these do. (Photo courtesy Craig Macaluso, Metairie, LA)

Plate 375
Trial Glaze Mixing Bowl.
"Cream of tomato" is how the owners describe this unusual shade of red; we understand there are a few more pieces around in this color.

Plate 374
Trial Glaze Fiesta Plates.
These 9" plates are in a dark persimmon and a rich golden caramel.

Plate 376
Rare Ice Pitcher.
Several pieces of this brown-mottled Fiesta red glaze have been found over the years — enough to suggest that HLC may have been at least toying with the idea of putting it into production, perhaps as competition for a line of dinnerware Stangl made that had a very similar glaze. Stangl's utilized solid turquoise on the inside of the bowls and cups as well on the top of the plates — a look HLC could have approximated by pairing the rusty red glaze with turquoise Fiesta.

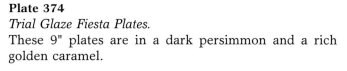

Plate 377
Trial Glaze Harlequin 9" Plates.
The owners describe the blue as being very similar to Skytone and the beige a good match for Jubilee.

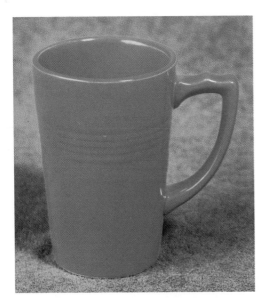

Plate 378
Harlequin Tumbler.
This has been fitted with a Riviera handle —
a one-of-a-kind employee's invention.

Plate 379
Chamberstick.
The imagination of the employee who created this unique chamberstick was really on overtime! It's made from the stem of a sweets compote, a demitasse saucer, and, of course, you recognize the familiar Fiesta ring handle.

 *Lamps*

Plate 380
Carafe Lamp.
These lamps are made with Fiesta and Harlequin components. The red lamps are both Fiesta. The first one was made from the spherical section and foot of the carafe with the stem of the sweets comport added for the neck. The hole the cord goes through on the bottom is factory glazed. The one in Plate 382 is made of casseroles, a sweets comport stem, and a small fruit bowl as the base. The body of the large cobalt lamp was fabricated from two Harlequin casseroles; once again the neck is a Fiesta sweets comport stem, and the base is a Fiesta fruit bowl. All are excellent examples of what HLC's inventive employees could do given a little time and access to the needed materials! The boudoir lamps made from syrup bottoms (Plates 383 and 385) were more than likely assembled by another company and sold commercially, since there are several in existence and bases are nearly always identical (the marble base is unusual). Both styles are sometimes found with hand-painted flowers. The cobalt Fiesta syrup-lamp has its original shade.

Plate 381

Plate 382

Plate 383

Plate 385

Plate 384
Syrup Lamp, left.
This example is quite different from the ones we've shown in past editions, this one has a wheel-cut "font" and a bobeche that is pierced and probably at one time was hung with crystal prisms. The wiring is original and appears typical of the '30s and '40s. The socket is Canadian, but since Canadian General Electric exported these to many places including the USA, that may not indicate that this lamp was assembled there.

Plate 386
A few years ago, these lamps were almost commonplace at outdoor shows and flea markets here in the Midwest. Here's a good way to make something both unique and useful from those stacks of saucers every collector seems to accumulate, proving that Fiesta collectors can be just as creative as HLC's employees were when inspired by Fiesta's wonderful colors and shapes. Try inverting a tumbler, adding a small vase cap or wooden piece and topping it off with a tulip-type glass shade for a darling bedside table lamp. Just remember to use a masonry bit in your drill.

We've always referred to these as the orange tree bowls because of their resemblance to Fenton's carnival glass pattern of the same name, and over the years some collectors have called them "peach tree." But according to Jo Cunningham's recently published book *Homer Laughlin, A Giant Among Dishes* (Schiffer, 1998) they're correctly named Apple Tree. The design is obviously by Rhead, as it is very similar to the stylized tree motif he used to decorate Ohio art pottery very early in his career. There are six sizes, they range from 5" to 10". Actual measurements vary a little as is normal with HLC products, but these bowl sets may exist in two styles. One collector has pointed out that his 10" bowl (which he says is actually 9¾") is much wider than normal at the bottom, heavier, and marked with an ink stamp rather than the standard embossed mark. He has a 7½" bowl with the same characteristics.

Another collector (the owner of nine of these bowls) measured capacity as well as dimension on each example in her collection. She has two 10" bowls with the ink stamp with minor variations (9¹⁵⁄₁₆", holding 100 fluid ounces and 9¹³⁄₁₆", holding 104 fluid ounces — the increase evidently due to thinner, slightly more flaring sides). Statistics for the other sizes (for you who enjoy statistics) are 9" (9¼", holding 80 fluid ounces), 8" (8⅛", holding 48 fluid ounces), 7" (7⅛", holding 32 fluid ounces), 6" (20 fluid ounces), and 5" (12 fluid ounces). All of the latter have the standard in-mold mark. The fact that the 7½" bowl we mentioned in the previous paragraph has the unusual ink stamp and obviously would not nest with the bowls having the embossed mark, supports the theory that there is probably a complete set of the ink-stamped bowls as well. Apple Tree bowls are most often glazed in turquoise, but they've also been found in ivory, yellow, and pumpkin. On rare occasions the ivory is decorated with stripes, as is the 5" bowl in Plate 387. It has three green stripes — one inside the rim, one outside the rim, and one on top.

Plate 387
Set of Six Apple Tree Bowls. (Photography by Jim Carpenter)

Plate 388
Ivory with Red Stripe.

Plate 389
Pumpkin Apple Tree Bowl.

Children's dishes were not made in any great amount; they're hard to find, and most collectors are avid in their search for them. You'll find some of these marked with an ink-stamped series of letters and numbers. For help in deciphering these codes, see the section called Dating Codes and English Measurements.

Plate 390
This display includes a wonderful Fiesta Tom and Jerry mug (obviously made for Gary) in ivory with the same comic animal decals as you see on the bowl and Laura-Ann's mug. In past editions, we've shown the Fiesta fruit bowl with this decal as well. The bowl in our photo is marked "Homer Laughlin Made in U.S.A. C 44 N8," indicating a 1944 production. The Little Orphan Annie mug was produced in the vellum glaze as a premium for the Ovaltine company. It's marked "Manufactured exclusively for the Wander Co. Chicago, Makers of Ovaltine." (Photo by Harvey Linn, Jr.)

Plate 391
This set is decorated with mamma rabbit and her family on a white background — note that the Fiesta Tom and Jerry is used again. The divided plate is the first of its kind we've seen.

Plate 392
Dick Tracy Plate, Mug, and Bowl.
Borrowing a plate from the Century line, this set is rare and very collectible because of the crossover interest in the character collectible field. These are especially sought after, collectors tell us, in California, due to the popularity of collectibles pertaining to the movie industry in that area. (Photography c Adam Anik)

Plate 393
Tom and the Butterfly Plate, Bowl, and Mug.

Plate 394
Cowboys, branding irons, and hats decorate this plate marked "Homer Laughlin Best China," indicating that this is a piece of restaurant ware.

Plate 396
This is decorated with the familiar green and white checks of the Ralston Purina Company; these were made by HLC as premiums for Ralston customers.

Plate 395
Here's a wonderful fifteen-piece set of Eggshell Nautilus, again decorated with the comic animal decals on an ivory background. The teapot is marked "Homer Laughlin Eggshell Made in U.S.A. G 42 (1942) N5." (Photo by Harvey Linn, Jr.)

Plate 397

Plate 398

Unknown Line.

What a shame we've never learned the official name of the line represented here. It's decorated with various scenes of children engaged in outdoor activities, and its shapes are Genesee and Empress. From the provenance provided by the owner, whose mother used these dishes when she was a child, and because we know these two shapes were standard during those years, we date this line 1910 – 1920. Other area companies produced lines with these decals, among them Edwin Knowles and the East Liverpool Pottery (ELPCO).

Plate 399

Plate 400

Nursery Rhymes Line.
Nursery Rhymes are the theme for this line. The shape is Yellowstone, and these pieces have a family provenance as well. They were given to the owner's mother by her grandfather, a glassblower who worked in many of the glass and pottery houses in the area. The stamp on the back dates this line to 1926. Shown are only three pieces from a nearly complete set.

Plate 401

Plate 402

159

Kitchen Kraft and OvenServe

As early as the 1930s, Homer Laughlin China was the leading manufacturer of a very successful type of oven-to-table kitchenware. These lines were called OvenServe and Kitchen Kraft. Offered in an extensive assortment of items, patterns, and decals, today's collectors find them most interesting to research and reassemble into matching sets.

The label on the right was found on a floral-embossed spoon and fork set in the rust glaze; examples of this line are shown on pages 162 and 163.

Guaranteed
To Withstand Changes of

Oven-Dinner Ware
"THE OVEN WARE FOR TABLE SERVICE"

The Homer Laughlin China Co.
Newell, W. Va.

Plate 403
Casserole in Metal Holder, Cake Plate, Medium Covered Jar, Stacking Refrigerator Set, Salt and Pepper Shakers, and Pie Server.
This tulip-decaled line is marked "Kitchen Kraft, OvenServe." Shown here is only a sampling of items that are available in these decaled lines.

Plate 404
Examples of floral-decaled Kitchen Kraft.

Plate 405

Sun Porch Individual Casserole and Salt and Pepper Shakers.

These choice pieces came out of a New Jersey basement where covered in soot they nestled together in a cardboard box stamped "4-Piece Range Set." Unfortunately the box did not survive, but as the picture shows, its 50-year old contents cleaned up to be brand, spanking "old." The individual casserole is this time used as a drip jar; one of the shakers has been turned around to show the decal on the back.

Plate 406

Sun Porch Tumblers.

Not Kitchen Kraft, of course, but shown here as a point of interest, these tumblers are decorated with a fired-on version of the Sun Porch decal. The matching teapot is on the Century shape and can be seen in Plate 422.

Plate 407

Here is an example of the elusive Kitchen Kraft underplate. This particular decal is very hard to find and sometimes varies from one piece to another. For instance, this variation was reported on a pie plate: there is cup and saucer in front of the jug, to its left flowers and a teapot. The lady has nothing in her hands and her hat is a different style, and red and blue, not yellow.

Plate 408

Blue Willow Covered Jar.

Plate 409
Kitchen Bouquet Pie Plate and Platter.

Plate 410
Kitchen Kraft Ashtray.
Hard to find in any color, it's shown here in pumpkin and ivory. These two are from a set of four purchased together back in the 1980s. One has a dating code that indicates a 1933 production. The rings in the bottom vary: two of that set have six (note the ivory example), while the others have only four around a 1½" plain center (like the one on the left). (Photo by Harvey Linn, Jr.)

Plates 411 through 415 contain examples of the OvenServe line embossed with the same floral pattern that decorates the handles of the Fiesta Kitchen Kraft spoon, fork, and server. The custard set in the wire rack shows a variety of available colors; yellow and rust are the most commonly encountered, and in addition to those shown, you may also find a piece or two in dark green or with brightly colored decals or a green wash over the embossed flowers.

Plate 411
We're assuming that this very rare item is a gravy boat; it's 3½" x 5½" long and it holds 12 ounces. It's shown here in two different glaze treatments.

Plate 412
Look at the fantastic, curdled glaze on this 11" bowl! It's the green of the Wells Art Glaze line. Very rare!

162

Plate 413
Custard Set in Wire Rack.

Plate 414
2½-Quart Casserole and Underplate.
This very attractive style is decorated with decals over the embossed flowers.

Plate 415
Batter Pitcher.
This piece is rare; it's shown in a very hard-to-find color — white.

The Kitchen Kraft below is decorated in an Art Deco leaf pattern (N–260), one of the Harmony lines we told you about in the chapter entitled The Story of Fiesta. This line was undiscovered until the sixth edition, and we were doubly excited to learn that a matching line of Kitchen Kraft had been produced. This, of course, is the line that coordinated with red Fiesta; in Plate 416 you'll see the casserole, mixing bowl, pie plate, spoon, fork, and server. More pieces are shown in Plate 417.

Plate 416
Casserole, Mixing Bowl, Pie Plate, Spoon, Fork, and Server.

Plate 417
Kitchen Kraft Jar, Nautilus Lug Cereal/Soup Bowl, 6½" and 7½" Plates, Cup and Saucer, Creamer and Sugar Bowl, and Large Vegetable Bowl.
It is interesting to note that collectors report finding several more Nautilus items than those that are listed in the Harmony assortment on page 10.

Plate 418
Art Deco Leaves, N-260.

Plate 419
Nautilus Cup with Fiesta Saucer, Kitchen Kraft Individual Casserole, Nautilus Fruit Bowl and 6½" Plate, 7½" Fiesta Plate, Kitchen Kraft Shakers and Jug with Yellow Lid. This was designed to go with yellow Fiesta. Collectors have termed this pattern Shaggy Flower; it's the decal the company identified as N-258.

Americana

This very attractive set was made exclusively for Montgomery Ward who offered it for sale in their catalogs from 1944 through 1956. Each piece (thirty-one in all) carries a different design patterned after a Currier and Ives print. The rose-pink decorations suggestive of mulberry historical Staffordshire ware were "printed from fine copper engravings," so states the ad in the 1944 catalog.

These pieces were available: cup and saucer; plates, 10", 8½", 7", 6", and 8" square; dessert/fruit bowl; demitasse cup and saucer; coupe soup; creamer and sugar bowl with lid; sauce boat and stand; egg cup; teapot; oval platters, 11", 13", 15"; round platter, 13"; oval vegetable bowl; round vegetable bowls, 8", 9"; and vegetable bowl lid, 9".

Plate 420

Century

These are only a few examples of the many different decal decorations applied to Century shapes. You'll find that many pieces carry the name of the line on the back, and the year of their manufacture is often indicated by a dating code. Some of the more attractive and accessible patterns are being reassembled into sets by today's collectors.

Wells Peacock Trademark.
The Wells family became involved with the company as early as 1889 when William Edwin Wells became Homer Laughlin's partner. Succeeding generations continued as leaders of the firm. This is the mark found on many pieces of the set in Plate 421.

Plate 421
Dinnerware with Stripes.
This is dated 1933/1934, probably made well before the striped Fiesta line. It's the first we've seen. Besides the platters, plates, and teapot shown, the partial set contained bowls in three sizes. Most items were marked with the Wells peacock in silver.

Plate 422

Teapot.
One line, Sun Porch (represented by this teapot and shown also in the chapter on Kitchen Kraft and OvenServe), is novel in that the decal depicts pieces of Fiesta on the table under the umbrella. It is interesting to note that this teapot is the only piece of Sun Porch ever found that is not Kitchen Kraft. There are bowls, a covered jar, a covered jug, a pie plate, an underplate, and a cake plate, but all are Kitchen Kraft. The collector who has them tells us he believes that this is an earlier line than Fiesta and suspects that Rhead may have modeled the carafe and bulb candlesticks after this decal.

Plate 423
English Garden is the name of this lovely dinnerware. It's dated 1933, and the casserole is marked with the colorful Wells trademark on page 167; note the inside decal on the casserole. Also shown are the egg cup; fast-stand gravy boat; plates, 10" and 8"; creamer and sugar bowl; butter dish; syrup jug with lid; and cream soup. Of special interest in this photo is the butter dish. This is actually the Century shape, one of only a few we've ever seen. In virtually every other instance, the one used in decaled lines utilizing Century is the Jade butter dish; you'll see more of this shape on one of the following pages.

Plate 424
6" Plate, Cup and Saucer, Deep Plate, Luncheon Plate, and Fruit Bowl.
For years people with a bit of disdain for inexpensive Depression-era dinnerware have remarked, "They used to give that stuff away at the movies." Well, here is a Century set that really was. Plates with the legend shown have been found in several Northeastern states and at least one in the South. These pieces are never marked on the back, but they are unmistakably HLC.

Dogwood

Dogwood is an especially lovely line of HLC dinnerware that was produced in the early 1960s. At least twenty items were made; see Suggested Values in the back of the book for a complete listing. Included were five sizes of plates. Among the hard-to-find items in this pattern are the 8" salad plate, the 10" dinner plate, the teapot, and the Kitchen Kraft mixing bowl set. The Dogwood decal has also been reported on Rhythm shapes; here the shape is Liberty.

Plate 425
Creamer, Sugar Bowl, and Sauce Boat.

Plate 426
Teapot, 10" Dinner Plate, 8" Salad Plate, Mixing Bowl Set, Teacup and Saucer, Oval Vegetable Bowl, 6" Oatmeal Bowl or 5" Fruit Bowl.
Note the hard-to-find items previously mentioned.

Historical America Subjects

Produced for the F. W. Woolworth Company who sold it through their retail stores, Historical America Subjects was aptly named. At least nineteen pieces were made, each decorated with a scene reproduced from the original works of Joseph Boggs Beale. All that has been reported to us has been in the rose-pink as shown here except for the 8" plate which has also been found in blue. The line, as far as we know, consisted of plates, 10", 9", 8", and 7"; rim soup, 8½"; dessert/fruit bowl, 5¾"; platters, 13" and 11"; round and oval vegetable bowls, 8¾" and 9½"; cup and saucer; cereal/soup bowl; creamer and sugar bowl; teapot; and gravy boat and undertray. Scenes bear titles such as "Betsy Ross and the Flag," "Lincoln's Gettysburg Address," "George Washington Taking Command of the Army," "The First Thanksgiving," and "Paul Revere." Though very hard to find, there's a lot of enthusiasm for this line, and prices are already higher than for most decaled dinnerware.

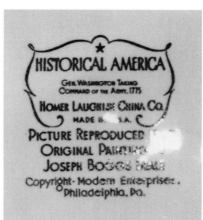

Historical America Subjects Mark.

Plate 427
Various Historical America Subjects Pieces.

Jade

Plate 428
La Hacienda Grouping.
La Hacienda is the pattern name; the shape is called Jade. According to the dating code in the backstamp, it was made circa 1935. Though we always thought the stick butter dishes were on the Century shape because they were consistently found in Century-based Mexican lines, here's proof that indeed they belong to the Jade line. Only the round butter dish shown in the Hacienda section and again in Century/English Garden is actually Century.

Plate 429
Unnamed Pattern.
This lovely but unnamed line has a backstamp that indicates a 1933 production date. Note the fast-stand gravy bowl and the 36s bowl directly behind the butter dish. Also shown in the photo is a plate with a Blue Willow decal and a saucer with a courting couple.

Nautilus

Here's the Nautilus shape again — it was shown in the Mexican lines and again as a basis for two of the Harmony lines. This time the pattern is called Old Curiosity Shop; though very hard to find, it has a lot of charm and is popular among HLC dinnerware collectors. Shown is the cup and saucer, 6½" plate, deep bowl, casserole with lid, fruit bowl, 11½" platter, deep plate, 9½" plates, gravy boat and liner, butter dish (Jade shape), and creamer and sugar bowl.

Plate 430
Cup and Saucer, 6½" Plate, Deep Bowl, Casserole with Lid, Fruit Bowl, 11½" Platter, Deep Plate, 9½" Plates, Gravy Boat and Liner, Butter Dish (Jade shape), and Creamer and Sugar Bowl.

Priscilla

This is one of the many beautiful patterns of dinnerware that has become very collectible. It's an extensive line and relatively easy to find. Two styles were produced — the regular line, simple round shapes on Eggshell (lightweight semiporcelain), and a second line that utilizes the Republic shape. Both are shown below. In addition to the dinnerware, you'll find matching Kitchen Kraft. Among the harder-to-find items are the tall teapot (shape designation unknown) shown in Plate 431 to the far left, the Republic teapot, and these Kitchen Kraft items: the 9½" fruit bowl (far right), coffeepot, and the tab-handled platter. A more complete listing is offered in the Suggested Values section. (Note: Other items may be found carrying the same mark but made by Universal China Company; these pieces are generally regarded as desirable enhancements to a Priscilla collection.)

Plate 431
Tall Teapot; Deep Plate, 8½"; Plates, 10" (the second is Republic); Kitchen Kraft Fruit Bowl; Republic Creamer and Sugar Bowl; and Republic Teapot.

Plate 432
Kitchen Kraft Jug; Coffeepot; Mixing Bowls; Casserole; Regular Teapot; and Republic Teapot.

Rhythm

Rhythm is a shape designed by Don Schreckengost. We're most familiar with it as one of the colored dinnerware lines, of course, but it was the basis of several decaled lines as well.

Plate 433
Rhythm Rose.
This is a lovely floral. It was produced from the mid-'40s through the mid-'50s and is marked with the gold stamp: Household Institute, Rhythm Rose.

Plate 434
Western Dinnerware.
While we once thought the Western dinnerware was a child's set, we've since heard from a lady who received some as a wedding gift. She tells us that in addition to the place setting, there were serving pieces such as a creamer and sugar bowl, vegetable bowls, and platter. From another source, we've learned that there was even an ashtray to match.

American Provincial Pattern.
American Provincial is the name of the pattern in these two plates. Note the variations in the decal as well as the decoration — some items are trimmed with a red stripe while other pieces have gold trim. The salt and pepper shakers are on the Jubilee shape. The large jug has never been reported in the solid colors of Rhythm.

Plate 435

Plate 436

Swing

Swing, introduced in 1938, was the first of HLC's shapes in the Eggshell weight. By '45 it was identified only as Eggshell, not to be confused with Eggshell Nautilus, a lighter-weight version of the Nautilus shape, or Eggshell Georgian, a lightweight rendering of a classic English shape. This line was decaled and/or pastel-striped and included a wide variety of pieces allowing for such unusual (for HLC) presentations as a breakfast-in-bed set. The shakers were also used with Virginia Rose and Rhythm. Because of its delicate appearance, pastels and floral treatments abound. And on rare occasions, you may find it in the Hacienda pattern, in blue-trimmed Mexicana, in Conchita, and in Mexicali.

Plate 437
Teapot.
This is the very rare Chinese Green Goddess teapot.

Plate 438
Plate.
This plate is from an appealing dinnerware line called Colonial Kitchen. On Eggshell Swing you may find a pattern stamped (on the back) Pueblo with a bare-breasted Indian woman making clay pots on a multicolored rug.

Plate 439
Casseroles.
These are two lovely floral-decorated casseroles. (Photography C. Adam Anik)

Plate 440
After Dinner (or Breakfast-in-Bed) Creamer, Cup and Saucer, and 6" Plate.
These are in an unnamed floral pattern.

176

Virginia Rose

Virginia Rose was the name given a line of standard HLC shapes which from 1929 until the early 1970s was used as the basis for more than a dozen patterns of decaled or embossed dinnerware. The designer was Fredrick Rhead, and the name was chosen in honor of the daughter of Joseph Mahan Wells, granddaughter of Wm. E. Wells. Virginia Rose was one of the most popular shapes ever produced. Even after it was discontinued for use in the home, the shape was adopted by the hotel china division at HLC and became a bestseller in the field of hotel and institutional ware. Shown here is only a sampling of the many floral patterns you may find on pieces marked Virginia Rose. Among the harder-to-find items are the double egg cup, coffee mug, 8" tray with handles, and the salt and pepper shakers. A matching line of Kitchen Kraft is also available. Some of it is limited as well. The 12" pie plate, salt and pepper shakers, cake plate and server, straight-sided casserole, and the 8" casserole with round sides are scarce. For a more complete listing of available items, see Suggested Values in the back of the book.

Plate 441
Plates, 10", 8", 6"; Soups, 8" (one flanged); Salt and Pepper Shakers; Egg Cup; Oatmeal Bowl, 6"; Deep Bowl, 5".

Plate 442
Kitchen Kraft Salt and Pepper Shakers and Casserole; 8" Tray.
The straight-sided casserole is harder to find than the style shown in Plate 443. The small tray is very scarce and may have been used as an undertray for the casserole.

Plate 443
Kitchen Kraft Covered Casseroles, 8½", 7½"; Daisy Chain Covered Casserole.
The casserole on the right is very rare. Like the mugs in Plate 446, the darker decal (the company's JJ-59) indicates 1930s production. This piece is marked DC-714 under the lid and carries the HLC Oven Serve logo.

Plate 444
Covered Vegetable; Cake Set; Platter, 15"; Plate, 8"; Sauce Boat and Liner (9½" Platter); Butter Dish; Creamer and Sugar Bowl; Cup and Saucer; Kitchen Kraft Casserole, 8".
This decal was cataloged as UR-128.

Plate 445
Water Pitcher, 7½"; Milk Pitcher, 5"; Kitchen Kraft Mixing Bowl Set.

Plate 446
Baltimore Coffee Mugs.
All are dated 1930; the pattern is JJ-59.

In the early 1900s in an attempt to enter the art pottery field, HLC produced a unique line of art china. It was marked in gold or black with an eagle and the name "Laughlin Art China." Perhaps as many as eighty-nine shapes were used, and several decorating techniques were employed. Most are decaled, but occasionally you will find a hand-decorated piece that may be artist signed. Their most extensive pattern, Currant (shown in the following plates), featured brown shaded backgrounds with decals of berries and vines.

Laughlin Art China Mark

Plate 447
8" Vase with Handles.

Plate 448
7" Vase.

Plate 449
2" x 10" Ruffled Salad Bowl, 9½" Plaque, 10" Scalloped Plate.

Plate 450
6½" x 12" "Fe Dora" Bread Tray.

Plate 451
Covered Dish.

Plate 452
6" Humidor, 6" Bulbous Pitcher, 12" "Orange" Bowl with Handles, and Straight-Sided 6½" Pitcher.

Plate 453
Demitasse or Hot Chocolate Set.

181

Plate 454
10" Pitcher.
Called "Dutch Jug" in old company records.

Plate 455
Geisha Jug.
(Photo by Craig Macaluso, Metairie, LA)

Plate 456
Sugar Baskets.
The gold-trimmed example is from a line called "Golden Fleece."

Plate 457
12" Vase.

Plate 458

9¾", 12", and 16" Vases and Chocolate or After-Dinner Pot.
Here's another style in an after-dinner pot — it's 10" tall. These items are
very rare.

Plate 459
14" Vase with Handles.

Plate 460
*"White Pets" Line. (right
and page 184).*
These pieces are hand-
painted, though they're
probably painted over a
decal — as you can see,
the same design was used
on more than one shape.
The vase with the dogs is 8";
the ewer is a magnificent
15½" tall. We have a snapshot in

183

our files of a 7" vase with a swan reflected in water and the tall trumpet-shaped 16" cylinder vase with the same dogs and cattails that you see here. The Mirror Cats (Plate 461) is a very hard-to-find design. Occasionally, one of these pieces will bear an artist's signature. A small stein has also been reported in this line, and there are sure to be other shapes.

Plate 461
(Photo by Jim Carpenter)

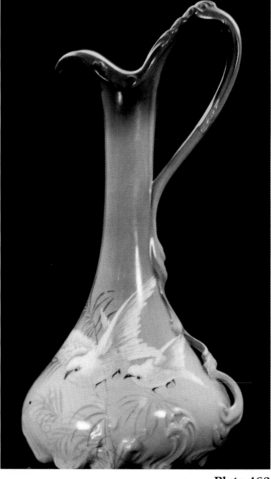

Plate 462

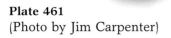

Plate 463

On these two pages are examples of Laughlin's Flow Blue, a rare and beautiful line much coveted by collectors of Art China.

Plate 464
Staghorn Mug with Monk.
(Photo by Jim Carpenter)

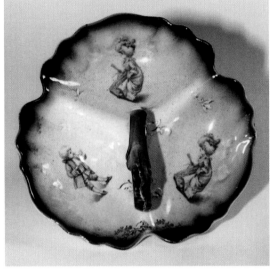

Plate 466
7", Three-part Candy Dish with child.

Plate 465
Large Tankard with Monk.

Plate 467
Cup and Saucer with child.

Plate 469
12" Vase.

Plate 468
Jardiniere.
This measures a huge 10" x 14½"; with its gold trim and deep color, it's a magnificent example of this type of ware.

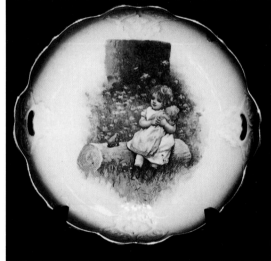

Plate 470
Plates with children (right).

Plate 471
5½ x 8½ Lady's Cuspidor.

Plate 472

186

Plate 473
Bowl.
One of the most beautiful examples of LAC we've seen, this bowl is unusual in shape as well as subject matter. The lady's breasts are exposed — as far as we know, this has never been seen on a piece from this line before.

Plate 474
Charger.
This matches the tankard shown in Plate 475 and is marked "An American Beauty, Semi-Vitreous China, 1900."

Plate 475
Large Tankard and Mugs.
This tankard has a second portrait on the back; it's very unusual to find a set complete with matching mugs.

Plate 476
Juno on Geisha Milk Jug.
Named for the queen of the gods of ancient Rome, wife and sister of Jupiter, the Juno line is very rare and highly collectible. This pitcher is a wonderful example — this decal is sometimes called "the lady and the peacock."

Plate 477
Juno Chocolate Pot, Demitasse Cup and Saucer.
Prime examples, both very rare — note the variation in the decals. What is characteristic to this line is the multi-hued shaded background.

Plate 478
Geisha Jugs with Fruit.
These are 6" Geisha jugs; the one with the peaches is marked Homer Laughlin Hudson 8 3 N.

Plate 480
Large Tankard.
This rare item is marked "American Floral."

Plate 479

Plate 481
Bowl.
This is a piece from a line marked "Laughlin's Holland." It was referred to by Homer Laughlin as their "orange bowl." This time it's decorated with a scene of three Dutch children watching a mother duck and her ducklings waddle by. This line is extremely rare!

Plate 482
6½" Jug.
Here's another piece from "Laughlin's Holland"; the shape is also found in the Dreamland series. This line is extremely rare!

Plate 483
Holland Rose Bowl and 15½" Ewer.
Not only is this a rare line, the rose bowl is a very rare piece in any pattern.

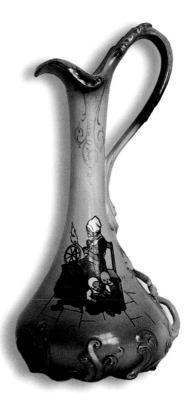

Plate 484
Large Tankard.
This item is very rare, especially with the patriotic decal.

Plate 485
Hand-painted Staghorn Mug.
The artwork is signed Millie Sims Leckie, leading us to believe that during the early 1900s when china painting was such a popular pastime with the ladies, some of these were sold as blanks to hobbyists.

Plate 486
Staghorn Stein.
This stein was commissioned by a hardware company. It reads "Berger Manufacturing Company Souvenir Mug, Canton, Ohio, Everything in Sheet Metal," on the front, and on the back "Ohio Hardware Association, February 27, 1928." We've also seen these mugs with a multicolored Jacobean design that is very attractive. This shape is probably one of the more commonly found pieces in the assortment.

Plate 487
Staghorn Stein.
This one is inscribed "Copyright 1905 by the H.M. Suter Publishing Company"; the name John E. Sheridan is signed on the diagonal near the player's elbow.

Plate 488
Silver Sienna Dutch Jug.
The characteristics of this line are the brown backgrounds that feature dog subjects and the silver bands. This piece is marked "Silver Sienna" in ink. It's extremely rare.

Dreamland

Children feeding a pet goat, doing laundry, playing badminton, and crying when their dog steals the "birdie" decorate this winsome but rare line made by Homer Laughlin in the early years after the turn of the century. It appears to be done in a technique called "pouncing" that was used by several of the larger art pottery manufacturers who operated in the same general area.

Plate 489
Vase.
This tiny vase is a mere 3½".

Plate 490
Tankard Set.
A wonderful tankard set on shapes that we have shown before marked Laughlin Art China. Another collector has this set without the brown shading at the bottom, and his is decorated with four different designs.

Plate 491
10½" Chop/Cake Plate.
Note the closed handles.

Plate 492
16" Vase.

Plate 493
Ruffled Salad Bowl and Jug.
This Art China shape was shown in Plate 449 in the Currant pattern. The little jug measures 6½".

Plate 494
Plaques.
These are the same basic plate with different designs.

Plate 495

Plate 496
10" Vase and 10" Cake Plate.
Note that this cake plate has open handles.

World's Fair: The American Potter

As a tribute to the American Potter, six pottery companies united their efforts and jointly built and operated an actual working kiln at the 1939–1940 World's Fair in New York City. A variety of plates, vases, figural items, and bowls were produced and marked with an ink stamp "The American Potter, 1939 (or '40), World's Fair Exhibit, Joint Exhibit of Capital and Labor."

The Homer Laughlin China Company entry, designed by Fredrick Rhead, is shown in Plate 499. In the center of each plate are the Trylon and Perisphere, adopted symbols of the Fair. These plates have found favor not only with collectors of Homer Laughlin but also with World's Fair enthusiasts, and as a result of the strong Art Deco influence imparted by Rhead into their design, Art Deco aficionados vie to own them too.

Plate 497
Yellow Vase.
This is about 7" in height — quite large as these vases go.

Plate 498
Assortment of World's Fair Items.
Potted, glazed, and fired right on the fairgrounds, these items come in many colors, sizes, and shapes. The Harlequin individual creamer (etched World's Fair on the side) is 2⅛", the yellow vase (far left) is 7½", and the cobalt vase (center back) is 6¼", to give you an idea of scale. All of these pieces are rare, and they all carry an ink stamp, "American Potter." You may also find bowls and ball-shaped candlesticks, but these are rare.

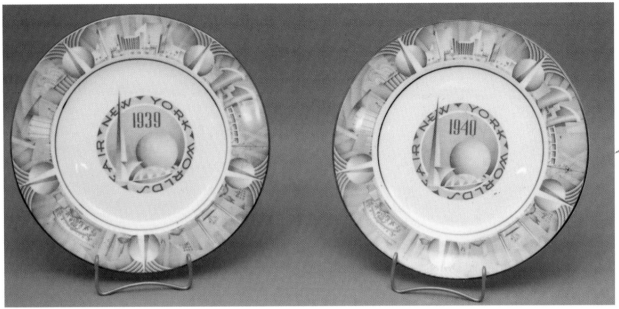

Plate 499

Plate 500

Plates and Ashtray Designed by Fredrick Rhead.
In Plate 499 you'll see the 1939 and the 1940 New York World's Fair plates. These are sought after not only by HLC and World's Fair collectors, but also by those who admire the wonderful Art Deco quality of the designs. Very rarely, one will bear this gold stamp: "Decorated by Charles Murphy, 150th Anniversary of George Washington as First President of the United States, 1789 – 1939." Plate 500 pictures souvenirs of the Golden Gate International Exposition of 1939 and 1940. They're marked "Golden Gate Intern. Expo., Copyright License 63C, Homer Laughlin, Souvenir."

Plate 501
Four Season Plates.
Each plate measures 4¼" in diameter. Spring shows a man fishing for trout; summer depicts a family picnicking; a man hunting with his dog represents autumn; and the winter plate has a skating scene. These sets are usually found in the colors shown, but a set with all four plates in turquoise has been reported, as well as a set in light green. Two autumn plates have been found in yellow and a winter in cobalt.

Plate 502
Cup and Saucer.
These are embossed with signs of the Zodiac — they're also rare.

Plate 503

Plate 503 and 504
(left and top of page 197)
George and Martha Washington Pitchers.
These were popular with fairgoers, since 1939 was the 150th anniversary of the inauguration of Washington as the first President of the United States. Martha is always the harder one to find. All shown here measure 5", but some are only 2" tall. They're usually ivory — examples in

cobalt are very rare. Mauve blue and Harlequin yellow have been reported as well as bisque. George and Martha toothpick holders and salt and pepper shakers were also made, but these are generally not marked. Three marks were used: "The American Potter, New York World's Fair," with the year on a raised disk superimposed over a Trylon; "First Edition For Collectors, New York's World's Fair, 1939"; or "Joint Exhibition of Capitol and Labor, American Pottery, NY WF, 1939."

Plate 504

Potter's Plates and Original Box.
Here are the easiest of the World's Fair items to find. There are two — The Potter at His Wheel and The Artist Decorating the Vase. They've been found in turquoise as shown, light green, and ivory. They're scarce in the latter two colors, and we've seen a couple in tan/mocha shades. One was marked "First Edition For Collectors Limited to 100 Pieces, #85." What is rare, though, is the box these plates came in, shown in Plate 505.

Plate 505

Plate 506

Plate 507
Edwin Knowles Marmalade.

Plate 508
Entries from five other companies.
Left to right: Cake set, "Cronin China Co., Minerva, O., National Brotherhood of Operative Potters"; Bowl, "Paden City Pottery, Made in USA," 10"; Plate, "Knowles, Joint Exhibit of Capital and Labor," 10¾"; Marmalade bottom (shown complete with lid in Plate 507), embossed with Trylon and Perisphere and "New York World's Fair," marked Edwin M. Knowles China Co., Semi-Vitreous," 3"; Pitcher, marked "Porcelier Trade Mark, Vitreous Hand Decorated China, Made in U.S.A." The Porcelier pitcher was part of a seven-piece set that included teapots in three sizes, a sugar bowl, creamer, and a larger water pitcher. Some are shown in Plates 509 – 511. All are hard to find, especially the ashtray.

Plate 509

Plate 510

Plate 511

Here are a few last items of interest we wanted to share with you.

Plate 513

Nude Vases and Donkey Ashtray.
Shown glazed in Fiesta red and ivory, one of the vases in Plate 513 is marked by hand under the glaze "GAW," more than likely the initials of its creator. Along with the donkey, these were discovered near Newell, the property of an HLC supervisor. Three more colors have been found — rose, maroon, and spruce, as well as one in ivory with a rose drip. We've seen a photograph of a green donkey ashtray and a mauve blue donkey figurine. The owner has two small vases she believes are HLC as well, identical in form (pilgrim flask shapes with angle handles), one in the red and the second in the mauve blue glaze. Both are commemoratives. The nude in Plate 512 is marked "USONA," a pottery that operated in the East Liverpool area during the 1930s through the '50s. Note differences in the mold. (Photo by Jim Carpenter)

Plate 512

Plate 514
Sit 'n Sip Set.
Pictured here with its original carton. These were marketed during the late '60s into the early '70s. Most, though not all, carry advertising messages. You'll often see a similar type of mug set in gift stores today, containing instructions to use the coaster as a lid to keep your coffee hot longer, as may have been the practice then.

Plate 515
Chip 'n Dip Plate.
Though we're not positive, this may well be an HLC product. It measures 12" in diameter and has a lot of good characteristics, leading us to suspect that it is. Do you have any information about it?

Plate 516
Bowl and Mug.
This is from the "other" Tom and Jerry set. But this one's not on Fiesta shapes, so it's not nearly as valuable as the one that is!

Plate 517
Lid.
This red lid fits the Kitchen Kraft stacking units perfectly, and that's about all we know about it. It may even have been designed for some other purpose — a hot plate, for instance, for the regular Fiesta line (the band of rings does seem out of step in Kitchen Kraft). This is the only one that's ever been reported.

Plate 518
Football Trophy.
This was designed by an HLC employee in the early '40s to commemorate Bill Booth, an Ohio State football star from East Liverpool (notice the "O" on his jersey). Booth was tragically killed in an automobile accident, and a very limited number of these trophies were dipped in the Fiesta glazes to present to his teammates. Besides the light green one shown here, a yellow one is on display along with other Fiesta experimental and production pieces at the Homer Laughlin museum, and we have reports of one in ivory and one in spruce green.

Plate 519

Though it's a little hard to believe considering the careful attention he paid to detail throughout the line, the syrup is the only piece of Fiesta that Rhead did not design. The mold was bought from the DripCut Company, who made the tops for HLC. (Other potteries, Vernon Kiln for one, also used this mold, and you'll find them in glass as well.) This blue one is molded of white ceramic and is marked "Drip-Cut, Heatproof, L.A., Cal." Decades ago a tea company filled syrup bases with tea leaves, added a cork stopper and their label, and unwittingly contributed to the frustration of today's collectors who have only a bottom. See the chapter entitled Commercial Adaptations and Ephemera for a photo.

Plate 520
Doll.
Her name is Delores, marked "Marin Tichlana, Made in Spain." She's made of hard plastic and vinyl and stands 15" tall — reminiscent of our Fiesta dancing girl logo.

Plate 521
Neon Clock.
This is contemporary, of course, but wonderful.

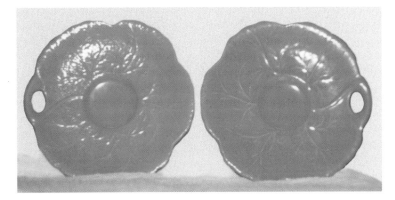

Plate 522
"Leaf Saucers."
Shown in Fiesta red, these were found in the East Liverpool/Newell area by an experienced collector who always thought they were made at HLC although they are unmarked; a saucer in cobalt has been found in the HLC morgue. Made also in green, they are 7" in diameter by ¾" high, a short-production premium go-along for Swanky Swigs.

Only in the first edition of this book were the suggested values based on our own buying and selling experiences. Since then we've always polled dealers and collectors from every area of the country, striving to arrive at an overall average. Opinions are always widely varied, but we have a formula we always follow: we throw out the high and low estimates (which are sometimes opposed by as much as 200%) and we average the others. Figures are never rounded off more than two dollars in either direction. We purposely shuffle the reports that have been sent in so we have no idea whose estimate we're reading. We try very hard to arrive at accurate prices that represent high average — "asking" prices of dealers who specialize, carry a large stock, and sell only quality merchandise. As we all know, there are always bargains to be had from other, less convenient resources, if we're willing to expend the effort to seek them out.

You may find entirely different prices realized on Internet auctions, but these are so often very erratic, and they can hardly be regarded as accurate. The egg cup that sells for $60.00 one week may not even bring reserve the next. One of our survey dealers noted that his maroon Harlequin high-lip creamer in excellent condition brought $75.00, while one in the same condition sold for $170.00 only a few weeks later. Prices depend on the merchandise in competition with it at that particular time, how many buyers might be online, and like any other auction, how badly the top bidder wants to own it. As one collector in our survey so aptly puts it: "Regarding Internet sales, there are two sides to every coin. With the 'Net, more and more individuals are selling and are willing to take less as they see good opportunity to sell their merchandise. This tends to hurt the established dealers and drive prices down. Collectors who want to buy rare items just wait (for a bargain) rather than pay dealer prices. As a result, though they're paying less, their collections become worth less when they sell. This has been very apparent at recent auctions — owners have been disappointed in what their collections bring. All of a sudden, it's virtually a buyer's market." (Regarding his observation: several large collections have been put up for auction, and as is always true, even though the demand may be steady, when the supply is greater, prices do go down.) He continues: "If current Internet and auction activities continue, values will go down." He expresses concern about how far this trend will continue before it corrects itself.

Another factor has come to bear on the market as well; at this point, it's not easy to interpret. Some see the influx of the Post86 Fiesta as a positive force that has generated renewed interest in the old, collectible Fiesta line. A collector who lives in the area observes: "Overall I believe there is strong demand for vintage Fiesta and many other HLC lines. The outlet (at the pottery) is always busy — there are auto plates from all over the country. As long as this continues, there will be high interest in Fiesta; prices need to reflect this." But not all agree. Others feel that new collectors may pass up a vintage gray sauce boat, for instance, since they can buy the same "look" for much less on the retail market. As one puts it: "At least for the time being, it seems to us that when the new Fiesta moved in, the old moved out. We believe the value of most old Fiesta has reached a plateau after rising for the last decade, with the exceptions of the rare pieces that the advanced collector is searching for."

With all things considered, this has been the most difficult survey we've ever attempted. Internet sales being what they are (common items often sell for 50% of book value), we expected for the first time to have to lower some of our prices. Many dealers we spoke with prior to the survey prepared us for this possibility. So it was much to our surprise when we didn't see this develop through our poll. It's been rather like listening to several people describe a traffic accident — everyone sees things a little differently!

Now more than ever, condition is the driving force, especially on Fiesta, though, of course, this applies to any type of dinnerware. As anyone who has attempted Internet selling knows, buyers have become sticklers for perfection. No one can fault them for their high standards, but it does make one wonder if some collectors have lost sight of the fact that Fiesta was handmade and reasonably should be expected to have the tiny flaws that represent the handmade nature of the ware (as opposed to machined products that are perfectly and routinely duplicated). If you were to examine ten pieces of Fiesta, as many as half would probably have glaze skips, a pit here or there or a glazed-over chip — maybe even part of a fingerprint. Of the other five, two might be considered flawless — even glazing, nothing off-round, perfectly molded and finished. For the sake of establishing a standard on which to base our pricing system, here is our criteria to define mint condition: no chips or cracks, no wear or scratches, no crazing, and no significantly detracting factory flaws. For those two absolutely pristine, flawless items out of the ten, expect to pay a premium. The three saggar pin marks that are evident on the underside of many pieces are characteristic and result from the technique employed in stacking the ware for firing. These should in no way be considered damage. Common items with scratches, wear, or tiny dings that we once discounted by 30% are now discounted by half; chips or hairlines will render them virtually worthless. A more desirable piece (one worth $75.00 and up) may bring 50% to 60% of its mint value if the damage is not particularly visual; a rare item may bring a higher percentage; one with a chip that is disfiguring or detracting, considerably less than 50%.

Decals when present must be complete, the colors well preserved, with very little wear. When decals are worn, faded, or otherwise damaged, items should be sharply discounted.

When buying odd lids and bases, remember that colors may vary, and some lids and openings will be just enough off-round that they will not properly fit together. If you do buy them separately, expect to pay 50% to 70% of listed values for lids and 30% to 40% for bases. For example, if a sugar bowl is listed at $20.00, its lid would be approximately $10.00 to $14.00 and its base $6.00 to $8.00.

Fiesta
Page 18 – 37

The first column of figures represents the range of values suggested for these colors: red, cobalt, and ivory. The second column contains values for turquoise (with exceptions), yellow, and light green. Collectors report that items discontinued in 1946 are generally harder to find in turquoise, since that color was not introduced until mid-1937, an entire year after the other colors. In the column on the far left, you'll notice that some of the items in the listings are followed by asterisks. These are the ones that were dropped in 1946. To evaluate these items in turquoise, use the first column of values (for red, cobalt, and ivory), generally the high end; for all other turquoise pieces, use the second column. Red Fiesta is at a premium right now, so use the high end of the range for red as well. (In fact, there is a trend at the moment for red to sell for 10% to as much as 25% over the high end; of course, this will bear watching.) The third column offers a range of values for the fifties colors — chartreuse, dark green, rose, and gray. You'll see that values in the column for medium green continue to soar. The last column, "As Specified," contains values for the specific colors mentioned in the listings on the far left.

While the middle-of-the-road market may be languishing, rare and very desirable Fiesta is always on the rise. The values we suggest for anything $500.00 and up should probably be regarded as minimum. It is impossible to set an accurate price range, even with the help of the advanced collectors and dealers who took part in our survey. Some of these items are so rare, even these veterans will seldom, if ever, have them in stock or see them on the market. When these rarities do come up for sale, they will naturally go to the bidder with the highest offer. With the Internet reaching such a wide audience, extremely rare items end up in the collections of those with the deepest pockets, regardless of book value. Bidding wars abound!

An original label such as the Kitchen Kraft label, the Royalchrome label, the Riviera label, etc., will add from $100.00 to $150.00 to the value of the item that carries it. Pieces that are rarely marked, for instance the cup, salt and pepper shakers, juice tumblers, etc., can increase in value by as much as 400% to 500% when they are marked. Double marked items (those with the ink stamp and the cast-indented mark) often sell at 25% over book.

There are fine points to collecting and price assessing that must be left up to the collector, since much of it is a matter of individual preference. Some collectors search out the medium green individual salad bowls that have no inside rings and the medium green cups that do and are willing to pay a premium to get them. Others find the issue to be of little consequence. We will leave this up to the individual.

NEV = No Established Value

(*) – Use the values in the first column to price this item in turquoise

Vintage Fiesta	Red, Cobalt, Ivory	Yellow, Turquoise, Light Green	1950s Colors	Medium Green	As Specified
Ashtray[1]	55.00 – 65.00	42.00 – 48.00	78.00 – 88.00	175.00 – 190.00	
Bowl, covered onion soup					
cobalt or ivory					650.00 – 725.00
red					675.00 – 750.00
turquoise[2]					7,500.00+
yellow or lt. green					600.00 – 650.00
Bowl, cream soup[3]	55.00 – 62.00	40.00 – 45.00	70.00 – 75.00	4,200.00+	
Bowl, dessert; 6"[4]	48.00 – 52.00	35.00 – 40.00	45.00 – 52.00	550.00 – 600.00	
Bowl, footed salad*	350.00 – 400.00	325.00 – 340.00			
Bowl, fruit; 11¾"*	300.00 – 340.00	250.00 – 275.00			
Bowl, fruit; 4¾"[5]	30.00 – 35.00	22.00 – 28.00	30.00 – 40.00	475.00 – 525.00	
Bowl, fruit; 5½"	30.00 – 35.00	22.00 – 28.00	32.00 – 40.00	70.00 – 80.00	
Bowl, individual salad; 7½"				100.00 – 120.00	
red, turquoise, or yellow					80.00 – 90.00
Bowl, mixing; #1*[6]	220.00 – 245.00	160.00 – 180.00			
Bowl, mixing; #2*[6]	120.00 – 130.00	100.00 – 115.00			
Bowl, mixing; #3*[6]	125.00 – 135.00	115.00 – 125.00			
Bowl, mixing; #4*[6]	150.00 – 160.00	120.00 – 130.00			
Bowl, mixing; #5*[6]	155.00 – 185.00	150.00 – 160.00			
Bowl, mixing; #6*[6]	250.00 – 275.00	200.00 – 215.00			
Bowl, mixing; #7*[6]	380.00 – 410.00	330.00 – 350.00			
Bowl, nappy; 8½"*	50.00 – 58.00	35.00 – 42.00	60.00 – 65.00	130.00 – 145.00	
Bowl, nappy; 9½"*	55.00 – 65.00	48.00 – 52.00			
Bowl, tricolator;					
any color					250.00 – 275.00
Bowl, unlisted salad;[7]					
yellow					95.00 – 110.00
ivory, red, or cobalt*					1,200.00+
Candle holders, bulb;					
pr*	125.00 – 140.00	90.00 – 110.00			
Candle holders, tripod;					
pr.*	600.00 – 650.00	450.00 – 485.00			
Carafe*	290.00 – 340.00	225.00 – 255.00			
Casserole[8]	200.00 – 225.00	130.00 – 165.00	275.00 – 300.00	900.00+	
Casserole, French;					
yellow					275.00 – 300.00
other standard color[9]					690.00 – 725.00
Casserole, promo;					
complete, standard color[10],					135.00 – 150.00
Coffeepot	240.00 – 255.00	175.00 – 195.00	325.00 – 350.00		
gray[11]					450.00 – 485.00
Coffeepot, demitasse*	485.00 – 550.00	375.00 – 425.00			
Comport, 12"*	180.00 – 200.00	140.00 – 150.00			
Comport, sweets*	90.00 – 100.00	75.00 – 80.00			
Creamer	25.00 – 35.00	18.00 – 22.00	35.00 – 40.00	80.00 – 90.00	
Creamer, ind.; in red					350.00 – 365.00
turquoise, or cobalt[12]					NEV
yellow					65.00 – 80.00
Creamer, stick-handled*	65.00 – 72.00	42.00 – 48.00			
Cup, demitasse	72.00 – 80.00	60.00 – 68.00	350.00 – 375.00		
Cup, see teacup					

Vintage Fiesta	Red, Cobalt, Ivory	Yellow, Turquoise, Light Green	1950s Colors	Medium Green	As Specified
Egg cup	68.00 – 72.00	55.00 – 60.00	150.00 – 160.00		
Lid, mixing bowls; #1 – 3[13] any color					750.00 – 770.00
Lid, mixing bowl; #4 any color					1,000.00 +
Lid, mixing bowls; #5 – 6[14]	NEV	NEV			
Marmalade*[15] maroon	275.00 – 325.00	220.00 – 245.00			1,000.00 – 1,200.00
Mug, Tom and Jerry	75.00 – 82.00	50.00 – 60.00	85.00 – 100.00	100.00 – 125.00	
Mustard*[16]	245.00 – 265.00	190.00 – 210.00			
Pitcher, disk juice; gray[17]					3,000.00 +
red					550.00 – 600.00
yellow					40.00 – 48.00
Harlequin yellow					52.00 – 60.00
celadon green[18]					200.00 – 240.00
any other color					NEV
Pitcher, disk water	160.00 – 170.00	100.00 – 125.00	270.00 – 280.00	1,200.00 +	
Pitcher, ice*	135.00 – 160.00	110.00 – 140.00			
Pitcher, 2-pt. jug	100.00 – 120.00	75.00 – 88.00	125.00 – 150.00		
Plate, cake*[19]	1,000 +	900.00 +			
Plate, calendar; 1954, 10"					40.00 – 45.00
1955, 9"					45.00 – 50.00
1955, 10"					40.00 – 45.00
Plate, chop; 13"[20]	45.00 – 60.00	35.00 – 42.00	80.00 – 100.00	325.00 – 375.00	
15"	65.00 – 80.00	42.00 – 50.00	125.00 – 145.00		
Plate, compartment; 10½"	38.00 – 45.00	35.00 – 40.00	65.00 – 75.00		
12"[10]	50.00 – 60.00	45.00 – 55.00			
Plate, deep	50.00 – 60.00	32.00 – 38.00	52.00 – 58.00	125.00 – 140.00	
Plate, 6"[21]	5.00 – 7.00	4.00 – 5.00	7.00 – 9.00	15.00 – 20.00	
Plate, 7"[21]	8.00 – 10.00	7.00 – 9.00	10.00 – 13.00	28.00 – 32.00	
Plate, 9"[21]	14.00 – 18.00	9.00 – 12.00	18.00 – 22.00	40.00 – 45.00	
Plate, 10"[21]	35.00 – 40.00	28.00 – 32.00	48.00 – 52.00	110.00 – 135.00	
Platter	40.00 – 45.00	30.00 – 35.00	52.00 – 58.00	160.00 – 175.00	
Salt & pepper shakers, pr.[22]	25.00 – 30.00	18.00 – 22.00	40.00 – 45.00	160.00 – 185.00	
Sauce boat[23]	75.00 – 85.00	40.00 – 48.00	72.00 – 80.00	160.00 – 180.00	
Sauce boat stand, see Fiesta Ironstone[24]					
Saucer	4.00 – 5.00	3.00 – 4.00	5.00 – 6.00	10.00 – 12.00	
Saucer, demitasse	18.00 – 22.00	15.00 – 18.00	90.00 – 110.00		
Sugar bowl with lid	52.00 – 58.00	42.00 – 48.00	68.00 – 75.00	175.00 – 225.00	
Sugar bowl, ind.; in turquoise					350.00 – 365.00
in yellow					115.00 – 125.00
Syrup *[25]	375.00 – 425.00	340.00 – 375.00			
Teacup	30.00 – 35.00	20.00 – 25.00	32.00 – 38.00	55.00 – 60.00	
Teapot, large *	225.00 – 260.00	185.00 – 210.00			
Teapot, medium	200.00 – 225.00	140.00 – 165.00	290.00 – 325.00	1,200.00 +	
Tom and Jerry, see Mug, Tom and Jerry					
Tom and Jerry bowl ivory w/gold letters					250.00 – 265.00
Tom and Jerry mug					

	Red, Cobalt, Ivory	Yellow, Turquoise, Light Green	1950s Colors	Medium Green	As Specified
ivory w/gold letters					55.00 – 65.00
Tom and Jerry bowl, not on Fiesta mold[26]					35.00 – 40.00
Tom and Jerry mug, not on Fiesta mold[27]					10.00 – 15.00
Tray, figure-8; cobalt turquoise, or yellow[28]					90.00 – 100.00 350.00 – 400.00
Tray, relish *					
Center insert	55.00 – 60.00	40.00 – 50.00			
Side insert	45.00 – 60.00	40.00 – 50.00			
Relish base	85.00 – 100.00	65.00 – 75.00			
Tray, relish; gold decorated					220.00 – 250.00
Tray, utility *	38.00 – 42.00	32.00 – 38.00			
Tumbler, juice;	40.00 – 45.00	35.00 – 40.00			
red					55.00 – 60.00
rose					60.00 – 65.00
chartreuse					
dark green					500.00 – 600.00
Jubilee colors except gray					100.00 – 125.00
gray					350.00+
maroon					NEV
Tumbler, water*	70.00 – 85.00	55.00 – 65.00			
Vase, bud*	100.00 – 125.00	72.00 – 85.00			
Vase, 8"*[29]	700.00+	600.00+			
Vase, 10"*[30]	950.00+	850.00+			
Vase, 12"*[31]	1,300.00+	1,100.00+			

#1. Sales report, medium green: $290.00.

#2. Prices realized at auction since our 8th edition: $11,000.00; $7,500.00 and very recently on eBay: $8,500.00.

#3. For medium green, reported sale March 2000: $6,000.00 in mint condition; earlier sales: $9, 500.00 and $7,800.00 (for one in very near mint condition).

#4. Sales report: medium green in near mint condition, $625.00.

#5. Sales report in medium green (near mint), $625.00.

#6. Turquoise bowls are scarce; use the high end of the range for pricing. Keep in mind our values are for mixing bowls in absolutely mint condition — no nicks inside or out.

#7. Though we have reports of two in colors other than yellow having sold for $3,000.00 each, our survey average is much lower — a good example of a rare item bringing whatever the market will bear; a cobalt example reportedly sold on eBay for $2,025.00.

#8. Medium green sales report: $1,300.00 in mint condition, $1,175.00 in near mint, lid only: $650.00.

#9. A cobalt base sold for $3,000.00. An ivory footed French casserole realized $6,250.00 on the Internet.

#10. These have been reported in Harlequin yellow, mauve blue, and spruce as well. Was the report of one in maroon correct? Collectors question its existence. Let us know if you have one. These colors are rare and will command much higher prices.

#11. Sales report for gray: $850.00 in near mint condition.

#12. These are extremely rare. One advisor suggested a price of $4,000.00+ on the cobalt; there were two sales reports on the turquoise: $4,200.00. and $6,500.00 (the latter in 1998).

#13. One person reported purchasing bowl lids #1 – #3 at less than half the suggested values.

#14. A value of $2,000.00 was recommended for ivory.

#15. Sales report for red, cobalt, and ivory, $360.00.

#16. Sales report for red: $375.00.

#17. Several expressed concern that the new gray disk pitcher has hurt the value of the old. Though in our survey the price still held, one suggested $1,200.00, a much lower value than our average.

#18. Sales report: $275.00 in near mint condition.

#19. Some feel that color is not a factor here.

#20. A medium green example brought $440.00 at auction in early 1999; another sold for $490.00.

#21. Several dealers have reported that they have to sell plates of any size from 25% to 50% below book to get them to move; prices listed above are survey averages.

#22. Sales report: one shaker in medium green, $140.00.

#23. Sales report: medium green, $250.00.

#24. Sales report in red (near mint): $295.00.

#25. Badly faded lids will detract from value.

#26. See Plate 516.

#27. See Plate 516.

#28. One respondent suggested a lower price for the tray in turquoise, $150.00 to $200.00. All others evaluated turquoise and yellow in the same range.

#29. Sales report: yellow, $850.00; light green turquoise and ivory, each $770.00.

#30. Sales report: red, yellow, and turquoise, $935.00 each.

#31. Some feel color is not significant in evaluating the large vases, while others say the red is hardest to find and most desirable. Sales report, red: $3,000.00, $1,870.00 (March 1999); ivory, $1,375.00 (March 1999); yellow, $1,155.00 (March 1999); green $750.00.

Kitchen Kraft
Page 38 – 43

Use the high side of the range to evaluate red and cobalt. Note: See Jubilee and Rhythm sections for information concerning the value of mixing bowls in the colors of those lines.

Bowl, mixing; 6" ....72.00 – 78.00
Bowl, mixing; 8" ....85.00 – 95.00
Bowl, mixing; 10" ....115.00 – 125.00
Cake plate...55.00 – 65.00
Cake server ....145.00 – 155.00
Casserole, individual ....150.00 – 160.00
Casserole, 7½" ....85.00 – 92.00
Casserole, 8½" ....105.00 – 115.00
Covered jar, large ....320.00 – 325.00
Covered jar, medium ....280.00 – 295.00
Covered jar, small..285.00 – 300.00
Covered jug..280.00 – 290.00
Fork ....125.00 – 135.00
Metal frame for platter..................................22.00 – 26.00
Pie plate, 9" ....45.00 – 48.00
   with advertising in gold ....55.00 – 65.00
Pie plate, 10" ....45.00 – 48.00
   in spruce green ....295.00 – 305.00
Platter..70.00 – 75.00
   in spruce green ....325.00 – 350.00
Salt & pepper shakers, pr...........................100.00 – 110.00
Spoon..135.00 – 145.00
Spoon, ivory, 12" ....500.00+
Stacking refrigerator lid ....75.00 – 85.00
   in ivory ....210.00 – 225.00
Stacking refrigerator unit ....48.00 – 58.00
   in ivory ....200.00 – 210.00

Ironstone
Page 43 – 44

Use the high side of the range to evaluate red Ironstone. Items with an asterisk (*) were made only in Antique Gold.

Ashtray, rare ....25.00 – 30.00
Coffee mug ....22.00 – 26.00
Coffee server* ....70.00 – 75.00
Covered casserole*...50.00 – 60.00
Creamer ....5.00 – 7.00
Fruit, small...5.00 – 7.00
Marmalade...45.00 – 55.00
Nappy, large...15.00 – 20.00
Pitcher, disk water* ....55.00 – 65.00
Plate, 7"...3.00 – 4.00
Plate, 10"...7.00 – 9.00
Platter, 13" ....18.00 – 22.00
Salad bowl, 10"*...50.00 – 65.00
Salt & pepper shakers, pr...............................10.00 – 14.00
Sauce boat ....25.00 – 30.00
Sauce boat stand..40.00 – 50.00
   in red ....150.00 – 200.00

Saucer ....1.50 – 2.00
Soup/cereal..7.00 – 9.00
Soup plate...10.00 – 14.00
Sugar bowl with lid.......................................12.00 – 16.00
Teacup..4.00 – 6.00
Teapot, medium* ....55.00 – 65.00

Amberstone
Page 44 – 46

NEV = No Established Value

Items marked with an asterisk (*) are decorated with the black Amberstone pattern. Collectors seem to prefer the plain brown hollow ware pieces over patterned items.

Ashtray, rare ....28.00 – 32.00
Bowl, jumbo salad...40.00 – 45.00
Bowl, soup/cereal..5.00 – 8.00
Bowl, vegetable..12.00 – 16.00
Butter dish* ....35.00 – 45.00
Casserole..52.00 – 58.00
Coffee server...58.00 – 62.00
Covered jam jar...50.00 – 55.00
Covered mustard...60.00 – 65.00
Creamer...7.00 – 8.00
Cup & saucer* ....6.00 – 8.00
Deep soup, 8"* ....10.00 – 12.00
Dessert dish..5.00 – 6.50
Jumbo mug..NEV
Pie plate*..32.00 – 38.00
Pitcher, disk water ....60.00 – 65.00
Plate, bread & butter* ....1.50 – 2.50
Plate, salad*..2.00 – 3.00
Plate, 10"*...5.00 – 7.00
Platter, oval* ....12.00 – 16.00
Platter, round serving* ....15.00 – 18.00
Relish tray, center handle* ....28.00 – 32.00
Salt & pepper shakers, pr...............................12.00 – 15.00
Sauce boat..18.00 – 22.00
   with Fiesta mark...30.00 – 35.00
Sauce boat stand..20.00 – 24.00
Sugar bowl with lid...8.00 – 9.50
Tea server ....55.00 – 60.00

Casualstone
Page 46

Items marked with an asterisk (*) are decorated with the gold Casualstone pattern. There is little interest in this pattern at this time.

Ashtray, rare ....12.00 – 15.00
Bowl, jumbo salad; 10"...................................35.00 – 38.00
Bowl, round vegetable....................................12.00 – 15.00
Bowl, soup/cereal..4.00 – 6.00
Butter dish, stick*...32.00 – 38.00

Casserole	40.00 – 45.00
Coffee server	40.00 – 45.00
Creamer	4.00 – 5.00
Cup & saucer*	6.00 – 8.00
Deep plate*	7.00 – 8.50
Dessert	4.50 – 5.50
Jumbo mug	12.00 – 18.00
Marmalade	40.00 – 45.00
Pie plate*	24.00 – 28.00
Pitcher, disk type	40.00 – 45.00
Plate, bread & butter*	2.50 – 3.50
Plate, dinner*	6.00 – 8.00
Plate, salad*	3.50 – 4.50
Platter, oval, 13"*	12.00 – 15.00
Platter, round*	12.00 – 15.00
Relish tray*	15.00 – 18.00
Salt & pepper shakers, pr.	7.00 – 8.50
Sauce boat	13.00 – 17.00
Sugar bowl with lid	7.00 – 8.50
Tea server	25.00 – 30.00

〰〰〰〰〰〰

Casuals
Page 47 – 48

Because it is reported to be harder to find than Hawaiian Daisy, use the high side of the range to evaluate Carnation.

Plate, 7"	8.00 – 12.00
Plate, 10"	12.00 – 14.00

Platter, oval	40.00 – 50.00
Saucer	5.00 – 6.00

〰〰〰〰〰〰

Striped and/or Decals
Page 48 – 51

Even after many surveys and pricing updates, there is still a wide range of opinions concerning how to evaluate striped Fiesta. Using red, ivory, and cobalt Fiesta prices as a basis, some felt it should be of equal value, one says 50% higher, and another thinks it should be three to five times as much. With this in mind, you be the judge!

As for decaled items, opinions ranged from 20% less than red, ivory, and cobalt up to 100% more. Decaled Fiesta is in short supply and market values are obviously hard to analyze. All of the following are Fiesta with the turkey decal:

Plate, 9½"	95.00 – 105.00
Plate, cake; KK	180.00 – 200.00
Plate, chop; 13"	110.00 – 135.00
Plate, chop; 15"	165.00 – 190.00

〰〰〰〰〰〰

Lustre
Page 52

Because items of this nature are so rare, we have not attempted to establish a market value.

〰〰〰〰〰〰

New Fiesta — Post86
Page 53 – 73

Many items, of course, are still on the market. We have attempted to list suggested values for only those secondary market pieces that may be of interest to collectors. For unused, mint condition apricot with good color and without flaws, collectors can generally use the current manufacturer's suggested retail price for other colors plus a percentage from 0% to 20%, depending on how badly they want the item. Remember that almost all stores discount Fiesta about 20% to 30% from the manufacturer's suggested retail price. Apricot in anything less than unused, mint condition is extrememly plentiful, having been a top selling color during the 1980s, and thus should attract little collector interest at anything higher than a fraction of (rather than a premium above) MSRP at this time. From our observations, the few apricot items we have listed below with values seem to be selling above these guidelines. The ranges we used are for mint condition factory firsts (the market abounds with seconds), and the high end represents perfect examples or those with only the most insignificant factory flaws. Sapphire was ony available in the items we've indicated a value for; a place setting included the 10½" dinner plate, the 7" salad plate, the 6⅞" 19-ounce, bowl, and the cup and saucer.

	Lilac	Apricot	Sapphire
Bowl, bouillon; 6¾"	40.00 – 50.00	7.00 – 9.00	
Bowl, chili; 18-oz	40.00 – 50.00		
Bowl, fruit; 5⅜", 6-oz.	30.00 – 40.00		
Bowl, medium; 6⅞", 19-oz.	35.00 – 45.00		
Bowl, pasta; 12"	65.00 – 80.00		
Bowl, rim soup; 9"	50.00 – 60.00		
Bowl, small; 5⅝", 14-oz.	25.00 – 35.00		
Bowl, stacking cereal; 6½"	35.00 – 45.00		
Bowl, vegetable; large, 39-oz.	65.00 – 85.00	15.00 – 20.00	30.00 – 40.00
Butter dish	50.00 – 65.00		
Candlestick, pyramid; ea.	225.00 – 275.00	25.00 – 32.00	

	Lilac	Apricot	Sapphire
Candlestick, round (bulb), ea.	45.00 – 65.00		
Carafe	NA		35.00 – 45.00
Casserole with lid	130.00 – 160.00		
Clock	NA		40.00 – 50.00
Coffee server, 36-oz.	175.00 – 200.00	30.00 – 40.00	
Creamer, covered sugar and tray set	80.00 – 95.00		
Creamer, individual	30.00 – 35.00		
Cup, A.D.	85.00 – 100.00	18.00 – 22.00	
Cup, jumbo, 18-oz.	400.00 – 55.00		14.00 – 18.00
Cup, regular	25.00 – 35.00		
Lamp	NA	90.00 – 100.00	
Mug, 10-oz.	35.00 – 45.00		
Napkin rings, 4-pc. set	80.00 – 100.00	30.00 – 40.00	
Pie baker, deep dish, 10⅛"	65.00 – 90.00	18.00 – 22.00	
Pitcher, disk; large	80.00 – 90.00		35.00 – 55.00
with anniversary logo	70.00 – 80.00		60.00 – 75.00
Pitcher, disk; mini	60.00 – 70.00	25.00 – 30.00	
Pitcher, disk; small (juice)	90.00 – 110.00		
Place setting, 5-pc.	160.00 – 180.00	40.00 – 50.00	75.00 – 90.00
Place setting of flatware, 5-pc.	40.00 – 60.00		
Plate, bread and butter; 6⅛"	25.00 – 35.00		
Plate, chop; 11¾"	55.00 – 65.00		
Plate, dinner; 10½"	40.00 – 50.00	9.00 – 12.00	
Plate, luncheon; 9"	40.00 – 50.00		
Plate, salad; 7"	30.00 – 40.00		
Platter, #6, 9⅝"	50.00 – 60.00		
Platter, #8, 11⅝"	60.00 – 75.00		
Platter, #10, 13⅝"	60.00 – 70.00		45.00 – 55.00
Salt and pepper shakers, pr.	45.00 – 55.00	18.00 – 22.00	
Sauce boat	55.00 – 70.00		
Saucer, A.D.; 4⅞"	20.00 – 25.00	7.00 – 10.00	
Saucer, jumbo; 6¾"	15.00 – 20.00		9.00 – 12.00
Saucer, regular	7.00 – 10.00		
Skillet	NA	20.00 – 30.00	
Sugar Caddy	35.00 – 45.00		
Sugar individual; with lid	45.00 – 60.00		
Teapot	100.00 – 130.00	30.00 – 40.00	
Tray, relish (corn-on-the-cob)	60.00 – 70.00		
Tray, round serving; with handles, 11"	325.00 – 350.00		40.00 – 50.00
Tumbler	30.00 – 40.00	10.00 – 15.00	15.00 – 20.00
Vase, bud; 6"	90.00 – 110.00	15.00 – 20.00	
Vase, medium, 9⅝"	325.00 – 400.00	35.00 – 45.00	85.00 – 135.00

Harlequin

Page 74 –83

Use the high side of the range to evaluate maroon, dark green, gray, and spruce green. Medium green Harlequin is even more scarce than medium green Fiesta, and as seasoned collectors vie with each other for these rarities, prices are soaring. Based on this activity, values are suggested individually for many medium green items; when no specific value is given, we suggest that you at least double the upper side of the high range. Colors represented by the lower end of the high range are chartreuse, rose, red, light green, and mauve blue. Those items marked with an asterisk are rare or non-existent in light green; no market value has been established for them.

NEV = No Established Value   * = Rare or nonexistent in medium green

Suggested Values 〜〜〜〜〜〜

	Low Range	High Range	Medium Green	As Specified
Ashtray, basketweave	35.00 – 40.00	52.00 – 60.00	110.00 – 115.00	
Ashtray, regular*	32.00 – 38.00	48.00 – 53.00		
Ashtray, saucer*	48.00 – 55.00	60.00 – 68.00		
ivory				110.00 – 120.00
Bowl, cream soup	22.00 – 25.00	28.00 – 32.00	900.00 +	
Bowl, fruit; 5½"	6.00 – 8.00	8.00 – 11.00	25.00 – 35.00	
Bowl, individual salad	22.00 – 28.00	36.00 – 42.00	72.00 – 80.00	
Bowl, mixing; Kitchen Kraft, 6"				
red or light green				80.00 – 90.00
Bowl, mixing; Kitchen Kraft, 8"				
mauve blue				100.00 – 125.00
Bowl, mixing; Kitchen Kraft, 10"				
yellow				100.00 – 125.00
Bowl, nappy; 9"	25.00 – 28.00	35.00 – 40.00	90.00 – 100.00	
Bowl, oval baker	22.00 – 27.00	35.00 – 42.00		
Bowl, 36s	22.00 – 28.00	35.00 – 40.00	115.00 – 125.00	
spruce green or maroon				85.00 – 95.00
Bowl, 36s oatmeal	12.00 – 16.00	22.00 – 28.00	45.00 – 50.00	
Butter dish, ½-lb.	90.00 – 115.00	120.00 – 135.00		
cobalt				250.00 – 300.00
Candle holders, pr.*	235.00 – 250.00	275.00 – 300.00		
Casserole	80.00 – 95.00	145.00 – 160.00	575.00 – 625.00	
Creamer, high-lip; any color				125.00 – 135.00
Creamer, individual*	16.00 – 20.00	30.00 – 35.00		
light green				65.00 – 70.00
Creamer, novelty	24.00 – 28.00	35.00 – 42.00	NEV	
Creamer, regular	10.00 – 14.00	15.00 – 20.00	65.00 – 75.00	
Cup, demitasse	38.00 – 42.00	90.00 – 110.00	350.00 – 400.00	
Cup, large (Epicure body)			NEV	
any color other than med green				165.00 – 185.00
Egg cup, double	15.00 – 20.00	25.00 – 28.00	1,000.00 – 1,200.00	
Egg cup, single*	20.00 – 25.00	30.00 – 35.00		
Marmalade*	200.00 – 225.00	250.00 – 265.00		
Nut dish, basketweave	12.00 – 15.00	18.00 – 20.00		
rose				25.00 – 30.00
light green				65.00 – 75.00
Perfume bottle, any color				120.00 – 140.00
Pie plate, ringed	NEV	NEV		
Pitcher, service water	70.00 – 75.00	90.00 – 105.00	2,000.00 +	
Pitcher, 22-oz. jug	40.00 – 50.00	65.00 – 70.00	750.00 – 800.00	
Plate, deep	15.00 – 20.00	25.00 – 30.00	80.00 – 90.00	
Plate, 6"	3.00 – 4.00	4.00 – 5.50	12.00 – 15.00	
Plate, 7"	5.00 – 6.00	6.00 – 8.00	14.00 – 16.00	
Plate, 9"	8.00 – 10.00	12.00 – 14.00	20.00 – 22.00	
Plate, 10"	22.00 – 26.00	35.00 – 40.00	95.00 – 110.00	
Platter, 11"	16.00 – 20.00	22.00 – 27.00	200.00 – 210.00	
Platter, 13"	20.00 – 24.00	30.00 – 34.00	275.00 – 300.00	
Relish tray, mixed colors*				320.00 – 335.00
base, turquoise only				80.00 – 85.00
insert, yellow				30.00 – 35.00
insert, red, spruce, or turquoise				80.00 – 85.00
insert, rose or mauve blue				40.00 – 45.00
Salt & pepper shakers, pr.	15.00 – 18.00	22.00 – 26.00	185.00 +	
Sauce boat	18.00 – 22.00	30.00 – 35.00	125.00 +	
Saucer	1.00 – 2.00	3.00 – 4.00	10.00 – 12.00	
Saucer, demitasse	12.00 – 18.00	25.00 – 30.00	175.00 +	
Spoon rest, see Rhythm				
Sugar bowl with lid	15.00 – 20.00	28.00 – 32.00	135.00 +	
Syrup*, in red or yellow				225.00 – 250.00
spruce or mauve				300.00 – 340.00
Teacup	7.00 – 9.00	9.00 – 11.00	35.00 – 45.00	
Teapot	85.00 – 90.00	145.00 – 155.00	NEV	
Tumbler	40.00 – 45.00	52.00 – 58.00		
ivory				85.00 – 110.00
Tumbler with car decal				60.00 – 65.00

Harlequin Animals
Page 84 – 85

Any animal in a standard color	175.00 – 195.00
Any animal in a non-standard color[32]	310.00 – 325.00
Mavericks, near to full-size with gold	40.00 – 50.00
smaller, of porcelain-type material	20.00 – 25.00

[32]Duck, turquoise, sold for $3,000.00 at auction.

Riviera and Ivory Century
Page 86 – 92

NEV = No Established Value

Batter set, standard colors	290.00 – 315.00
with decals	170.00 – 185.00
red	NEV
ivory, with covered sugar bowl and 11½" square platter	NEV
Bowl, baker; 9"	25.00 – 30.00
Bowl, cream soup; with liner, ivory	75.00 – 80.00
liner only	20.00 – 25.00
Bowl, fruit; 5½"	12.00 – 14.00
cobalt	34.00 – 38.00
Bowl, nappy; 7¼"	25.00 – 30.00
Bowl, oatmeal; 6"	38.00 – 42.00
Bowl, utility; ivory	48.00 – 52.00
Butter dish, ¼-lb.	135.00 – 150.00
ivory	175.00 – 185.00
turquoise	290.00 – 315.00
cobalt	250.00 – 280.00
Butter dish, ½-lb, other Riviera colors	120.00 – 130.00
cobalt, ½-lb	300.00 – 325.00
Casserole	110.00 – 120.00
Creamer	11.00 – 13.00
Cup & saucer, demi; ivory	80.00 – 90.00
Jug, covered	130.00 – 145.00
Jug, open	90.00 – 100.00
Jug, open; 4½", ivory	NEV
Pitcher, juice; yellow	120.00 – 135.00
Pitcher, juice; mauve blue	210.00 – 225.00
Plate, compartment	NEV
Plate, deep	22.00 – 25.00
Plate, 6"	7.00 – 9.00
Plate, 7"	10.00 – 14.00
cobalt	35.00 – 45.00
Plate, 9"	16.00 – 20.00
Plate, 10"	55.00 – 65.00
Platter, 11½"	22.00 – 25.00
Platter, 11¼", closed handles	24.00 – 28.00
Platter, 12", cobalt	70.00 – 80.00
Platter, 15"	55.00 – 65.00
Salt & pepper shakers, pr.	18.00 – 20.00
Sauce boat	22.00 – 27.00
Sauce boat, fast-stand	75.00 – 85.00
Saucer	4.00 – 5.00
Sugar bowl with lid	18.00 – 20.00
Syrup with lid	160.00 – 180.00

Teacup	8.00 – 11.00
Teapot	155.00 – 165.00
Tidbit, 2-tier, ivory	70.00 – 75.00
Tumbler, handled	70.00 – 75.00
ivory	135.00 – 145.00
(These have been reported in spruce green, NEV)	
Tumbler, juice	52.00 – 55.00

Carnival
Page 93

Use the low range of values for these colors: gray, light green, yellow, and dark green. The high side represents values for cobalt, red, ivory, and turquoise.

Fruit, small	5.00 – 7.00
Oatmeal 35s	4.00 – 6.00
Plate, 6½"	2.00 – 3.00
Saucer	1.00 – 2.00
Teacup	4.00 – 6.00

Epicure
Page 94 – 95

NEV = No Established Value

Interest in this line is growing, a trend that is in keeping with the popularity of other manufacturer's '50s lines. Gray seems to be the favorite of many collectors, so use the high side of the range to evaluate your gray Epicure.

Ashtray	NEV
Bowl, cereal/soup	30.00 – 35.00
Bowl, covered vegetable	80.00 – 90.00
Bowl, fruit	20.00 – 24.00
Bowl, nappy, 8¾"	32.00 – 38.00
Casserole, individual	85.00 – 95.00
Coffeepot, 10"	190.00 – 215.00
Creamer	18.00 – 22.00
Gravy bowl	40.00 – 45.00
Ladle, 5½"	75.00 – 85.00
Nut dish, 4"	32.00 – 38.00
Pickle (small oval platter)	50.00 – 60.00
Plate, 6½"	7.00 – 9.00
Plate, 8"	18.00 – 22.00
Plate, 10"	30.00 – 35.00
Platter, large	28.00 – 32.00
Salt & pepper shakers, pr.	22.00 – 26.00
Sugar bowl with lid	25.00 – 30.00
Teacup & saucer	22.00 – 28.00
2-tier tidbit	100.00 – 125.00

Five Petal Daisy
Page 95
Use Tango prices to evaluate this line. (See page 213.)

Jubilee
Page 96

NEV = No Established Value

   After years of confusion, we now realize that the only gray 10" mixing bowl known to man came from one of the Jubilee three-piece bowl sets. There are no gray 6" or 8" bowls.

Bowl, cereal/soup	6.00 – 8.00
Bowl, fruit	4.00 – 5.00
Bowl, mixing; KK, 6"	90.00 – 110.00
Bowl, mixing; KK, 8"	100.00 – 120.00
Bowl, mixing; KK, 10"	125.00 – 150.00
gray	200.00 – 250.00
Bowl, nappy; 8¾"	7.00 – 9.00
Casserole	35.00 – 45.00
Coffeepot	45.00 – 55.00
Creamer	5.00 – 6.50
Cup & saucer	4.00 – 6.50
Cup & saucer, AD	12.00 – 15.00
Egg cup	7.00 – 11.00
Fiesta juice tumbler, see Fiesta pricing	
Fiesta juice pitcher, see Fiesta pricing	
Plate, 6"	1.50 – 2.50
Plate, 7"	3.00 – 4.50
Plate, 9"	5.00 – 7.00
Plate, 10"	8.00 – 10.00
Plate, calendar; cream, 1953	20.00 – 25.00
Plate, chop	14.00 – 17.00
Platter, 11"	8.00 – 10.00
Platter, 13"	10.00 – 14.00
Salt & pepper shakers, pr.	6.00 – 10.00
Sauce boat	9.00 – 12.00
Sugar bowl with lid	7.00 – 10.00
Teapot	42.00 – 48.00

Pastel Nautilus
Page 97

   This is another '50s line that is enjoying increased popularity.

Bowl, cream soup	9.00 – 11.00
Bowl, flat soup (deep plate)	7.00 – 10.00
Bowl, footed oatmeal; 6"	6.00 – 8.50
Bowl, fruit; 5"	5.00 – 6.50
Bowl, tab-handled soup/cereal	9.00 – 12.00
Bowl, oval vegetable	9.00 – 12.00
Bowl, round nappy	9.00 – 12.00
Casserole with lid	40.00 – 45.00

Creamer	7.00 – 8.50
Cup & saucer	10.00 – 12.00
Egg cup, double.	12.00 – 15.00
Gravy boat	12.00 – 16.00
Plate, 6"	2.50 – 3.50
Plate, 7"	5.00 – 6.50
Plate, 8"	5.00 – 6.50
Plate, 9"	6.00 – 8.00
Plate, 10"	9.00 – 12.00
Platter, 13"	12.00 – 16.00
Platter, 11"	9.00 – 12.00
Platter/gravy boat liner, 9"	9.00 – 12.00
Sugar bowl with lid	10.00 – 15.00

Rhythm
Page 98 – 101

Bowl, footed cereal/chowder	9.00 – 13.00
brown, black, cobalt, or white	20.00 – 25.00
Bowl, fruit; 5½"	5.00 – 6.50
Bowl, mixing; KK, 6"	90.00 – 110.00
Bowl, mixing; KK, 8"	100.00 – 120.00
Bowl, mixing; KK, 10"	150.00 – 160.00
Bowl, nappy	9.00 – 14.00
Bowl, salad; large	55.00 – 65.00
Bowl, soup	8.00 – 12.00
Casserole lid	50.00 – 60.00
(bottom is nappy)	
Creamer, 2¾"	7.00 – 9.00
Cup & saucer	9.00 – 12.00
Cup & saucer, AD; scarce	200.00 – 235.00
Plate, 6"	5.00 – 6.00
Plate, 7"	6.00 – 8.00
Plate, 8", very rare	20.00 – 25.00
Plate, 9"	7.00 – 10.00
Plate, 10"	10.00 – 14.00
Plate, calendar	10.00 – 14.00
Plate, snack	28.00 – 32.00
maroon	120.00 – 135.00
Platter, 11½"	12.00 – 14.00
Platter, 13½"	14.00 – 18.00
Salt & pepper shakers, pr.	10.00 – 15.00
Sauce boat	10.00 – 15.00
cobalt	18.00 – 22.00
Sauce boat stand	10.00 – 14.00
Spoon rest, colors other than white, turquoise, or dark green	200.00 – 235.00
white	110.00 – 125.00
dark green	350.00 – 375.00
turquoise	400.00 +
Sugar bowl with lid	18.00
Teapot	50.00 – 60.00
3-tier tidbit	38.00 – 42.00

Seller's Line
Page 102

Very rare, NEV.

~~~~~~~~

Serenade
Page 102 – 103

Bowl, fruit	7.00 – 11.00
Bowl, lug soup	25.00 – 30.00
Bowl, nappy, 9"	20.00 – 25.00
Casserole	65.00 – 75.00
Casserole base, Kitchen Kraft	55.00 – 65.00
matching lid	90.00 – 100.00
complete	145.00 – 165.00
non-standard color	300.00 – 350.00
Creamer	12.00 – 18.00
Pickle dish	15.00 – 20.00
Plate, 6"	4.00 – 5.00
Plate, 7"	5.00 – 7.00
Plate, 9"	9.00 – 12.00
Plate, 10"	18.00 – 22.00
Plate, chop	22.00 – 28.00
Plate, deep	25.00 – 30.00
Platter, 12½"	15.00 – 20.00
Salt & pepper shakers, pr.	14.00 – 18.00
Sauce boat	18.00 – 22.00
Sugar bowl with lid	15.00 – 20.00
Teacup & saucer	12.00 – 15.00
Teapot	85.00 – 100.00

~~~~~~~~

Skytone/Suntone
Page 104 – 105
Use values for Jubilee to price these lines.

~~~~~~~~

Tango
Page 105

Use the high side of the range to evaluate red, spruce green, and maroon items. Though many collectors like the shapes and colors of this line, dealers tell us that because it's so hard to find, most don't really attempt to collect it, and unless they can offer several items for sale at once, it's hard to sell. So while they may do well to sell the lone plate at 50% of book price, a lot of several items or an incomplete set might bring from 25% to 50% more than our suggest values.

Bowl, fruit; 5¾"	5.00 – 7.00
Bowl, nappy; 8¾"	9.00 – 12.00
Bowl, oval baker; 9"	9.00 – 12.00

Casserole	60.00 – 70.00
Creamer	6.00 – 8.00
Cup & saucer	7.00 – 9.00
Plate, 6"	3.00 – 4.00
Plate, 7"	3.00 – 4.50
Plate, 9"	6.00 – 8.00
Plate, 10"	9.00 – 11.00
Plate, deep	8.00 – 11.00
Platter, 11¾"	9.00 – 12.00
Salt & pepper shakers, pr.	10.00 – 15.00
Saucer	1.50 – 2.50
Sugar bowl with lid	15.00 – 20.00

~~~~~~~~

Wells Art Glaze
Page 106 – 108

Batter set, 3-pc.	200.00 – 235.00
Bowl, cream soup	25.00 – 30.00
Bowl, fruit; 5"	12.00 – 15.00
Bowl, nappy; 8"	22.00 – 28.00
Bowl, oatmeal 36s	22.00 – 28.00
Bowl, oval baker; 9"	22.00 – 28.00
Casserole	65.00 – 75.00
Coffeepot, individual	125.00 – 145.00
Covered jug, 9"	130.00 – 140.00
Covered jug, with decals	70.00 – 80.00
Covered muffin	70.00 – 80.00
Cream soup stand	12.00 – 17.00
Creamer	20.00 – 25.00
Creamer, individual	20.00 – 24.00
Cup, bouillon; with handles	22.00 – 26.00
Cup, coffee; 4¾"	19.00 – 23.00
Cup & saucer	19.00 – 23.00
Cup & saucer, AD	30.00 – 35.00
Egg cup, double	22.00 – 26.00
Nut dish/butter pat	12.00 – 15.00
Pickle dish with handles	22.00 – 28.00
Plate, 6"	6.00 – 9.00
Plate, 7"	10.00 – 14.00
Plate, 9"	14.00 – 18.00
Plate, 10"	22.00 – 28.00
Plate, chop; with handles	25.00 – 32.00
Plate, deep	18.00 – 22.00
Plate, square, 6"	15.00 – 18.00
Platter, oval, 11½"	22.00 – 28.00
Platter, oval, 13½"	30.00 – 35.00
Platter, oval, 15½"	40.00 – 45.00
Sauce boat	25.00 – 30.00
Sauce boat, fast-stand	32.00 – 38.00
Sauce boat liner with handles	18.00 – 22.00
Sugar bowl, individual, open	16.00 – 22.00
Sugar bowl with lid	22.00 – 26.00
Syrup	120.00 – 135.00
Syrup, with decals	62.00 – 68.00
Teapot, Empress, rare	325.00 – 350.00
Teapot, regular	95.00 – 115.00

Mexican Decaled Lines
Mexicana, Hacienda, Conchita, and Max-i-cana
Page 109 – 118

To simplify the problem of evaluating these lines, we have compiled a general listing that basically will apply to the first three patterns mentioned above (on Century shapes) and Max-i-cana on Yellowstone. Not all of these items have been found in every pattern. Letter codes have been used to indicate pieces that so far are known to exist in only the coded patterns: H — Hacienda; Me — Mexicana; Ma — Max-i-cana. Remember that prices given below are for pieces with mint decals. Examples with worn or scratched decals are worth no more than chipped ones.

Bell (H)	90.00 – 98.00
Bowl, baker; 9"	28.00 – 32.00
Bowl, cream soup; rare (H, Ma, Me)	60.00 – 68.00
Bowl, deep, 2½" x 5" (Me)	40.00 – 44.00
Bowl, fruit; 5"	12.00 – 14.00
Bowl, lug soup; 4½" (Ma, Me)	38.00 – 42.00
Bowl, oatmeal; 6"	28.00 – 32.00
Bowl, vegetable; 8½"	25.00 – 30.00
Bowl, vegetable; 9½"	28.00 – 32.00
Butter dish, ½-lb. (H, Ma)	135.00 – 150.00
round (H)	220.00 – 235.00
Casserole	135.00 – 145.00
Creamer	15.00 – 20.00
Creamer, large (Ma)	22.00 – 26.00
Cup & saucer	18.00 – 22.00
Egg cup, rolled edge (Me, Ma)	40.00 – 45.00
Egg cup, torpedo shape (Me, Ma)	32.00 – 38.00
Plate, 6"	5.00 – 7.00
Plate, 7"	12.00 – 14.00
Plate, 9"	18.00 – 22.00
Plate, 9½" (10")	42.00 – 46.00
Plate, deep, 8"	22.00 – 25.00
Platter, 10"	30.00 – 34.00
Platter, oval or square well, 11½"	35.00 – 40.00
Platter, oval or square well, 13½"	48.00 – 52.00
Platter, square well, 15"	48.00 – 52.00
Sauce boat	30.00 – 35.00
Sauce boat liner (Me, Ma)	28.00 – 32.00
Sugar bowl with lid	28.00 – 32.00
Sugar bowl, large (Ma)	28.00 – 33.00
Syrup jug, covered, Century (H, Me)*	375.00 – 425.00
Tall covered jug, Century, (H, Me)*	425.00 – 475.00
Teapot, rare (H, Me)	145.00 – 165.00
Tumbler, fired-on design, 6-oz	10.00 – 13.00
Tumbler, fired-on design, 8-oz	14.00 – 17.00
Tumbler, fired-on design, 10-oz	15.00 – 20.00

*Jugs with missing lids are worth one-third to one-half as much as those with lids.

Kitchen Kraft Conchita & Mexicana

Bowl, mixing; 6"	30.00 – 35.00

Bowl, mixing; 8"	35.00 – 40.00
Bowl, mixing; 10"	40.00 – 50.00
Cake plate, 10½"	35.00 – 40.00
Cake server	65.00 – 75.00
Casserole, individual	90.00 – 105.00
Casserole, 7½"	80.00 – 85.00
Casserole, 8½"	82.00 – 88.00
OvenServe, Handy Andy	55.00 – 62.00
Metal base	15.00 – 20.00
Covered jar, large	155.00 – 175.00
Covered jar, medium	135.00 – 145.00
Covered jar, small	125.00 – 135.00
Covered jug	160.00 – 175.00
Fork	70.00 – 75.00
Pie plate	32.00 – 38.00
Refrigerator stack unit	45.00 – 50.00
Lid	50.00 – 60.00
Salt & pepper shakers, pr.	50.00 – 60.00
Spoon	65.00 – 75.00
Underplate, 9"	40.00 – 45.00
Underplate, 6" (rare)	45.00 – 50.00

Max-i-cana Fiesta

This line is so rare that even very advanced collectors tell us they've never seen a piece.

Cup & saucer	52.00 – 58.00
Fruit, 5½"	40.00 – 45.00
Nappy, 8½"	65.00 – 72.00
Plate, 6"	16.00 – 20.00
Plate, 10"	45.00 – 52.00
Platter	68.00 – 72.00

Miscellaneous Mexican Lines

After carefully studying the results of our survey, we found very little difference between the average of the values suggested for Mexican Decaled Lines and the values offered for the less-familiar lines such as Mexicali Virginia Rose. So in order to simplify this section of the price guide, we suggest that for any Mexican decal on any shape other than Century — Swing, Nautilus, Virginia Rose, Liberty, and Harlequin are shown in this issue — use the Mexican Decaled Lines values, placing the top of the value range for the miscellaneous lines at its low end (for the flat pieces) to about the middle range (for the molded hollow ware). The harder-to-find items such as the butter dish, egg cup, and casserole, for instance, will bring just as much in one Mexican decaled line as another.

Go-Alongs
Page 119 – 130

NEV = No Established Value

Collectors report a lot of interest in excellent-to-mint condition go-alongs.

Plate 270: Pitcher with fired on figures..............40.00 – 45.00
Plate 271: Tumblers, each ....12.00 – 16.00
Plate 272: Coaster set..16.00 – 20.00
Plate 273: Boxed ensemble ....NEV
Tumblers fired on design 6 oz..............9.00 – 12.00
Tumblers fired on design 8 oz...........12.00 – 16.00
Tumblers fired on design 10 oz. ....15.00 – 18.00
Plate 274: Tumblers, each ....20.00 – 25.00
Plate 275: Ensemble go-alongs, part of boxed ensemble ...NEV
Plate 276: Sherbet ....15.00 – 18.00
Plate 277: Rattan tumbler holders, each ....10.00 – 20.00
Plate 278: Quikut flatware set, mint in box ....100.00 – 115.00
Plate 279: Chef's Set Quickcut, MIB..............................NEV
Plate 280: Metal frame for Fiesta jam set (cream
soup) ....85.00 – 100.00
Metal frame for Fiesta marmalade, very
rare..100.00 – 125.00
Metal frame for Fiesta chop plate..........50.00 – 60.00
Plate 281: Metal frame for Fiesta double tidbit set
with folding stand.......................125.00 – 140.00
Plate 282: Metal frame for Fiesta promotional
casserole.......................................$40.00 – 45.00
Plate 283: Metal frame for Fiesta salad service set,
very rare......................................125.00 – 145.00
Not shown: Metal frame for Fiesta mustard &
marmalade....................................90.00 – 100.00
Metal frame for Fiesta cake plate..........45.00 – 50.00
Metal revolving base for Fiesta relish
tray...32.00 – 38.00
Metal frame for Fiesta condiment set
(mustard and shakers), very rare.............110.00 – 120.00
Plate 284: Metal handle for Fiesta mixing bowl-ice
bucket ....70.00 – 80.00
Plate 285: Fiesta 3-tier tidbit tray (in mixed
colors)...100.00 – 120.00
(Add 10% for each plate in red or
cobalt — 20% for each plate in the '50s colors)
Plate 286: Frame for Fiesta ice-lip pitcher &
tumblers (watch for repros)............90.00 – 100.00
Plate 287: Ash stand.......................................125.00 – 150.00
Plate 288: Century nut dish in ivory ....55.00 – 62.00
Plate 289: Century 2-tier tidbit tray in ivory..........70.00 – 75.00
Plate 290: Harlequin nut dish ....45.00 – 52.00
Plate 291: Metal holder for Harlequin tumbler..........22.00 – 25.00
Not shown: Metal holder for Kitchen Kraft
platter ....22.00 – 28.00
Metal holder for Kitchen Kraft pie
plate ....18.00 – 23.00
Metal holder for Kitchen Kraft casse-
role..18.00 – 23.00
Plate 292: Fiestawood salad bowl ....100.00 – 125.00
Plate 293: Metal holder for Fiesta nappy ....16.00 – 20.00
Metal dripolator insert for Fiesta
teapot...12.00 – 19.00
Metal frame for Fiesta jam set ....80.00 – 90.00
Wireware holder for Fiesta juice set............85.00 – 92.00
Sta Bright Flatware, 3-pc. setting.........16.00 – 20.00
Fiestawood tray with glass insert ....120.00 – 130.00

Glass insert for Fiestawood tray..........22.00 – 28.00
Plate 294: Fiestawood hors d'oeuvres tray..........100.00 – 115.00
Plate 295: Wooden tray/metal base for Fiesta chop
plate...70.00 – 75.00
Plate 296: Fiestawood hors d'oeuvres tray..........100.00 – 110.00
Plate 297: Metal Kitchenware bread box ....60.00 – 70.00
Metal Kitchenware garbage can ....75.00 – 85.00
Plate 298: Metal Kitchenware canister set, 4-pc...100.00 – 115.00
Metal Kitchenware napkin holder ....52.00 – 64.00
Plate 299: Wastebasket.....................................60.00 – 70.00
Plate 300: Metal Kitchenware bread box ....85.00 – 95.00
Not shown: Metal Kitchenware stool ....135.00 – 145.00
Metal Kitchenware 3-tier vegetable
bin ....85.00 – 92.00
Plate 301: Popcorn set in original box.............................NEV
5-pc popcorn bowl set, excellent paint....85.00 – 95.00
Plate 302: Metal 3-part tidbit set, excellent
paint...72.00 – 77.00
Plate 303: Hankscraft egg cup...............................6.00 – 8.00
Hankscraft egg poacher with glass
insert..50.00 – 60.00
Plate 304: Fiestacraft paper, MIB ....25.00 – 35.00
Plate 305: Paper tablecloth, napkins..................15.00 – 20.00
Plate 306: Cabinet...NEV
Plate 308: Sheet of decals.................................60.00 – 70.00
Plate 309: Japan tea set: pot, sugar & creamer, 6 plates,
6 cups & saucers.........................100.00 – 125.00
Not shown: Luncheon set, tablecloth & 4 napkins,
circa 1930s–'40s, color & design
compatible ....40.00 – 50.00

~~~~~~

Commercial Adaptations and Ephemera
Page 131 – 142

NEV = No Established Value

Plate 310 and Plate 311: Fiesta price lists
Undated (1936) ....100.00 – 125.00
1936 – 1939......................................45.00 – 75.00
1940 – 1949......................................45.00 – 65.00
1950 – 1959......................................25.00 – 45.00
1960 – 1968......................................15.00 – 25.00
Plate 312: Harlequin price list ....125.00 – 175.00
Plate 313: Riviera price list..NEV
Plate 314: Jubilee price list ....35.00 – 40.00
Plate 315: Epicure price list...............................90.00 – 105.00
Plate 317: Fiesta store display, complete (variations exists
large and small) NM ....1,400.00 – 1,650.00
Plate 318: Fiesta carton for dinnerware set.......120.00 – 130.00
Plate 319: Fiesta carton, dancing girl logo, small to
large ....45.00 – 52.00
Plate 320: Fiesta carton (no dancing girl logo)........32.00 – 37.00
Not shown: Fiesta carton for juice set (no dancing girl
logo) ....38.00 – 42.00
Plate 321: Harlequin reissue 45-pc set, MIB ....NEV
Riviera 16-pc set, MIB ....NEV
Plate 322: Amberstone packaging ....Add 100% minimum
to value of item

Plate 323:   Ensemble ad from Christmas catalog....200.00 – 250.00
Plate 324 – Plate 326: Ensemble ads, full page from newspaper,
    depending on the ad and its condition......600.00 – 1,200.00
Plate 327 – Plate 328: Ensemble ad, insert flyer, 2 sides printed,
    very rare...3,000.00
Plate 329:   Fiesta ashtray, commemorative or
    advertising......................................70.00 – 80.00
Plate 330:   Kitchen Kraft pie plate with
    advertising......................................75.00 – 85.00
    In spruce green ....310.00 – 335.00
Plate 331:   Fiesta plate, Lazarus Anniversary ....52.00 – 58.00
    Mug...75.00 – 85.00
Plate 332:   Fiesta fruit bowl, Lazarus Anniver-
    sary ....42.00 – 48.00
Plate 333:   Fiesta tumbler, Lazarus Anniversary ....70.00 – 85.00
Plate 334:   Fiesta egg cup, Lazarus Anniversary ..60.00 – 70.00
Plate 335:   Fiesta syrup with Dutchess tea.......175.00 – 200.00
Plate 336:   Can label ....12.00 – 15.00
Plate 337:   Seed package ....12.00 – 15.00
Plate 338:   Can label ....12.00 – 15.00
Plate 339:   Rolled Oats box ....50.00 – 75.00
Plate 340:   Can label ....12.00 – 15.00
Plate 341:   National Dairy Council punch-outs, as
    shown (watch for repros) ....130.00 – 140.00
    each cutout ....5.00 – 25.00
Plate 342:   Flour sack...NEV
Plate 343:   Ice cream parlor decoration ....25.00 – 35.00
Plate 344:   Restaurant menu...............................NEV
Plate 345:   Fiesta Tom & Jerry mugs in white (or
    color inside), 1-color advertising..........40.00 – 45.00
    2-color advertising ....50.00 – 55.00
    3-color advertising ....60.00 – 65.00
    4-color advertising ....70.00 – 75.00
    Fiesta Tom & Jerry mugs in color with
    advertising......................................80.00 – 85.00
    Fiesta Tom & Jerry mugs, color inside, no
    advertising......................................30.00 – 35.00
    Matching Sit n' Sip coasters ....30.00 – 35.00
Plate 346:   Buick Sit n' Sip coasters....................30.00 – 35.00
Plate 347:   Buick ashtray....................................75.00 – 82.00
Plate 348:   Buick Tom & Jerry mugs...................75.00 – 80.00
Plate 349:   New Fiesta mug ....5.00 – 8.00
Not shown: Ads from 1960s ....15.00 – 40.00

~~~~~~~~~~

Experimentals, Samples, Trials, and Inventions
Page 147 – 153

 Most of the items shown in this chapter are one of a kind or at least extremely rare, making them difficult if not impossible to evaluate. Many who took part in this survey indicated they had little or no experience in buying or selling these pieces. On our previous survey, to leave you with at least a reference point, the average suggested price for the maroon mug in Plate 61 was $1,000.00 to 1,200.00, though one estimate placed it at several hundred dollars higher. (These are from a set of fifteen which along with a large bowl was

dipped at the factory as a special gift for a supervisor.) Prices exceeding $8,000.00 were suggested for the ivory individual teapot, French casserole, and footed mixing bowl.

~~~~~~~~~~

Lamps
Page 153 – 154

Fiesta lamp with fabricated body......................600.00 – 800.00
Harlequin lamp with fabricated body ....400.00 – 550.00
Syrup lamp base, undecorated ....240.00 – 260.00
Syrup lamp base, hand painted......................250.00 – 270.00
 with original shade, add ....30.00 – 35.00

~~~~~~~~~~

Apple Tree Bowls
Page 155

 Add 10% for colors other than turquoise, 30% for striped examples.

Set of six..250.00 – 275.00

~~~~~~~~~~

Children's Sets
Page 156 – 159

NEV = No Established Value

Plate 390:   Animal characters on Fiesta shapes, each
    pc ....200.00 – 250.00
    on HLC shapes other than Fiesta, each
    pc..50.00 – 65.00
    Little Orphan Annie mug...................75.00 – 90.00
Plate 391:   Rabbit family on Fiesta mug ....150.00 – 200.00
    divided plate ....75.00 – 90.00
Plate 392:   Dick Tracy set
    Plate ....135.00 – 150.00
    Soup/cereal ....145.00 – 160.00
    Mug..145.00 – 160.00
Plate 393:   Tom & the Butterfly set
    Plate ....52.00 – 58.00
    Bowl..65.00 – 70.00
    Mug..65.00 – 70.00
Plate 394:   Western China plate ....75.00 – 90.00
Plate 395:   Eggshell Nautilus set, very rare......................NEV
Plate 396:   Ralston bowl....................................40.00 – 45.00
Plate 397:   Bowl, fruit; Empress shape, 5"...........35.00 – 50.00
    Bowl, coupe, Empress shape, 8".........65.00 – 85.00
    Cup, Empress shape ....45.00 – 60.00
Plate 398:   Plate, Empress shape, 9" ....45.00 – 60.00
Not shown: Plate, Empress shape, 6" ....35.00 – 40.00

Plate 399:   Pitcher, Genesee shape, ca 1915,
　　　　　　3½" ....115.00 – 135.00
Plates 400 & 402: Plate, Yellowstone shape,
　　　　　　6½" ....35.00 – 45.00
Plate 401:   Platter, Yellowstone shape, 9" ....65.00 – 75.00

Kitchen Kraft
Page 160 – 162

Add at least 50% to these values for the more collectible lines such as Sun Porch.

Bowl, mixing; 6" ....22.00 – 26.00
Bowl, mixing; 8" ....22.00 – 28.00
Bowl, mixing; 10" ....35.00 – 40.00
Cake plate...32.00 – 38.00
Cake server..40.00 – 45.00
Casserole, individual ....60.00 – 70.00
Casserole, 6" ....38.00 – 42.00
Casserole, 8½" ....40.00 – 45.00
　　Metal base...................................15.00 – 20.00
Covered jar, large ....110.00 – 125.00
Covered jar, medium...........................90.00 – 105.00
Covered jar, small ....75.00 – 85.00
Covered jug....................................100.00 – 110.00
Pie plate...35.00 – 40.00
Platter..40.00 – 45.00
　　Metal base...................................20.00 – 25.00
Salt and pepper shakers, pr. ....40.00 – 45.00
Spoon...38.00 – 42.00
Stacking refrigerator lid.......................30.00 – 35.00
Stacking refrigerator unit ....22.00 – 28.00
Underplate..20.00 – 25.00

Embossed OvenServe Lines
Page 162 – 163
Add 50% when decals are present.

Ashtray ....50.00 – 60.00
Batter pitcher....................................65.00 – 75.00
Bean pot, 4x4½" ....10.00 – 12.00
Bean pot, 4¼x5½" ....12.00 – 15.00
Bowl, 4"...4.00 – 5.50
Bowl, fruit; 5½" ....8.00 – 10.00
Bowl, mixing; 6¼" ....10.00 – 14.00
Bowl, mixing; 7¼" ....12.00 – 18.00
Bowl, mixing; 8½" ....20.00 – 25.00
　　11½" ....50.00 – 60.00
Bowl, oval baker; 6½" ....7.00 – 8.50
Bowl, oval baker; 8½" ....10.00 – 14.00
Bowl, oval baker; 11" ....18.00 – 22.00
Bowl, ramekin; handled, 4½"....................5.00 – 6.00
Bowl, tab-handled soup; 7" ....9.00 – 12.00
Casserole, 6" ....12.00 – 15.00

Casserole, 7½" ....22.00 – 28.00
Casserole, 8½" ....28.00 – 32.00
Casserole, 10" ....40.00 – 45.00
Cup, 3¾", rare ....20.00 – 25.00
Custard cup, 3½" ....4.00 – 5.00
Pie plate, 9" ....16.00 – 20.00
　　10½" ....22.00 – 28.00
Plate, 7" ....5.00 – 7.00
Plate, 10" ....9.00 – 12.00
Platter, deep, oval, 8" ....12.00 – 14.00
Platter, deep, oval, 12" ....15.00 – 18.00
Saucer, 5¾" ....5.00 – 8.00

Harmony Lines
Page 164 – 165
For Kitchen Kraft items not listed here, use the high side of the range of values suggested for Kitchen Kraft above.

Bowl, cereal/soup................................12.00 – 14.00
Bowl, fruit; 5½"....................................6.00 – 8.00
Bowl, mixing; KK, 10"...........................35.00 – 40.00
Bowl, nappy; 9" ....15.00 – 18.00
Bowl, oval baker; 10" ....16.00 – 22.00
Cake server, KK ....50.00 – 55.00
Casserole, KK, 8"................................45.00 – 50.00
Cup & saucer......................................8.00 – 12.00
Fork, KK ....50.00 – 55.00
Pie plate, KK, 10" ....35.00 – 40.00
Plate, 6"...3.00 – 4.00
Plate, 7"...6.00 – 9.00
Plate, 9"...9.00 – 12.00
Spoon, KK..50.00 – 55.00

Americana
Page 166

Bowl, coupe soup................................14.00 – 16.50
Bowl, cream soup ....70.00 – 80.00
Bowl, dessert/fruit..................................6.00 – 9.00
Bowl, oval vegetable; 8½" ....22.00 – 27.00
Bowl, round vegetable; 8" ....22.00 – 27.00
Bowl, round vegetable; 9" ....22.00 – 27.00
Bowl lid, 9" ....42.00 – 48.00
Creamer..12.00 – 15.00
Cup & saucer ....15.00 – 18.00
Cup & saucer, AD ....28.00 – 32.00
Egg cup..22.00 – 28.00
Plate, 6"...3.00 – 4.00
Plate, 7"...5.00 – 7.00
Plate, 8" square ....12.00 – 15.00
Plate, 8½"..12.00 – 15.00
Plate, 10" ....20.00 – 28.00
Platter, 11"..15.00 – 20.00
Platter, 13"..22.00 – 27.00

Platter, 15" ....65.00 – 75.00
Platter, round, 13" ....35.00 – 40.00
Sauce boat ....12.00 – 15.00
Sauce boat stand ....45.00 – 60.00
Sugar bowl with lid...18.00 – 25.00
Teapot ....90.00 – 110.00

Century
Page 167 – 168

Because it is impossible to list every Century-based dinnerware line produced by HLC, we offer these suggestions to help you determine approximately how much you should expect to pay. Note that values are rising for the more desirable lines such as Sun Porch and English Garden.

Use values under Mesican Decaled Lines (pages 213 – 214) following these guidelines.

1) For place-setting items (plates, cups and saucers, small bowls, etc.) purchased one at a time in a very simple pattern, use half of these prices.

2) For place-setting items purchased one at a time in a more desirable pattern (for example, Sun Porch, English Garden, etc.), use 75% of these prices.

3) For larger serving pieces or purchases of larger lots of a very simple pattern, use 75% of these prices.

4) For larger serving pieces or purchases of larger lots of a more desirable pattern, use 100% of these prices.

Dogwood
Page 169

Values are given for pieces with excellent gold trim.

Bowl, cereal; 6" ....10.00 – 12.00
Bowl, fruit; 5¾" ....6.00 – 8.00
Bowl, mixing; KK, 6½"......................................35.00 – 45.00
Bowl, mixing; KK, 8¾"......................................35.00 – 45.00
Bowl, mixing; KK, 10½".....................................35.00 – 45.00
Bowl, oval vegetable; 9½" ....20.00 – 25.00
Bowl, round vegetable; 8¾" ....20.00 – 25.00
Bowl, soup; 8"..12.00 – 15.00
Creamer...12.00 – 15.00
Cup & saucer ....10.00 – 12.00
Plate, 6"...4.00 – 5.00
Plate, 7"...10.00 – 12.00
Plate, 8", scarce..12.00 – 15.00
Plate, 9"...8.00 – 10.00
Plate, 10", scarce..12.00 – 15.00
Platter, 11¾" ....20.00 – 25.00
Platter, 13½" ....25.00 – 35.00
Sauce boat ....20.00 – 28.00
Sauce boat liner, 8½" ....25.00 – 30.00
Sugar bowl with lid...10.00 – 12.00
Teapot...75.00 – 85.00

Historical America Subjects
Page 170
To evaluate this line, use suggested prices for Americana. (See page 217.)

Jade
Page 171
Values for decaled Jade may be computed by using the suggestions under Century.

Nautilus
Page 172
Values for decaled Nautilus (other than Harmony) may be computed by using the suggestions under Century.

Priscilla
Page 173

Reports from dealers are that Priscilla sells well for them. This line was also made by Universal China; theirs are marked like HLC's, and Priscilla aficionados find that these pieces add dimension to their collections. Values are given for pieces with excellent gold trim.

Bowl, fruit; 5" ....7.00 – 8.00
Bowl, fruit; KK, 9½", scarce...............................32.00 – 38.00
Bowl, mixing; small, KK, 6" ....35.00 – 40.00
Bowl, mixing; medium, KK, 8"............................38.00 – 42.00
Bowl, mixing; large, KK, 10" ....40.00 – 45.00
Bowl, oval vegetable; 9" ....20.00 – 25.00
Bowl, round vegetable; 8" ....20.00 – 25.00
Bowl, soup; 8"..12.00 – 15.00
Cake plate, KK, 11" ....20.00 – 25.00
Casserole, round, KK, 8½" ....35.00 – 40.00
Coffeepot, KK ....90.00 – 100.00
Creamer...15.00 – 20.00
Cup & saucer ....12.00 – 15.00
Pie plate, KK, 9½"...25.00 – 30.00
Pitcher, water; KK...32.00 – 38.00
Plate, 6" ....6.00 – 7.00
Plate, 7" ....8.00 – 10.00
Plate, 8" ....9.00 – 10.00
Plate, 9" ....9.00 – 10.00
Plate, 10" ....12.00 – 15.00
Platter, tab-handled, made by Universal..............25.00 – 30.00
Platter, 9"...20.00 – 25.00
Platter, 13½" ....28.00 – 32.00
Sauce boat ....20.00 – 25.00

Sugar bowl with lid..20.00 – 25.00
Teapot, regular..85.00 – 90.00
Teapot, Republic, hard to find............................85.00 – 90.00
Teapot, tall, hard to find, made by Universal..........85.00 – 90.00

Rhythm
Page 174 – 175

Plate 433: Rhythm Rose
   Bowl, mixing; KK, small ....12.00 – 15.00
   Bowl, mixing; KK, medium................15.00 – 18.00
   Bowl, mixing; KK, large.....................22.00 – 28.00
   Cake plate, KK, 10½"..........................18.00 – 22.00
   Cake server, KK.................................38.00 – 42.00
   Casserole, KK, 8½" ....38.00 – 42.00
   Coffeepot, KK...................................38.00 – 42.00
   Creamer ....7.00 – 9.00
   Cup & saucer, AD............................15.00 – 18.00
   Pie plate, KK, 9½".............................18.00 – 20.00
   Pitcher, jug type, KK..........................38.00 – 42.00
   Plate, 6"..3.00 – 5.00
   Plate, 9"...7.00 – 9.00
   Plate, deep, 8"..................................12.00 – 14.00
   Platter, 13"......................................15.00 – 18.00
   Sauce boat ....12.00 – 14.00
   Sugar bowl with lid...........................12.00 – 14.00
   Underplate, KK, 6" ....10.00 – 12.00
   Underplate, KK, 9" ....12.00 – 15.00
Plate 434: Western
   Bowl, fruit......................................15.00 – 20.00
   Bowl, vegetable ....20.00 – 25.00
   Cup & saucer....................................18.00 – 22.00
   Plate, 9"...18.00 – 25.00
Plates 435 – 436: American Provincial
   Spoon rest....................................100.00 – 125.00
Use the Rhythm Rose prices to evaluate other American Provincial.

Swing
Page 175 – 176
NEV = No Established Value

Plate 437: Green Goddess teapot, very rare.......................NEV
 Values for other pieces of Swing dinnerware lines may be computed by using the suggestions under Century.

Virginia Rose
Page 177 – 179
NEV = No Established Value
 Values are given for pieces with excellent gold or silver trim.

Bowl, covered vegetable; 9"..............................100.00 – 125.00

Bowl, deep, 5"..18.00 – 22.00
Bowl, fruit; 5½"..5.00 – 8.00
Bowl, mixing; KK, 6"..35.00 – 45.00
Bowl, mixing; KK, 8"..40.00 – 48.00
Bowl, mixing; KK, 10"..40.00 – 50.00
Bowl, oatmeal; 6"...12.00 – 15.00
Bowl, oval vegetable; 8", scarce............................30.00 – 35.00
Bowl, oval vegetable; 9"......................................20.00 – 25.00
Bowl, oval vegetable; 10"....................................28.00 – 32.00
Bowl, vegetable; 7½", scarce................................28.00 – 32.00
Bowl, vegetable; 8½"..22.00 – 28.00
Bowl, vegetable; 9½"..30.00 – 35.00
Butter dish, ½-lb..125.00 – 175.00
Cake plate, KK, scarce..70.00 – 80.00
Cake server, KK, scarce.......................................75.00 – 85.00
Casserole, Daisy Chain, DC-714 ....NEV
Casserole, KK, OvenServe:
 Round sides, 8", scarce.................................90.00 – 115.00
 Straight sides, scarce..................................150.00 – 175.00
Creamer..15.00 – 20.00
Cup & saucer..12.00 – 15.00
Egg cup, double ....60.00 – 75.00
Mug, coffee...50.00 – 65.00
Pie plate, KK, 9½"..35.00 – 42.00
Pie plate, KK, large, scarce..................................40.00 – 50.00
Pitcher, milk; 5"...65.00 – 80.00
Pitcher, water; 7½"...150.00 – 175.00
Plate, 6"...7.00 – 8.00
Plate, 7"...11.00 – 14.00
Plate, 8", scarce...15.00 – 18.00
Plate, 9"...8.00 – 10.00
Plate, 10"...12.00 – 15.00
Plate, deep, 1" flange ....15.00 – 20.00
Plate, deep, no flange...15.00 – 20.00
Platter/gravy liner, 9"...28.00 – 32.00
Platter, 10½", scarce...30.00 – 35.00
Platter, 11½"..20.00 – 25.00
Platter, 13"...28.00 – 35.00
Platter, 15½"..40.00 – 50.00
Salt & pepper shakers:
 KK, scarce, pr. ....160.00 – 185.00
 Regular, scarce, pr......................................125.00 – 150.00
Sauce boat ....25.00 – 30.00
Sugar bowl with lid..22.00 – 28.00
Tray with handles, 8" ....28.00 – 35.00

Laughlin Art China
Page 180 – 190

Plate 447: Vase, with handles, Currant, 8"..........125.00 – 140.00
Plate 448: Vase, Currant, 7"............................110.00 – 125.00
Plate 449: Bowl, ruffled, Currant, 2" x 10".........165.00 – 180.00
   Plate, Currant, 9½"............................75.00 – 85.00
   Plate, scalloped, Currant, 10"..........90.00 – 110.00
Plate 450: Bread tray, Fe Dora, Currant,
   12½"..90.00 – 110.00
Plate 451: Covered dish, Currant....................210.00 – 235.00
Plate 452: Humidor, wooden lid, Currant,

5" x 6" ....225.00 – 250.00
Pitcher, bulbous, Currant,
4½" x 5"..............................125.00 – 145.00
Orange bowl with handles, Currant,
12"..............................190.00 – 215.00
Pitcher, straight sides, Currant,
6½"..............................140.00 – 155.00
Plate 453: Chocolate pot, Currant..................295.00 – 325.00
Chocolate cup & saucer, Currant ....110.00 – 125.00
Plate 454: Pitcher, Dutch Jug, Currant, 10".....165.00 – 185.00
Plate 455: Pitcher Geisha Jug, large...............125.00 – 140.00
Plate 456: Sugar basket, Golden Fleece..........240.00 – 265.00
Sugar basket, Currant....................200.00 – 225.00
Plate 457: Vase, Currant, 12" ....210.00 – 230.00
Plate 458: Vase, Currant, 9¾" ....165.00 – 185.00
Vase, slim form, Currant, 12" ....155.00 – 175.00
Vase, slim form, Currant, 16" ....250.00 – 275.00
Chocolate/AD pot, Currant, 10"......300.00 – 325.00
Plate 459: Vase, with handles, Currant,
14".................................325.00 – 350.00
Plate 460: Bread tray, White Pets....................175.00 – 190.00
Plate 461: Pitcher, Geisha Jug, Mirror Cats, large.350.00 – 400.00
Plate 462: Ewer, White Pets, 15½" ....425.00 – 450.00
Plate 463: Vase, with handles, White Pets, 8"......275.00 – 300.00
Plate 464: Mug, Staghorn, Flow Blue, with
Monk...............................180.00 – 200.00
Plate 465: Tankard, Flow Blue, monk playing
violin, lg ....275.00 – 300.00
Plate 466: Bonbon, gold trim, Flow Blue.........180.00 – 200.00
Plate 467: Chocolate cup & saucer, gold trim, Flow
Blue..................................180.00 – 200.00
Plate 468: Jardiniere, with handles, gold trim, Flow Blue,
10" x 14"......................................700.00 – 750.00
Plate 469: Vase, Flow Blue, with lady, 12" ......350.00 – 385.00
Plate 471: Cuspidor, lady's, gold trim Flow Blue,
5½" x 8".................................360.00 – 385.00
Plate 470 & 472: Plates, Flow Blue, each ....180.00 – 200.00
Plate 473: Bowl, lady with breasts exposed ....350.00 – 375.00
Plate 474: Charger, American Beauty, 10".......150.00 – 165.00
Plate 475: Tankard, American Beauty ....360.00 – 390.00
Mug, American Beauty ....125.00 – 140.00
Plate 476: Pitcher, Geisha Jug, Juno...............375.00 – 400.00
Plate 477: Chocolate pot, Juno........................375.00 – 400.00
Cup and saucer, AD; Juno..............195.00 – 225.00
Plate 478 & 479: Pitcher, Geisha Jug, Fruit 6"...165.00 – 185.00
Plate 480: Tankard, American Floral...............345.00 – 360.00
Plate 481: Orange bowl, Holland, rare............475.00 – 500.00
Plate 482: Jug, Holland, 6½"..........................425.00 – 475.00
Plate 483: Rose bowl, Holland, very rare........475.00 – 525.00
Ewer, Holland 15½" ....625.00 – 725.00
Plate 484: Tankard, American eagle & flags ....380.00 – 400.00
Plate 485: Stein, Staghorn, hand painted.........125.00 – 150.00
Additional Art China, not shown:
Creamer (matches Currant Sugar
basket) ....110.00 – 130.00
Creamer (matches Golden Fleece sugar
basket) ....125.00 – 150.00
Stein, Staghorn, Currant ....85.00 – 95.00
Plate, Currant, 7"..............................45.00 – 55.00
Plate, White Pets, child and donkey .....150.00 – 165.00
Rose bowl, Currant, 4"....................165.00 – 180.00

Stein, Staghorn, White Pets ....180.00 – 200.00
Tankard, Currant, shape as shown in Plate
404 ....225.00 – 250.00
Vase, Juno, gold trim, 12" ....360.00 – 385.00
Vase, White Pets, with cats, shape as shown in
Plate 459, 14"................................425.00 – 450.00
Plate 486: Stein, Staghorn, advertising ....220.00 – 245.00
Plate 487: Stein, Staghorn, football player.......325.00 – 350.00
Plate 488: Pitcher, Dutch Jug, Silver Sienna....375.00 – 400.00

~~~~~~~~~

Dreamland
Page 191 – 193

Plate 489: Vase, Dreamland, 3½" ....225.00 – 250.00
Plate 490: Stein, Dreamland ....245.00 – 265.00
Tankard, Dreamland ....400.00 – 450.00
Plate 491: Chop/Cake plate, Dreamland..........250.00 – 300.00
Plate 492: Vase, Dreamland, 16" ....425.00 – 475.00
Plate 493: Ruffled, salad bowl, Dreamland .....275.00 – 325.00
Jug, Dreamland, 6½" ....275.00 – 325.00
Plate 494: Plaque, Dreamland........................225.00 – 250.00
Plate 496: Vase, Dreamland, 10" ....300.00 – 350.00
Cake plate, open handles, Dreamland..250.00 – 300.00

~~~~~~~~~

World's Fair: The American Potter
Page 194 – 198
NEV = No Established Value

Plate 497 & 498: Vase, under 5"..........................70.00 – 110.00
Vase, 5"..200.00 – 225.00
Vase, 6"..250.00 – 300.00
(add 20% for cobalt)
Vase, 7" to 8"...............................350.00 – 400.00
Candle holder, each, rare ....200.00 – 250.00
Bowl, extremely rare......................250.00 – 300.00
Individual creamer, standard
color ....100.00 – 125.00
hard-to-find colors ....150.00 – 175.00
Plate 499: Plate HLC World's Fair, either
year ....250.00 – 275.00
Plate 500: Plate, Golden Gate Expo, either
year ....200.00 – 225.00
Ashtray, Golden Gate Expo ....125.00 – 150.00
Plate 501: Bowl, Four Seasons, each ....90.00 – 100.00
Plate 502: Cup & saucer, Zodiac ....100.00 – 125.00
Plate 503: Pitchers, George and Martha Washington,
cobalt, 5", extremely rare.............................NEV
Plate 504: Pitcher, Martha Washington, ivory,
5" ....75.00 – 80.00
George etc. ....40.00 – 50.00
Plate 505 – 506: Plate, Potters; either view
Tan..60.00 – 70.00
Turquoise...45.00 – 50.00
Ivory or green ....120.00 – 140.00

	Box only	75.00 – 100.00
Plate 507:	Marmalade, complete, Edwin Knowles, very rare	300.00 – 400.00
Plate 508:	Cake set, Cronin China Co.	125.00 – 150.00
	Bowl, Paden City Pottery, 10"	125.00 – 150.00
	Plate, Knowles, 10¾"	100.00 – 135.00
	Marmalade (see Plate 427 for complete example)	
	Juice Pitcher, Porcelier	175.00 – 200.00
Plate 509:	Ashtray, Porcelier	125.00 – 130.00
Plate 510:	Teapot, large, Porcelier	290.00 – 325.00
	Teapot, medium, Porcelier, not shown	285.00 – 320.00
	Teapot, small, Porcelier	325.00 – 350.00
Plate 511:	Creamer, Porcelier	125.00 – 150.00
	Water pitcher, Porcelier	250.00 – 300.00
	Sugar bowl, not shown	150.00 – 175.00

Miscellaneous
Page 199 – 201

NEV = No Established Value

Plate 513:	Nude vase	350.00 – 385.00
	Donkey ashtray	550.00 – 600.00
Plate 514:	Sit 'n Sip, see Commercial Adaptations for pricing information.	

Plate 515:	Chip & dip, 12"	NEV
Plate 516:	Tom & Jerry bowl	35.00 – 40.00
	Tom & Jerry mug	10.00 – 15.00
Plate 517:	Lid	NEV
Plate 518:	Bill Booth football	1,100.00 – 1,400.00
Plate 520:	Doll	50.00 – 65.00
Plate 522:	Leaf saucers, 7"	NEV

Values for Our Early Editions

The earlier editions of our Fiesta book have themselves become sought-after collectibles. However, online auctions have made far more available than we once thought existed, and values have gone down dramatically. Remember that condition is important, and values are given for copies in very fine condition.

First Edition	100.00 – 150.00
Second Editon	60.00 – 85.00
Third Edition	40.00 – 65.00
Fourth Edition	30.00 – 40.00
Fifth Edition	25.00 – 30.00
Sixth Edition	20.00 – 25.00

COLLECTOR BOOKS

Informing Today's Collector

For over two decades we have been keeping collectors informed on trends and values in all fields of antiques and collectibles.

DOLLS, FIGURES & TEDDY BEARS

4707	A Decade of **Barbie Dolls** & Collectibles, 1981–1991, Summers	$19.95
4631	**Barbie Doll** Boom, 1986–1995, Augustyniak	$18.95
2079	**Barbie Doll** Fashion, Volume I, Eames	$24.95
4846	**Barbie Doll** Fashion, Volume II, Eames	$24.95
3957	**Barbie** Exclusives, Rana	$18.95
4632	**Barbie** Exclusives, Book II, Rana	$18.95
4557	**Barbie**, The First 30 Years, Deutsch	$24.95
5672	The **Barbie Doll** Years, 4th Ed., Olds	$19.95
3810	**Chatty Cathy** Dolls, Lewis	$15.95
5352	Collector's Ency. of **Barbie** Doll Exclusives & More, 2nd Ed.,Augustyniak	$24.95
2211	Collector's Encyclopedia of **Madame Alexander** Dolls, Smith	$24.95
4863	Collector's Encyclopedia of **Vogue Dolls**, Izen/Stover	$29.95
5598	**Doll Values**, Antique to Modern, 4th Ed., Moyer	$12.95
56101	**Madame Alexander** Collector's Dolls Price Guide #25, Crowsey	$9.95
5612	**Modern Collectible Dolls**, Volume IV, Moyer	$24.95
5365	**Peanuts Collectibles**, Podley/Bang	$24.95
5253	Story of **Barbie**, 2nd Ed., Westenhouser	$24.95
5277	**Talking Toys** of the 20th Century, Lewis	$15.95
1513	**Teddy Bears & Steiff** Animals, Mandel	$9.95
1817	**Teddy Bears & Steiff** Animals, 2nd Series, Mandel	$19.95
2084	**Teddy Bears, Annalee's & Steiff** Animals, 3rd Series, Mandel	$19.95
5371	**Teddy Bear** Treasury, Yenke	$19.95
1808	Wonder of **Barbie**, Manos	$9.95
1430	World of **Barbie** Dolls, Manos	$9.95
4880	World of **Raggedy Ann** Collectibles, Avery	$24.95

TOYS, MARBLES & CHRISTMAS COLLECTIBLES

2333	Antique & Collectible **Marbles**, 3rd Ed., Grist	$9.95
5353	**Breyer Animal** Collector's Guide, 2nd Ed., Browell	$19.95
4976	**Christmas Ornaments**, Lights & Decorations, Johnson	$24.95
4737	**Christmas Ornaments**, Lights & Decorations, Vol. II, Johnson	$24.95
4739	**Christmas Ornaments**, Lights & Decorations, Vol. III, Johnson	$24.95
4649	Classic Plastic **Model Kits**, Polizzi	$24.95
4559	Collectible **Action Figures**, 2nd Ed., Manos	$17.95
3874	Collectible **Coca-Cola Toy Trucks**, deCourtivron	$24.95
2338	Collector's Encyclopedia of **Disneyana**, Longest, Stern	$24.95
4958	Collector's Guide to **Battery Toys**, Hultzman	$19.95
5038	Collector's Guide to **Diecast Toys** & Scale Models, 2nd Ed., Johnson	$19.95
4651	Collector's Guide to **Tinker Toys**, Strange	$18.95
4566	Collector's Guide to **Tootsietoys**, 2nd Ed., Richter	$19.95
5169	Collector's Guide to **TV Toys** & Memorabilia, 2nd Ed., Davis/Morgan	$24.95
5360	**Fisher-Price Toys**, Cassity	$19.95
4720	The Golden Age of **Automotive Toys**, 1925–1941, Hutchison/Johnson	$24.95
5593	Grist's Big Book of **Marbles**, 2nd Ed.	$24.95
3970	Grist's Machine-Made & Contemporary **Marbles**, 2nd Ed.	$9.95
5267	**Matchbox Toys**, 1947 to 1998, 3rd Ed., Johnson	$19.95
4871	**McDonald's** Collectibles, Henriques/DuVall	$19.95
1540	Modern **Toys** 1930–1980, Baker	$19.95
3888	**Motorcycle Toys**, Antique & Contemporary, Gentry/Downs	$18.95
5368	**Schroeder's Collectible Toys**, Antique to Modern Price Guide, 6th Ed.	$17.95
2028	**Toys**, Antique & Collectible, Longest	$14.95

FURNITURE

1457	American **Oak** Furniture, McNerney	$9.95
3716	American **Oak** Furniture, Book II, McNerney	$12.95
1118	Antique **Oak** Furniture, Hill	$7.95
2271	Collector's Encyclopedia of **American** Furniture, Vol. II, Swedberg	$24.95
3720	Collector's Encyclopedia of **American** Furniture, Vol. III, Swedberg	$24.95
5359	Early **American** Furniture, Obbard	$12.95
1755	Furniture of the **Depression Era**, Swedberg	$19.95
3906	**Heywood-Wakefield** Modern Furniture, Rouland	$18.95
1885	**Victorian** Furniture, Our American Heritage, McNerney	$9.95

3829	**Victorian** Furniture, Our American Heritage, Book II, McNerney	$9.95

JEWELRY, HATPINS, WATCHES & PURSES

1712	Antique & Collectible **Thimbles** & Accessories, Mathis	$19.95
1748	Antique **Purses**, Revised Second Ed., Holiner	$19.95
1278	Art Nouveau & Art Deco **Jewelry**, Baker	$9.95
4850	Collectible **Costume Jewelry**, Simonds	$24.95
3722	Collector's Ency. of **Compacts**, Carryalls & Face Powder Boxes, Mueller	$24.95
4940	**Costume Jewelry**, A Practical Handbook & Value Guide, Rezazadeh	$24.95
1716	Fifty Years of Collectible **Fashion Jewelry**, 1925–1975, Baker	$19.95
1424	**Hatpins** & Hatpin Holders, Baker	$9.95
1181	100 Years of Collectible **Jewelry**, 1850–1950, Baker	$9.95
4729	**Sewing Tools** & Trinkets, Thompson	$24.95
5620	Unsigned Beauties of **Costume Jewelry**, Brown	$24.95
4878	Vintage & Contemporary **Purse Accessories**, Gerson	$24.95
3830	Vintage **Vanity Bags** & Purses, Gerson	$24.95

INDIANS, GUNS, KNIVES, TOOLS, PRIMITIVES

1868	Antique **Tools**, Our American Heritage, McNerney	$9.95
5616	Big Book of **Pocket Knives**, Stewart	$19.95
4943	Field Guide to Flint **Arrowheads & Knives** of the North American Indian	$9.95
3885	**Indian Artifacts** of the Midwest, Book II, Hothem	$16.95
4870	**Indian Artifacts** of the Midwest, Book III, Hothem	$18.95
5685	**Indian Artifacts** of the Midwest, Book IV, Hothem	$19.95
5687	**Modern Guns**, Identification & Values, 13th Ed., Quertermous	$14.95
2164	**Primitives**, Our American Heritage, McNerney	$9.95
1759	**Primitives**, Our American Heritage, 2nd Series, McNerney	$14.95
4730	Standard **Knife** Collector's Guide, 3rd Ed., Ritchie & Stewart	$12.95

PAPER COLLECTIBLES & BOOKS

4633	**Big Little Books**, Jacobs	$18.95
4710	Collector's Guide to **Children's Books**, 1850 to 1950, Jones	$18.95
5596	Collector's Guide to **Children's Books**, 1950 to 1975, Jones	$19.95
1441	Collector's Guide to **Post Cards**, Wood	$9.95
2081	Guide to Collecting **Cookbooks**, Allen	$14.95
5613	Huxford's **Old Book** Value Guide, 12th Ed.	$19.95
2080	Price Guide to **Cookbooks** & Recipe Leaflets, Dickinson	$9.95
3973	**Sheet Music** Reference & Price Guide, 2nd Ed., Pafik & Guiheen	$19.95
4654	**Victorian Trade Cards**, Historical Reference & Value Guide, Cheadle	$19.95
4733	**Whitman Juvenile Books**, Brown	$17.95

GLASSWARE

5602	Anchor Hocking's **Fire-King** & More, 2nd Ed.	$24.95
4561	Collectible **Drinking Glasses**, Chase & Kelly	$17.95
4642	Collectible **Glass Shoes**, Wheatley	$19.95
5357	Coll. **Glassware** from the 40s, 50s & 60s, 5th Ed., Florence	$19.95
1810	Collector's Encyclopedia of **American Art Glass**, Shuman	$29.95
5358	Collector's Encyclopedia of **Depression Glass**, 14th Ed., Florence	$19.95
1961	Collector's Encyclopedia of **Fry Glassware**, Fry Glass Society	$24.95
1664	Collector's Encyclopedia of **Heisey Glass**, 1925–1938, Bredehoft	$24.95
3905	Collector's Encyclopedia of **Milk Glass**, Newbound	$24.95
4936	Collector's Guide to **Candy Containers**, Dezso/Poirier	$19.95
4564	**Crackle Glass**, Weitman	$19.95
4941	**Crackle Glass**, Book II, Weitman	$19.95
4714	**Czechoslovakian Glass** and Collectibles, Book II, Barta/Rose	$16.95
5528	Early American **Pattern Glass**, Metz	$17.95
5682	**Elegant Glassware** of the Depression Era, 9th Ed., Florence	$19.95
5614	Field Guide to **Pattern Glass**, McCain	$17.95
3981	Evers' Standard **Cut Glass** Value Guide	$12.95
4659	**Fenton** Art Glass, 1907–1939, Whitmyer	$24.95
5615	Florence's **Glassware Pattern Identification** Guide, Vol. II	$19.95
3725	**Fostoria**, Pressed, Blown & Hand Molded Shapes, Kerr	$24.95
4719	**Fostoria**, Etched, Carved & Cut Designs, Vol. II, Kerr	$24.95

3883	**Fostoria Stemware**, The Crystal for America, Long/Seate	$24.95
5261	**Fostoria Tableware**, 1924 – 1943, Long/Seate	$24.95
5361	**Fostoria Tableware**, 1944 – 1986, Long/Seate	$24.95
5604	**Fostoria**, Useful & Ornamental, Long/Seate	$29.95
4644	**Imperial Carnival Glass**, Burns	$18.95
3886	**Kitchen Glassware** of the Depression Years, 5th Ed., Florence	$19.95
5600	Much More Early American **Pattern Glass**, Metz	$17.95
5690	Pocket Guide to **Depression Glass**, 12th Ed., Florence	$9.95
5594	Standard Encyclopedia of **Carnival Glass**, 7th Ed., Edwards/Carwile	$29.95
5595	Standard **Carnival Glass** Price Guide, 12th Ed., Edwards/Carwile	$9.95
5272	Standard Encyclopedia of **Opalescent Glass**, 3rd Ed., Edwards/Carwile	$24.95
5617	Standard **Pressed Glass**, 2nd Ed., Edwards/Carwile	$29.95
4731	**Stemware Identification**, Featuring Cordials with Values, Florence	$24.95
4732	**Very Rare Glassware** of the Depression Years, 5th Series, Florence	$24.95
4656	**Westmoreland Glass**, Wilson	$24.95

POTTERY

4927	**ABC Plates & Mugs**, Lindsay	$24.95
4929	**American Art Pottery**, Sigafoose	$24.95
4630	**American Limoges**, Limoges	$24.95
1312	**Blue & White Stoneware**, McNerney	$9.95
1958	So. Potteries **Blue Ridge Dinnerware**, 3rd Ed., Newbound	$14.95
1959	**Blue Willow**, 2nd Ed., Gaston	$14.95
4851	Collectible **Cups & Saucers**, Harran	$18.95
1373	Collector's Encyclopedia of **American Dinnerware**, Cunningham	$24.95
4931	Collector's Encyclopedia of **Bauer Pottery**, Chipman	$24.95
4932	Collector's Encyclopedia of **Blue Ridge Dinnerware**, Vol. II, Newbound	$24.95
4658	Collector's Encyclopedia of **Brush-McCoy Pottery**, Huxford	$24.95
5034	Collector's Encyclopedia of **California Pottery**, 2nd Ed., Chipman	$24.95
2133	Collector's Encyclopedia of **Cookie Jars**, Roerig	$24.95
3723	Collector's Encyclopedia of **Cookie Jars**, Book II, Roerig	$24.95
4939	Collector's Encyclopedia of **Cookie Jars**, Book III, Roerig	$24.95
5040	Collector's Encyclopedia of **Fiesta**, 8th Ed., Huxford	$19.95
4718	Collector's Encyclopedia of **Figural Planters & Vases**, Newbound	$19.95
3961	Collector's Encyclopedia of **Early Noritake**, Alden	$24.95
1439	Collector's Encyclopedia of **Flow Blue China**, Gaston	$19.95
3812	Collector's Encyclopedia of **Flow Blue China**, 2nd Ed., Gaston	$24.95
3431	Collector's Encyclopedia of **Homer Laughlin China**, Jasper	$24.95
1276	Collector's Encyclopedia of **Hull Pottery**, Roberts	$19.95
3962	Collector's Encyclopedia of **Lefton China**, DeLozier	$19.95
4855	Collector's Encyclopedia of **Lefton China**, Book II, DeLozier	$19.95
5609	Collector's Encyclopedia of **Limoges Porcelain**, 3rd Ed., Gaston	$24.95
2334	Collector's Encyclopedia of **Majolica Pottery**, Katz-Marks	$19.95
1358	Collector's Encyclopedia of **McCoy Pottery**, Huxford	$19.95
3837	Collector's Encyclopedia of **Nippon Porcelain**, Van Patten	$24.95
2089	Collector's Ency. of **Nippon Porcelain**, 2nd Series, Van Patten	$24.95
1665	Collector's Ency. of **Nippon Porcelain**, 3rd Series, Van Patten	$24.95
4712	Collector's Ency. of **Nippon Porcelain**, 4th Series, Van Patten	$24.95
1447	Collector's Encyclopedia of **Noritake**, Van Patten	$19.95
1037	Collector's Encyclopedia of **Occupied Japan**, 1st Series, Florence	$14.95
1038	Collector's Encyclopedia of **Occupied Japan**, 2nd Series, Florence	$14.95
2335	Collector's Encyclopedia of **Occupied Japan**, 5th Series, Florence	$14.95
4951	Collector's Encyclopedia of **Old Ivory China**, Hillman	$24.95
5564	Collector's Encyclopedia of **Pickard China**, Reed	$29.95
3877	Collector's Encyclopedia of **R.S. Prussia**, 4th Series, Gaston	$24.95
5618	Collector's Encyclopedia of **Rosemeade Pottery**, Dommel	$24.95
1034	Collector's Encyclopedia of **Roseville Pottery**, Huxford	$19.95
1035	Collector's Encyclopedia of **Roseville Pottery**, 2nd Ed., Huxford	$19.95
4856	Collector's Encyclopedia of **Russel Wright**, 2nd Ed., Kerr	$24.95
4713	Collector's Encyclopedia of **Salt Glaze Stoneware**, Taylor/Lowrance	$24.95
3314	Collector's Encyclopedia of **Van Briggle Art Pottery**, Sasicki	$24.95
4563	Collector's Encyclopedia of **Wall Pockets**, Newbound	$19.95
2111	Collector's Encyclopedia of **Weller Pottery**, Huxford	$29.95
3876	Collector's Guide to **Lu-Ray Pastels**, Meehan	$18.95
3814	Collector's Guide to **Made in Japan Ceramics**, White	$18.95

4646	Collector's Guide to **Made in Japan Ceramics**, Book II, White	$18.95
2339	Collector's Guide to **Shawnee Pottery**, Vanderbilt	$19.95
1425	**Cookie Jars**, Westfall	$9.95
3440	**Cookie Jars**, Book II, Westfall	$19.95
4924	Figural & Novelty **Salt & Pepper Shakers**, 2nd Series, Davern	$24.95
2379	Lehner's Ency. of **U.S. Marks** on Pottery, Porcelain & China	$24.95
4722	**McCoy Pottery**, Collector's Reference & Value Guide, Hanson/Nissen	$19.95
1670	**Red Wing Collectibles**, DePasquale	$9.95
1440	**Red Wing Stoneware**, DePasquale	$9.95
1632	**Salt & Pepper Shakers**, Guarnaccia	$9.95
5091	**Salt & Pepper Shakers** II, Guarnaccia	$18.95
2220	**Salt & Pepper Shakers** III, Guarnaccia	$14.95
3443	**Salt & Pepper Shakers** IV, Guarnaccia	$18.95
3738	**Shawnee Pottery**, Mangus	$24.95
4629	Turn of the Century **American Dinnerware**, 1880s–1920s, Jasper	$24.95
3327	**Watt Pottery** – Identification & Value Guide, Morris	$19.95

OTHER COLLECTIBLES

4704	Antique & Collectible **Buttons**, Wisniewski	$19.95
2269	Antique **Brass & Copper** Collectibles, Gaston	$16.95
1880	Antique **Iron**, McNerney	$9.95
3872	Antique **Tins**, Dodge	$24.95
4845	Antique **Typewriters & Office Collectibles**, Rehr	$19.95
5607	Antiquing and Collecting on the **Internet**, Parry	$12.95
1128	**Bottle** Pricing Guide, 3rd Ed., Cleveland	$7.95
4636	**Celluloid** Collectibles, Dunn	$14.95
3718	Collectible **Aluminum**, Grist	$16.95
4560	Collectible **Cats**, An Identification & Value Guide, Book II, Fyke	$19.95
4852	Collectible **Compact Disc** Price Guide 2, Cooper	$17.95
5666	Collector's Encyclopedia of **Granite Ware**, Book 2, Greguire	$29.95
4705	Collector's Guide to **Antique Radios**, 4th Ed., Bunis	$18.95
5608	Collector's Gde. to Buying, Selling, & Trading on the **Internet**, 2nd Ed., Hix	$12.95
3880	Collector's Guide to **Cigarette Lighters**, Flanagan	$17.95
4637	Collector's Guide to **Cigarette Lighters**, Book II, Flanagan	$17.95
4942	Collector's Guide to **Don Winton Designs**, Ellis	$19.95
3966	Collector's Guide to **Inkwells**, Identification & Values, Badders	$18.95
4947	Collector's Guide to **Inkwells**, Book II, Badders	$19.95
5621	Collector's Guide to **Online Auctions**, Hix	$12.95
4862	Collector's Guide to **Toasters** & Accessories, Greguire	$19.95
4652	Collector's Guide to **Transistor Radios**, 2nd Ed., Bunis	$16.95
4864	Collector's Guide to **Wallace Nutting Pictures**, Ivankovich	$18.95
1629	**Doorstops**, Identification & Values, Bertoia	$9.95
4717	Figural **Nodders**, Includes Bobbin' Heads and Swayers, Irtz	$19.95
5683	**Fishing Lure** Collectibles, 2nd Ed., Murphy/Edmisten	$29.95
5259	**Flea Market Trader**, 12th Ed., Huxford	$9.95
4945	**G-Men and FBI Toys** and Collectibles, Whitworth	$18.95
5605	**Garage Sale & Flea Market Annual**, 8th Ed.	$19.95
3819	**General Store** Collectibles, Wilson	$24.95
5159	Huxford's Collectible **Advertising**, 4th Ed.	$24.95
2216	**Kitchen Antiques**, 1790–1940, McNerney	$14.95
4950	The **Lone Ranger**, Collector's Reference & Value Guide, Felbinger	$18.95
2026	**Railroad** Collectibles, 4th Ed., Baker	$14.95
5619	**Roy Rogers and Dale Evans** Toys & Memorabilia, Coyle	$24.95
5367	**Schroeder's Antiques Price Guide**, 18th Ed., Huxford	$12.95
5007	**Silverplated Flatware**, Revised 4th Edition, Hagan	$18.95
1922	Standard **Old Bottle** Price Guide, Sellari	$14.95
5694	Summers' Guide to **Coca-Cola**, 3rd Ed.	$24.95
5356	Summers' Pocket Guide to **Coca-Cola**, 2nd Ed.	$9.95
3892	**Toy & Miniature Sewing Machines**, Thomas	$18.95
4876	**Toy & Miniature Sewing Machines**, Book II, Thomas	$24.95
5144	Value Guide to **Advertising Memorabilia**, 2nd Ed., Summers	$19.95
3977	Value Guide to **Gas Station Memorabilia**, Summers & Priddy	$24.95
4877	Vintage **Bar Ware**, Visakay	$24.95
4935	The W.F. Cody **Buffalo Bill** Collector's Guide with Values	$24.95
5281	**Wanted to Buy**, 7th Edition	$9.95

Schroeder's ANTIQUES Price Guide